Travel, Tourism and the Moving Image

TOURISM AND CULTURAL CHANGE

Series Editors: Professor Mike Robinson, *Ironbridge International Institute for Cultural Heritage, University of Birmingham, UK* and Dr Alison Phipps, *University of Glasgow, Scotland, UK*

TCC is a series of books that explores the complex and ever-changing relationship between tourism and culture(s). The series focuses on the ways that places, peoples, pasts and ways of life are increasingly shaped/transformed/created/packaged for touristic purposes. The series examines the ways tourism utilises/makes and re-makes cultural capital in its various guises (visual and performing arts, crafts, festivals, built heritage, cuisine, etc.) and the multifarious political, economic, social and ethical issues that are raised as a consequence.

Understanding tourism's relationships with culture(s) and vice versa is of ever-increasing significance in a globalising world. This series will critically examine the dynamic interrelationships between tourism and culture(s). Theoretical explorations, research-informed analyses and detailed historical reviews from a variety of disciplinary perspectives are invited to consider such relationships.

Full details of all the books in this series and of all our other publications can be found on http://www.channelviewpublications.com, or by writing to Channel View Publications, St Nicholas House, 31–34 High Street, Bristol BS1 2AW, UK.

TOURISM AND CULTURAL CHANGE: 45

Travel, Tourism and the Moving Image

Sue Beeton

CHANNEL VIEW PUBLICATIONS
Bristol • Buffalo • Toronto

Library of Congress Cataloging in Publication Data
Beeton, Sue.
Travel, Tourism and the Moving Image/Sue Beeton.
Tourism and Cultural Change: 45
Includes bibliographical references and index.
1. Tourism and motion pictures. 2. Tourism – Decision making. I. Title.
G155.A1B3836 2015
910'.019–dc23 2015008251

British Library Cataloguing in Publication Data
A catalogue entry for this book is available from the British Library.

ISBN-13: 978-1-84541-528-0 (hbk)
ISBN-13: 978-1-84541-527-3 (pbk)

Channel View Publications
UK: St Nicholas House, 31–34 High Street, Bristol BS1 2AW, UK.
USA: UTP, 2250 Military Road, Tonawanda, NY 14150, USA.
Canada: UTP, 5201 Dufferin Street, North York, Ontario M3H 5T8, Canada.

Website: www.channelviewpublications.com
Twitter: Channel_View
Facebook: https://www.facebook.com/channelviewpublications
Blog: www.channelviewpublications.wordpress.com

Copyright © 2015 Sue Beeton.

All rights reserved. No part of this work may be reproduced in any form or by any means without permission in writing from the publisher.

The policy of Multilingual Matters/Channel View Publications is to use papers that are natural, renewable and recyclable products, made from wood grown in sustainable forests. In the manufacturing process of our books, and to further support our policy, preference is given to printers that have FSC and PEFC Chain of Custody certification. The FSC and/or PEFC logos will appear on those books where full certification has been granted to the printer concerned.

Typeset by Techset Composition India (P) Ltd, Bangalore and Chennai, India.
Printed and bound in Great Britain by Short Run Press Ltd.

Contents

Figures	ix
Tables	xi
Acknowledgements	xiii

	Introduction: The Birth of This Book...	1
	The Development of the Moving Image Around the World	3
	Reading This Book	3
1	Mise-en-Scène	6
	Why the 'Moving Image'?	8
	Travel and Tourism	9
	Glancing at the Gaze and its Mediation/Mediatisation	13
	Understanding Audiences	16
	Film-Induced Travel and Tourism	21
	Theoretical Framework	30
	Conclusion	35
	Part 1: From Static to Moving Images	**37**
2	From Panoramas to Phantom Rides	39
	Panorama, Pictures and Travel	40
	Virtual (Vicarious) Travel of the Late 19th and Early 20th Centuries	48
	Short, Sweet and Silent: The Movies of the Early 20th Century	55
	From Talking Audiences to Talking Pictures	58
	Conclusion: Active Audiences, Active Tourists	59
3	The Emotions of Motion 1: Travel, War and Unrest in the Era of the Moving Image	61
	A Typology of War Films	63

v

	War in the Age of the Moving Image: Travel Lectures, Newsreels, Movies and TV	65
	Conclusion	73
4	The Emotions of Motion 2: War Propaganda, National Cinema and Travel	75
	The Ascendancy of Hollywood	75
	The Role of Moving Images in Propaganda and Distraction	77
	The Rise of National Cinemas (1914–1926)	86
	War Movies, Escapism and Tourism	86
	Conclusion	89
5	Travel in the Era of Modern Warfare and Moving Images	90
	The Spy Movies of the Cold War (circa 1947–1991)	92
	Modern Warfare, Film and Travel	98
	Anti-War Films	102
	Emotional and Economic Recovery via Film and Travel	103
	'Unreal Unrest'	105
	Conclusion: Travel, Warfare and Moving Images	106

Part 2: Travelling In, On and Through the Landscape: Voyeur or Flâneur? — **107**

6	Badlands and Beauty: Landscape, Travel and Place in the Western	111
	Landscapes, Moviescapes and Mythscapes	114
	The Power of the Small Screen: TV Westerns	118
	Conclusion: Some Practical Implications for Tourism	123
7	Simply a Story? The Cultural Pervasiveness of the Western	125
	Movie Ranches	125
	Did it Really Go Away? The Resurgence of the Western	132
	The Western as a Reference Point	133
	From Frontiers to Pioneers: Australian Journeys	134
	Tourism Subtexts	139
8	Travel and Transformation: Road Movies and Touristic Journeys	141
	Elements of the Road Movie	144
	The Road, Travel and Tourism	147
	The Other Road Movies: Europe and Australia	148
	Tourism Subtexts	154

9	Baddies in the Old and New Worlds: Bushrangers, Gangsters and Crime On Screen	158
	The Australian Bushranger: Replicating the American Western?	158
	Mysteries and Detectives	167
	Gangsters, Mafioso and Triads	170
	Tourism Subtexts	173

Part 3: Imagining Places: Illusions and Dreams — 177

10	Creating Place	179
	Animation and Fantasy	180
	Development of the (Studio) Theme Park	181
	Authenticity?	190
	A Framework for Studio Theme Park Development	195
11	Spaces and Places: Travelling for/to the Moving Image	197
	Follow That Star: Film Tourism Precincts	197
	Film Museums, Art and Events	201
	Illusions, Dreams and Travel	208
12	Conclusion: Manifestations of Tourism Through Film and Television: Making (Some) Meaning from Moving Images and Moving People	210
	Small Screens, Big Reactions: TV, Computers and Mobile Technology	213
	Computers and Mobile Technology	217
	Being Watched While Travelling	221
	So What Does It All MEAN?	222
	The Future: A Never-ending Story …	225
	References	227
	Index	238

Figures

Figure 1.1	Stages in the development of a para-social relationship	20
Figure 1.2	Model of film-induced tourism knowledge development	22
Figure 1.3	Modelling the relationship between audience and tourist activity	29
Figure 3.1	Tourists with the coconuts at Doune Castle	71
Figure 4.1	Photo of the *Gone with the Wind* mill and signage noting the connection with the movie	88
Figure 5.1	Modelling the relationship between audience and tourist activity	91
Figure 6.1	Tourists at Ford Point, Monument Valley	115
Figure 6.2	My Monument Valley moment	121
Figure 7.1	The Movie Ranch, Kattemingga, Australia	131
Figure 7.2	*Man from Snowy River* fans	137
Figure 7.3	With Tom Burlinson	137
Figure 7.4	The guest book	138
Figure 7.5	Good Morning Australia!	138
Figure 7.6	The girl from Snowy River?	139
Figure 8.1	Modelling the relationship between audience and tourist activity	156
Figure 9.1	Modelling the relationship between audience and tourist activity	174
Figure 10.1	The park bench where Disney dreamed Disneyland	183
Figure 10.2	Creating place: Hogwarts Experience, Universal Studios. Clockwise from top left: Dumbledore's welcome (his hologram can be seen on the balcony); the paintings; ancient murals and paintings; The Sorting Hat; Harry, Ron and Hermione appear as holograms	187
Figure 10.3	Studio theme park model	193

Figure 10.4	Filming advertisements in theme parks (Universal, Orlando)	194
Figure 10.5	Studio theme park development	196
Figure 11.1	Tourists at Hong Kong's Avenue of Stars	198
Figure 11.2	Modelling the relationship between audience and tourist activity	208
Figure 12.1	Havana, Cuba – images of the imagination and reality. From the left, we can see a photo of a lovingly cared for car, women posing for tourists in the World Heritage heart of Havana, and finally the ruined residences one block away	212
Figure 12.2	Cuban musician, Ahmando Aguist	212
Figure 12.3	Double entendre: The Goathland Hotel with its fictional Aidensfield Arms signage	214
Figure 12.4	Privacy earthworks and signage for the *Sea Change* cottage	215
Figure 12.5	*Neighbours* tour guide, tourists and the Ramsey Street sign	216
Figure 12.6	Modelling the relationship between audience and tourist activity	224

Tables

Table 1.1	Typology of audience activity	18
Table 1.2	Typology of audience and tourist activity	19
Table 1.3	Forms and characteristics of tourism and the moving image	32
Table 3.1	Typology of war films	64
Table 6.1	Western themes and styles	113
Table 8.1	Road movies and westerns	145
Table 8.2	'Place' as a character in Australian road movies and American/spaghetti westerns	152
Table 9.1	Dominant tourism images in the Kelly movie eras	162
Table 9.2	Australian bushranger and settler movies and TV series' relationship with landscape	165
Table 10.1	Pearce's model of authenticity	192

Acknowledgements

Thanks to the Australian Centre for the Moving Image in Melbourne for introducing me to the concept and story of the moving image and allowing me to volunteer there during the Tim Burton blockbuster exhibition, enabling me to develop an in-depth understanding of the moving image in all its forms.

Many colleagues and some of my idols in the travel literature field have also encouraged, challenged and supported my endeavours, in particular Gary Best, Jennifer Laing, Glen Croy, Sue Turnbull, Keith Hollinshead, Pico Iyer and Rolf Potts. Over the years, my Masters students have presented me with a great sounding board for my thoughts and ideas, and I am forever thankful to them, in particular Madelene McWha.

While I am responsible for any errors or omissions, the constructive feedback from the series editors and anonymous reviewers as well as Warwick Frost as a critical reader have all contributed significantly to the quality of this publication.

Introduction: The Birth of This Book ...

> *You'll go back to the lower country ... and EARN THE RIGHT TO LIVE*
> *UP HERE!*
> *Like your father did!*
> *The Man from Snowy River*, 1982

Many of the 'early' academic studies of tourism (primarily from the 1960s onwards) were undertaken by academics from a variety of disciplinary backgrounds, including geography, economics, marketing and psychology through to sociology and anthropology. Each brought a range of perspectives and strong disciplinary knowledge to this 'new' field of study, contributing in many and varied ways, which they continue to do. Ultimately, such interest led to specialised tourism educational programmes being established at universities, which led to a significant change in academic research and knowledge in the field.

By the late 20th century, the study of tourism took an interesting turn, where we have students graduating from schools of tourism with undergraduate degrees in 'tourism' as opposed to the more social science based disciplines. This includes the *Bachelor of Tourism, Bachelor of Business (Tourism Management)* and *Bachelor of Arts (Tourism)* programmes, among others. Some of these graduates went on to further study in tourism and are now among our academic leaders, teachers and researchers. Consequently, many students are coming out of their courses as 'tourism specialists' with only a cursory understanding of other disciplines and their relevance to tourism. Philip Pearce *et al.* (2011) refer to those who have travelled such educational routes as 'Generation T' (*Gen T*). While one can argue that such a limited disciplinary background is a limitation, it actually presents *Gen T* with opportunities to explore tourism from a range of academic disciplinary perspectives.

I am one such person. Coming to tourism and academia a little 'later in life' and with a tourism *industry* background, I had no underpinning academic disciplinary knowledge, but a great and eclectic thirst for understanding the tourism phenomenon. Whether such a situation is optimal, I will leave others to decide, but I do know that I continue to be inspired by my eclectic interests that seem to revolve around the social sciences as well as a more pragmatic approach, informed by a lifelong interest in people, groups and cultures.

In fact, I came to academic life because of a movie. In the 1980s and 1990s I began guiding horseback tours in the Victorian High Country and working with the small business operators and communities in those rural areas. These tours became extremely popular (and viable) after the release of the iconic Australian movie, *The Man from Snowy River* (1982). As a guide, I witnessed people trying to ride like a bushman, careering down mountainsides and generally playing out scenes from the movie. Also, for a time, I was part of the (fictional?) life of these resilient, resourceful people of whom we, as Anglo-Australians, are so proud and which, for many, still possess a high level of authenticity. In order to continue working with these small business operators and other practitioners, I returned to study to enhance my knowledge of tourism and develop my research skills as a consultant. At the time it did not occur to me that I would end up as an academic studying the relationship between film and tourism. To be honest, I was barely aware that this was an option until well after my return to university, when I began to understand the opportunities presented by academic research and thought.

Initially, it was relatively easy to study the film tourism phenomenon, as very few people had actually done so, giving me an enormous amount of leeway (and, some may say, licence). However, as I have continued to work in this area over the ensuing 15–20 years (including my practical experience), I find I am leaning more and more towards thinking about the disciplines of cinema (and media) studies, psychology, anthropology and sociology to inform my work and help me understand 'why' we do what we do. This is incredibly exciting, challenging and even frightening for one who has no grounding knowledge of any of these disciplines. However, I believe that my lifelong obsession with observing people and society, in an attempt to make some sense of 'life', provides me with some intrinsic, on-the-ground knowledge, as does my experience as *Gen T*, a tourist, academic and guide.

So, in this book I work towards merging a selection of the great work from those disciplines with my more specific knowledge of film-induced tourism. I do hope that I have been successful, at least in part, but I also trust that others will continue to work in the areas I identify in this book and continue to progress our understanding and knowledge.

I dedicate this book to all of my *Generation T* friends, colleagues and students.

The Development of the Moving Image Around the World

The aim of this book is not to provide a definitive review of the development of the moving image in all parts of the world; rather it is to provide markers that illustrate the relationship between tourism and the moving image, dispelling the popularly held myth that film-related tourism is a recent phenomenon. Consequently, the focus is primarily on developments in the USA, UK, Europe and Australia, for a number of reasons. First, my own background is clearly Western, which helps me to interpret some of those cultural nuances. Also, much of the development of the moving image and tourism run parallel in these Western, developed countries, particularly when we consider the pervasiveness of Hollywood. As we move further into discussing some of the more modern forms of the moving image and tourism, I do make a slight shift towards incorporating additional perspectives, including a discussion of Asian popular culture and tourism, which has become an area in which I will be doing further studies with my Asian colleagues. Due to this 'Western' and historical perspective, there are undoubted colonialist undertones to much of the work cited and my personal interpretation, which is a perspective from which I cannot extricate myself.

Reading This Book

While the book can be read from cover to cover, developing its argument relating to audiences, tourists and moving images, it is possible to dip in and out of the work as required. Specific themes are introduced in each chapter, particularly related with the various 'fashions' (or developments) with regard to the moving image and tourism, which often reflect each other. While it is presented primarily chronologically, the work does not slavishly follow this line when there are direct thematic links outside what can be a restrictive (and at times conflicting) temporal perspective.

Most of the research I relate here is auto-ethnographic, where I reflect on personal lived experiences within a framework based on psychological, media and communication theory. This theory considers the audience of a moving image experience (such as film) to be an active participant, rather than simply a passive bystander. I have developed a circular, iterative model based on these theories and the research of myself and others in the field, which is first introduced in Chapter 1 and which is returned to a number of times throughout the book. A particular caveat regarding my study is that the majority of my research is based on fictional moving image experiences, and while I acknowledge the role of non-fictional works in tourism, I only occasionally stray into that area.

Following the first chapter, which sets the scene by outlining the premise of the book and provides a brief history of the relevant aspects of tourism referred to throughout the book, along with communication and moving image studies, are three broad thematic sections. The first, 'From Static to Moving Images', begins with a discussion of the very early era of the moving image, which begins prior to the advent of cinema and continues through to the silent moving picture era. There are a number of parallels with the emerging area of cinema as mass entertainment and that of mass tourism, which permeates much of the book. There are also interesting links between some of the early technology and cinema and tourism today noted in Chapter 2. Chapters 3 and 4 consider the role of film and travel during wartime, and the rise of national cinemas along with this era's focus on domestic tourism as a way to recover from war and deprivation, both emotionally and economically. The next chapter takes the war stories and images into the era of the Cold War as well as discussing the introduction of modern warfare and television. I argue that many of these images present places in exotic and often appealing ways, especially the more romanticised spy movies, which all contribute to our responses to these places when we travel, or even consider travelling.

The following part, 'Travelling In, On and Through the Landscape: Voyeur or Flâneur?', looks at the role that landscape plays in the western movie genre in Chapters 6 and 7, which include some personal experiences related not only to the American western, but also to Italian spaghetti westerns. Subsequent chapters discuss landscape and travel in the road movie genre and then various crime genres including the Australian bushranger, detective stories and American gangsters.

Part 3, 'Imagining Places: Illusions and Dreams', looks at how certain places, such as movie ranches and some studios have been created, not only to film movies and television, but also to cater to tourists, while the theme park is purely a tourist construct yet inhabits the world of the moving image. The popularity of animation in Asia as well as the West provides additional travel and tourism possibilities, especially as technology improves to create places where we can engage with our imaginary friends. Chapter 11 continues the discussion to look at film tourism precincts, museums and moving image related events, such as artistic installations and festivals.

Before I attempt to make some sense of all of the discussions regarding active audiences and active tourists in the last chapter, we look at the pervasiveness of the small screens from TV to computers and mobile technology, followed by some other aspects of the moving image that are influencing our travel experiences. However, this book is does not 'end' with any great statements or ultimate conclusions, but presents a number of paths that future researchers, students and writers, including myself, can follow.

1 Mise-en-Scène[1]

> *The moving image has evolved over centuries: Chinese shadow plays and eerie magic lantern shows in Renaissance Rome led to the invention of cinema in the 1890s. As time passed, Hollywood and Bollywood boomed, man's first steps on the moon were televised and a videogame character named Mario won our hearts. Today, the Web and the mobile phone are transforming the moving image anew.*
> Australian Centre for the Moving Image, 2011 (http://www.acmi.net.au/screen_worlds_about.htm)

Travel and tourism involve moving from one place to another – from an origin to a destination (home to away), from the familiar to the new; and/or from one state to another – from being stressed to relaxed, bored to stimulated, tired to invigorated, from desire to fulfilment, or even from anticipation to disappointment. Certainly, travel itself can be a conduit for learning, knowing, thinking and belonging (Amad, 2006: 101). Furthermore, we have created ways in which images 'move' (as in a film), which can create similar emotional responses in the viewer as those the traveller experiences while touring. Whenever (and wherever) these worlds intersect and interact, whether physically, metaphorically or emotionally, the results can be extremely powerful and intense.

The premise that informs the work in this book is that the moving image has been (and remains) a powerful emotional and physical presence as well as a mirror of the culture of the time in which it exists and, along with travel and tourism, that it can also be an agent of change. To paraphrase the aim outlined in the Introduction, the myth so often proliferated by students and academics alike, that film related tourism is a recent phenomenon (see Gjorgievski & Trpkova, 2012; Rewtrakunphaiboon, 2009), needs to be seriously reconsidered. Certainly, formal study of this relationship is relatively recent, as outlined in this chapter, yet travel and tourism has been linked inextricably with the moving image since its 19th-century inception.

As with various aspects of travel, the concept of the *moving image* can be considered in various ways; that is, the images move, the place of screening moves, enabling one to view one place in another (for example, watching an IMAX movie of Antarctica in New York) and, finally, (moving) images move people emotionally. By studying the effects of these moving images on contemporary culture, travel and leisure, we can situate the traveller within this discussion.

Throughout this book I examine various forms of the moving image and its concomitant travel and tourism themes, links, subtexts and connotations, bringing together research from a range of disciplines including cinema studies, communications and sociology as well as anthropology, considering it through a tourism lens, being my own background and perspective. Furthermore, research into the moving image itself (especially film) has shifted from what began as a more linear study of the technology and structure of films (primarily taking a supply-side perspective) towards considering the place and role of the audience (Popple & Kember, 2004). This provides us with a number of synergies with tourism studies, which has also moved from a more singular quantitative, economics-based field to incorporate more research into *why* tourists do things and not simply *what* they do, particularly in terms of its influence on, and being influenced by, cultural change. Notably, the view that audiences and tourists are passive consumers is being challenged, and forms the basis of much of the work introduced in this book.

While the direct observational elements of film-induced tourism have been well covered in the tourism literature, particularly in relation to destination marketing and management, there is little published work relating to the less quantifiable elements of this phenomenon such as travel and tourism and moving images in the cultural context 'of the day', particularly from the perspective of tourism academia. As Connell (2012: 19) concludes:

> Clearly, film tourism research within the cognate area of Tourism Studies has reached a tipping point. As a research community, we are now aware that film tourism occurs, that it is part of a range of motivators in the tourism destination decision-making process, that it creates a range of impacts, and has been adopted by savvy tourism marketers and businesses seeking uniqueness and novelty. ... It is an apposite time to move on from this point to prompt a more critical understand of film tourism, and in this shift, it will be essential to draw from cultural geography, social psychology, media studies and film theory approaches in future research.

Such disciplinary and thematic developments can also be represented visually, which is covered later in this chapter and has been based on ongoing studies outlined in various knowledge-based reviews (Beeton, 2010a, 2011). Running tangentially to Connell's and my own state-of-the-art reviews, others have taken the field of the moving image, travel and tourism further inwards, with researchers including Reijnders (2011) talking about their personal relationship with film and TV, tourism and the tourist's imagination, further internalising the experience of travel.

In addition, there have been some thought-provoking approaches published in the sociological and anthropological literature that assist to inform this work. As a case in point, Friedberg (1993) considers the link between film and tourism from a postmodern perspective, especially in terms of the subjective effects each has on their respective audiences and travellers/tourists, proposing that 'tourism produces an escape from boundaries' (Friedberg, 1993: 59). A further social sciences example is Strain's (2003) anthropological work on entertainment, cinema and tourism, where she notes that:

> the institutions of cinema, tourism, and anthropology all began their processes of development in the late nineteenth century ...: tourists provided information for early armchair anthropologists; anthropologists used film as a data-collecting tool; popular films were financed by tourist bureaus and tourist footage was integrated into popular films; anthropological texts charted out new tourist areas; and anthropologists and tourists were protagonists in popular films. (Strain, 2003: 19)

However, Blom (2007) argues that there are significant differences between anthropology and 'film culture', as the former presents a culture from an outsider's (*etic*) perspective, where he sees early non-fiction documentary film focusing more on the local inhabitants, presenting a non-mediated product. While this may have been true in certain cases, such as the early Icelandic travel films that Blom discusses, both anthropology and documentary film have changed significantly, with the anthropologist often claiming an *emic* insider's perspective, while film presents a more mediated and interpretive product.

Clearly, the study of film, travel and tourism is complex and continually developing, and I delve further into the development of knowledge and interdisciplinary literature in the section on 'Film-Induced Travel and Tourism' later in this chapter. However, a full review is not possible in a few paragraphs, so relevant literature is also discussed in the appropriate place throughout the book, providing the reader with a more comprehensive and relevant analysis.

Why the 'Moving Image'?

When we consider what I have in earlier publications termed 'film-induced tourism' (also referred to as cinematic tourism, movie-induced tourism, TV tourism, tele-tourism, and so on), it relates to both films that are consciously developed with tourism in mind, such as travelogues and their progeny, the TV travel show, through to other film genres, both fiction and non-fiction, where encouraging tourism is not a primary aim (Beeton, 2000, 2005a). That said, in 2007 the Australian Minister for Tourism, Fran Bailey, proposed that Tourism Australia commission and fully fund a soap opera aimed specifically at the flagging Japanese tourism market (Travel Today, 2007). Fortunately, this did not come to fruition, as it would have cost more than the organisation's entire annual tourism marketing budget, and there were serious concerns that the Japanese viewers would be aware that the series was not a fictional piece of entertainment, but a ruse to encourage them to visit, subsequently rejecting it in today's media-savvy world. Today, we see a more sophisticated approach to the use of film for destination marketing in the numerous collaborations between film and tourist commissions, as well as local governments and organisations.

Due to the various technological and creative developments we are witnessing today, I prefer to use the term *moving image* rather than film as it is more inclusive and representative of my own interests and the developing field of *contents tourism*, which is discussed later as well as in Beeton *et al.* (2013). The relationship between such popular media and tourism is between more than simply movies and TV – as noted earlier, the moving image in all its forms has the potential to move us, and can include computer/video games, film studio theme park 'reality' experiences and even holograms. This is a broad sphere, but so is the moving picture's influence on our cultural perspectives as well as our travel and tourism experiences – just because a programme was not made to promote tourism does not mean that it doesn't. More often than not, these 'accidental' or incidental tourism promotions become the most powerful forms of promotion, as viewers tend to resent and often reject overt promotional material in today's media-savvy age. That said, there remains a significant place and role for the travelogue or travel programme, as demonstrated in a number of the discussions in this publication.

Travel and Tourism

Much of the work in the ensuing chapters assumes a basic knowledge of tourism, particularly its 'story' over the past few centuries. However, I trust that this is being read by those with an interest in, but limited knowledge of, the tourism phenomenon. In order to provide all readers with an understanding of the tourism framework in which this study is situated, a brief historical outline follows, along with an introduction to the *tourist gaze* and the concept of mediation/mediatisation. But first, we consider the use of the terms *tourist* and *traveller*.

Travel or tourism: Travellers or tourists?

The debate continues as to what are the similarities and differences between the terms *travel* and *tourism* as well as *travellers* and *tourists*. While those in the tourism studies field tend to refer to tourism and tourists as relating to all travellers for pleasure or leisure (which includes those with the desire to develop knowledge and self as well as hedonistic pleasures), other disciplines tend to be far more precise and discriminatory. Amad (2006) is a case in point, describing travel as 'the practice of a privileged subject undertaking a demanding voyage in search of active experiences' and tourism as 'the practice of democratized masses signed up for recreational tours in search of distracting experiences' (Amad, 2006: 100), indicating a 'high art/low art' form of discrimination between these terms. Yet, within the field of tourism studies, such a description of 'tourism' relates more to the phenomenon of *mass tourism*, while Amad's so-called 'traveller' tends to be considered an *independent tourist*. The conceit that gaining knowledge or an understanding of others and oneself somehow belongs to an endeavour of a higher order than mere *tourism* is one I do not accept. One rarely travels without learning something and experiencing some pleasure.

After some discussion of the distinctions between the explorer, the traveller and the tourist, popular travel writer Donald Horne concludes that 'we might leave the word "tourist" with the more open meaning it has had for a couple of centuries, while recognising that the tourist experience can be enlightening, silly, deadening or depraved, according to circumstances' (Horne, 1992: 155).

While I acknowledge the existence of these different perspectives, I find the argument between 'traveller and tourist' somewhat moot; as John Urry points out, 'it is travel which is the absolute precondition for the emergence of mass tourism' (Urry, 1988: 35). However, the reader does need to understand the author's perspective in order to engage with the work. As the research underpinning this book progressed, I came to be more comfortable using the term 'traveller' in a broader sense as opposed to a more specific 'tourist'. Certainly, many film genres and stories are more related to a journey (or travelling), rather than the more traditional touristic activities. What viewers do afterwards, such as visiting film sites, is broadly considered to be 'tourism', yet they are travelling to get there, often inspired by travel-based narratives, where the journey can be more important than the destination.

Historical developments and contemporary popular media

Providing an historical synopsis of an activity as complex and nuanced as tourism is problematic, as we continue to uncover historical perspectives of the phenomenon, even as, through our desire to present a contained homogenous meta-story, we run the risk of reinforcing the current 'present mindedness and superficiality' (Walton, 2005: 6) of the topic. While this brief outline is selective and tends to focus on the accepted notions of the major social developments of the past few centuries as they relate to tourism, I also acknowledge the shifting sands on which such understanding is built, and hope that the discussions in this book contribute to broadening and even slightly altering our perspective on tourism.

From the times of antiquity (and even prior) there is evidence of travel by a wealthy elite for leisure and pleasure (tourism) as opposed to war and trade (conquering and commerce). It would seem that once a society obtained the time and money to travel they did so, which has been seen by some as a cultural/economic form of invasion and conquering (Amad, 2006). For example, travel was prevalent in Roman Augustan society (44 BC–AD 69) with a formalised itinerary comprising visiting a series of what they considered to be the important tourist sites, including tours of Greece, Asia Minor and Egypt. Travel writers such as Pausanias provided citizens with pre-travel information set out in voluminous guidebooks, including his *Guidebook of Greece* (Lomine, 2005). Such an itinerary and use of travel writing is close to how many of us travel today, whether on an organised tour or independently. Some of these earlier tourists also participated in a form of graffiti, with places bearing witness to scratchings such as 'Gaius Numidius Eros was here in year 28 of Caesar, returning from India, in the month Phamenoth' (Braund, 1985: 277). With a nod to the popular media of the day (literature), professional tour guides at Troy were identifying the places referred to in Homer's *Iliad*, including where Paris pronounced his judgement (Lomine, 2005: 74).

During the 13th and 14th centuries, religious pilgrimages became organised through the production of guidebooks and the development of a network of hospices to serve their needs. These pilgrims often wanted to participate in a mixture of broad cultural activities as well as their religious devotion and, by the 15th century, there were regular pilgrimage-based tours from Venice to the Holy Land (Urry, 2002). In his 1670 publication, *Voyage to Italy*, English Roman Catholic priest and tutor Richard Lessels coined the term 'The Grand Tour', when referring to the habit of upper class young men (often landed gentry) voyaging to France and Italy with a tutor in order to 'finish their education' of the world, *in the world*, through exposure to the cultural legacy of the Renaissance and classical antiquity. From the 17th century, the popular media of that time, literature and art, informed and developed the *Grand Tour* to incorporate more places than the initial focus on France and Italy, including Greece, Switzerland and Germany. At the time, this was the only way that people could view the major (and minor) works of art, architecture and other cultural artefacts, and there were entrepreneurs willing to capitalise on this opportunity. However, the experience was far broader than simply a 'high' cultural education, with the young lords receiving 'tutelage' in carousing and socialising away from the social constraints of their homeland. They also purchased a large range of souvenirs, from statues and furniture to personal portraits. This notion of a *Grand Tour* as a way to complete one's worldly education is not only found back then, but is also reflected today in the young backpackers' educational and hedonistic tours of the world, often taken as a rite of passage before settling in to further study, professional work or marriage.

Lasting from a few months to years, the *Grand Tour* remained the territory of the privileged elite until the changes in recreational possibilities produced by the Industrial Revolution. The Industrial Revolution of the 18th and 19th centuries had a profound effect on where and how people lived, with mass migration to the cities to work in the factories occurring simultaneously with the creation of mining and mill towns: how they worked, with half day and then a full day of no work being introduced; how they lived, which for many workers was in crowded insanitary conditions, but began to improve for a growing middle class of merchants, supervisors and managers; how they travelled, with the development of trains and steamships; and how they re-created, with new forms of entertainment coming out of the scientific developments, such as moving pictures. The development of a middle class who had the time and money to travel, along with a desire to return to a rural 'idyll' as a counterpoint to the busy, crowded and polluted cities and towns, increased the desire to travel for recreational purposes. The *Grand Tour* shifted from its classical style based on high cultural artefacts to a *Romantic Grand Tour*, focusing more on scenic beauty and an appreciation of the sublime (Urry, 2002).

Again, the popular media of the day played a major role, reflecting and enhancing the desire to return to a simpler, healthier, rural life as a counterpoint to the noisy, polluted industrial towns through the art, poetry and literature of the *Romantic Movement*. Creative people such as English poets Wordsworth and Samuel Taylor Coleridge, and artists such as Turner and Constable articulated this, while in France the paintings of Géricault and Delacroix as well as the plays, poems and novels of Victor Hugo all promoted the rural idyll. As a result, such popular media played a significant role towards influencing people's desire to travel, also informing them on where *and how* to travel. As the media became more developed and accessible through the innovations and inventions of the Industrial Revolution, we see the rise of the professional travel journalist encouraged by publishers such as Samuel Beeton who was among the first to understand that 'informative features on tourism could help to sell magazines' (Steward, 2005: 44). Beeton's innovation and perception as a publisher is also evident in his presentation of the famous *Mrs Beeton*'s cookery books, where together they pioneered what has now become the standard format of presenting the ingredients of the recipes separately from the preparation and cooking instructions.

At the same time, transport was becoming more open and accessible to larger numbers of people through improved roads, increased safety and the development of the steam train and steamship. In fact, the railways around the world took an active interest in promoting tourism to the places their trains travelled to, with many early tourism posters featuring such sites (Horne, 1992). To support the increasing number of tourism travellers, the railways also constructed lavish accommodation and recreation resorts at places such as Niagara Falls in North America, at the seaside in the UK (where visitors from the polluted mining towns could 'take the air'), and even Mount Buffalo in Australia, where the only accommodation was the Victorian Railways owned and operated chalet. Steamships also promoted travel to exotic places, with shipping lines such as the Orient and Pacific Steam Navigation Companies publishing the *Orient Line Guide* in 1882, and future editions celebrating not only where the ships sailed to, but also the changes in seafaring technology and the development of specialised cruise ships (MacKenzie, 2005).

Accordingly, the transport developments made places more accessible, the popular media made them more desirable, while work patterns gave more people the time and money to travel, with a concomitant rise in travel and tourism around the (developed) world. It is this historical correlation with the moving image that informs the following chapters, demonstrating the relationship between moving images and moving people.

Glancing at the Gaze and its Mediation/Mediatisation

The Latin term *curiositas* helps us to understand the concept of the 'gaze', whether in medicine (where its genesis lies), film or tourism. Variously defined, *curiositas* historically represented a fascination with the spectacle, containing notions of anxiety, care, refinement and elaboration along with curious enquiry, and was considered in the medieval period to be a temptation and vice, a *lust of the eyes*, invoking demons. Seen as a potential threat to Christian orthodoxy, it was received with suspicion and hostility by the Church (Zacher, 1976). However, over time the meaning of *curiositas* moved away from denoting a religious Christian 'sin' to come to be viewed as a legitimate secular motive for travelling the world, and the notions of curiosity and *spectacle* were accepted as an integral part of the experience. As Adler explains, '[t]he virtuosi came in time to be known as "curious travellers," travel handbooks marking objects for their attention as "curiosities," and designing itineraries which might "gratify the curiosity by degrees"' (Adler, 1989: 15).

Today, the term *curiosity* is used to describe an inquisitiveness and eagerness for knowledge, and in turn links us to the concept of *the gaze*. The *medical gaze*, described by Foucault (1976) in relation to the socially organised and systematised gaze of a medic, is what we can now refer to as a *curious* gaze. However, the use of the gaze has expanded to incorporate other fields that can also be seen to contain elements of *curiositas*, including film (moving images) and tourism. Friedberg (1993: 4) notes that, in direct response to the 19th-century development of transport, architecture, urbanisation and visualisation through photography and film, which 'brought the past to the present, the distant to the near, the miniscule to its enlargement', a *mobilised virtual gaze* became apparent. Friedberg goes on to argue that film is not actually a direct gaze between the viewer and the subject (object), but a received perception that has been already mediated, becoming a 'virtual' gaze.

When we take the 'mobilised' elements of this gaze, it incorporates the cultural physical activities of walking and travelling as well as the more sedentary activity of viewing a film, where on the one hand the person moves, while on the other, it is the image that moves.

Echoing elements of the aforementioned *virtual mobile gaze* and further systematising while at the same time broadening the concept of the gaze, sociologist John Urry coined the term, *tourist gaze*. This was clearly differentiated by its tourism context and resonated with the activity of tourists gazing upon sites and sights and often taking representations of this gaze home for others to gaze upon. Yet, as can be seen even from this brief discussion, the notion of gazing and its relation to curiosity is far more complex. In the second edition of his 1990 seminal work, *The Tourist Gaze: Leisure and Travel in Contemporary Societies,* Urry explains that 'this book then is about how in different societies and especially within different social groups in diverse historical periods the tourist gaze has changed and developed' (Urry, 2002: 1).

He explains that so-called 'gazes' vary in terms of the social group and historical period being studied as well as being constructed 'through difference' (Urry, 2002: 1). That is, a gaze must have a counterpoint with which it can be compared and contrasted, such as the domestic non-tourist activities of home and work versus the seemingly more exotic experiences of the tourist. As noted at the beginning of this chapter, the notion of tourism is one of difference and movement – from one place to another, one state to another, and so on. In this manner, tourists objectify and subsequently interpret their experience. In the third edition (*The Tourist Gaze 3.0*), Urry confirms that 'the gaze is a socially organised and systematized, as is the gaze of the medic' (Urry & Larsen, 2011: 1).

While Urry categorises the tourist gaze into three comparative areas, namely 'the romantic/collective ... authentic/inauthentic ... [and] ... historic/modern' (Urry, 2002: 75), we have seen Friedberg and others refer to a *mediated* mobile or virtual gaze to describe a more imaginary stroll (flâneurie) through imaginary places and times, as in some films. The flâneur, one who 'walks the city in order to experience it' (Baudelaire, 1986[1863]) is often seen in tourism, which is examined further in Part 2. Consequently, the notion of developing a visualisation of the travel experience into a *gaze* parallels the development of tourism in terms of the use of visual media such as painting, sketching, photography and film as a way to describe the experience, recall emotions and fantasise.

Along with the development of mass media and its role in 'making meaning' for the viewer, the tourist gaze itself is becoming increasingly mediatised, for the independent as well as the mass tourist (Beeton *et al.*, 2005). As Jansson (2002) argues, the more organised tourism becomes, the more mediatised and simulated it also becomes through the use of guidebooks, travel magazines, tourist brochures and moving images. This notion is supported by Griffiths (2006: 246) reference to a 'technologically mediated tourist gaze' as illustrated by the 3D IMAX film, *Across the Sea of Time* (1996), which applies the developing technologies of film and photographic media to its story.

While Urry's earlier editions of *The Tourist Gaze* (1990, 2002) did not go into any depth regarding the moving image when describing his version of the *gaze* (apart from a brief mention of the democratising role of television in terms of the role that *vision* plays in the development of tourism), he does note that, from around the middle of the 19th century, 'tourism and photography became welded together' (Urry, 2002: 149) both as an act of the tourist and that of the promoter or recorder. In *The Tourist Gaze 3.0*, he and co-author Larsen note that 'major films and soap operas often cause tourist flows where few roamed before the location was made visible upon the silver screen' (Urry & Larsen,

2011: 116); however, connections between the tourist gaze and media gaze do not appear to be explicit. Jansson further notes that 'the tourist gaze has become more and more intertwined with the consumption of media images' (Jansson, 2002: 431), while Beeton develops this linkage to include moving pictures, arguing that 'film has become the singular most influential form of creative art today, reaching mass populations never before envisaged or possible' (Beeton, 2005a: 6). These three statements move our gaze from still images to today's mass-media forms of the moving image.

However, the very act of gazing changes what is being looked at, tending to transfer it to a *thing* that is being observed in isolation through the world of the viewer, rather than in relation to its own world of existence. As Horne (1992: 6) notes, '[h]owever sympathetic we are as tourists ... [w]e create a new culture – the culture of tourist-observed objects and people'. The gaze of the poet, writer, artist or cameraman (still or moving), also creates something new that often further influences our gaze as a tourist. And so the cycle continues. ...

Despite the fact that this discussion of the gaze and notions of mediation/mediatisation has been extremely brief and does not come to any definitive conclusion or meta-description of the concepts, it serves as a point from which we can begin to view the complex relationships between moving images and tourism. It also illustrates the numerous divergent yet, in many ways, connected perspectives that can emerge in any such value-laden discourse.

Understanding Audiences

There is an extensive body of work in the fields of psychology, communication and media studies relating to understanding (film) audiences and their reactions, responses and activities. It is not my aim to summarise all of the trends in the literature, but rather to introduce some theories that point towards a potential connection between film and tourism as outlined below, with the inferred links and framework further developed throughout the book.

While there remain those who consider audiences to be primarily passive, non-critical consumers of mass media, research into audience participation in the communications field has moved from a focus on studying 'passive' spectators absorbing all with which they were presented towards a more inclusive analysis of involved, active audiences (Eco, 1986; Evans, 2007; King & Krzywinska, 2002; Stranieri, 2000). Turnbull (2009) supports this, arguing that they not only actively engage with the media, but also often create their own ways in which to do this, which could be through tourism. Evans (2007) argues that this is not a binary active/passive dichotomy, finding that audiences often engage actively and passively simultaneously. Certainly, researchers now tend to see audiences as engaging actively with what they are viewing, whether undertaking the experience as a group at the cinema or individually on one's television, personal computer or other personal viewing apparatus. This can be conceptualised as an emotional connection while viewing the media, but can also extend to consider a more active participatory role before, during and especially after viewing a movie, television programme or other form of moving image. The clearest link here with tourism relates to certain types of engagement (usually in the public arena) after viewing, which is discussed throughout this book. However, there remain other, less demonstrable and private connections between the moving image and tourism which we also consider as the narrative of this book unfolds.

Nevertheless, the concept that an audience's emotional interaction moves from the private and personal out into a more public arena is not new, with psychologists Horton and Wohl in 1956 presenting the notion of *para-social relationships* between actors and audience. They describe this as a one-sided relationship where one person believes they know the other, while the second party has no knowledge of the first. Such relationships occur with fans and their idols, and can relate closely to movies and other forms of the moving image. Horton and Wohl explain this concept by stating that:

> [o]ne of the striking characteristics of the new mass media – radio, television, and the movies – is that they give the illusion of a face-to-face relationship with the performer. The conditions of response to the performer are analogous to those in a primary group. The most remote and illustrious men are met *as if they* were in the circle of one's peers; the same is true of a character in a story who comes to life in these media in an especially vivid and arresting way. We propose to call this seeming face-to-face relationship between spectator and performer a *para-social relationship*. (Horton & Wohl, 1956: 218)

In spite of its resonance with today's celebrity-obsessed society, Horton and Wohl's work was virtually ignored until the growth of interest in communication and media studies during the 1970s (Giles, 2002). Studies since then have examined viewers' para-social interaction (PSI) with soap opera characters (Auter & Davis, 1991; Cohen, 1999; Geraghty, 1991; Rubin & Perse, 1987), TV newscasters (Levy, 1979; Rubin *et al.*, 1985), children's TV characters (Reeves & Greenberg, 1977) and TV performers (Feilitzen & Linn, 1975; Turner, 1993) as well as reality show participants and talk-back radio

Table 1.1 Typology of audience activity

Audience orientation	Communication sequence		
	Before exposure	During exposure	After exposure
Selective	Selective exposure-seeking		
Involved		Decoding and interpreting	
'Using'			Social utilities

Source: Levy and Windahl (1984: 54).

personalities (Rubin & Step, 2000). The concept can also relate to the actors in other forms of the moving image, particularly film stars and celebrities in general (Dietz *et al.*, 1991; Stever, 2009; Wohlfeil & Whelan, 2012) and even animated characters (see Chapter 10 for more on animation, attraction and tourism). While some film tourism researchers, such as Kim (2011), are beginning to consider this rich heritage of audience research from the communication and media studies fields in relation to tourism, at the time of writing there was little published material, suggesting an extremely rich vein of material yet to be explored.

As a way to conceptualise audience interaction, Rosengren and Windahl (1972) identified two dimensions of PSI, from imagining oneself being in the action to identifying with fictional characters by talking about them as if they are real. It is not such a great stretch to see audiences visiting places to re-enact (or act out) the action or character they have identified with on the screen. Through ensuing studies of mass media audiences and communication in relation to television viewing, Levy and Windahl (1984) developed a typology of audience activity (Table 1.1) which acknowledges that there are activities that occur after exposure to the media.

While they have not related this to corporeal activities such as travel and tourism, there are certain tourism-related synergies with what they refer to as the realm of 'social utilities'. What Levy and Windahl are primarily referring to in relation to the audience orientation of 'using' social utilities is that viewers may reflect on, discuss and integrate information after their exposure to the media. Throughout this book, I argue that audiences go even further in this post-exposure phase, often undertaking activities that have been influenced by the prior media exposure, participating in active re-creations and interpretations along with a more internal emotional engagement or experience. Therefore, I propose that the typology be reconfigured to reflect the tourism linkages, as in Table 1.2.

Table 1.2 Typology of audience and tourist activity

Audience orientation	Communication sequence		
	Before film exposure	During film exposure	After exposure
Selective	Selective exposure-seeking	Reinforcing existing norms	
Involved		Decoding and interpreting	Internal/involved utilities: • sacred journeys/pilgrimage; • emotional tourism experiences.
'Using'			Social utilities: • talking (or social networking) about film experience; • undertaking tourism activities with others; • re-creation; • sharing (talking or social networking about) emotional tourism experiences.

Source: Adapted from Levy and Windahl (1984).

In a somewhat prescient statement, Horton and Wohl (1956) pre-empted today's studies of film inducing fans to travel to re-enact scenes and experiences from their favourite shows by noting that:

> If we have emphasized the opportunities offered for playing a vicarious or actual role, it is because we regard this as the key operation in the spectator's activity, and the chief avenue of the program's meaning for him [sic]. (Horton & Wohl, 1956: 221)

In a review of the PSI literature, Giles presents the stages of the development of para-social relationships, which is reproduced in Figure 1.1. In terms of travel to film sets and sites, we can add a dimension to this model, or incorporate visits to the physical places as 'other encounters', 'imagined interaction' or even 'attempt to contact' if the visit is to a hot set where filming is occurring. However, in most cases the locational site visits would come into 'imagined interaction'. A nice example of this was when I was studying the Australian TV series, *Sea Change* (1998–2000), as related in *Film-Induced*

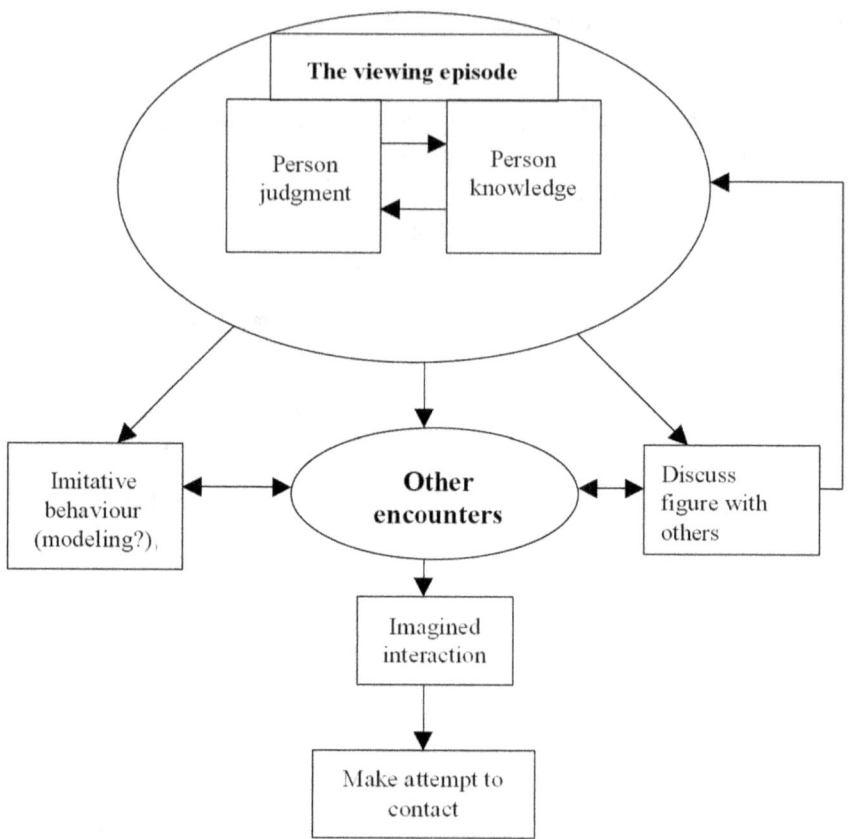

Figure 1.1 Stages in the development of a para-social relationship
Source: Giles (2002: 297).

Tourism (2005a). I was interviewing a couple staying in the cottage that had been the home of the romantic lead and, at the end of the interview, the husband commented to me that his wife had been 'pretending to be Sigrid' all weekend. Sigrid Thornton was the actor, not the character, so she was not only imagining an interaction, but also being the celebrity, linking with Celebrity Worship Syndrome as well as PSI.

Hills (2002, 2005), in his studies on fans, also brings in notions of PSI, which is discussed in the section on Fans later in this chapter, while Gilles Deleuze (1989) observes that, when viewers recollect (or even perceive) their cinematic experience, 'the physical and the mental, or rather the images, continually followed each other, running behind each other and referring back to each other around a point of indiscernibility' (Deleuze, 1989: 69). It is this personal, active, iterative practice that has further informed my understanding of the ways in which audiences respond to moving images, and then later in recollection, which includes when visiting film sets, locations and sites.

Such concepts of audience involvement and their subsequent tourism activity (both emotional and physical) are discussed throughout this publication, playing a key role in helping us to understand the complex relationships between tourism and the moving image. This model is further developed in the following section.

Film-Induced Travel and Tourism

In the introduction to a special edition on Film Tourism in the journal *Tourism Planning and Development*, I discussed the advance of film tourism not only in relation to the articles presented in that edition, but also in a more general overview of the literature (Beeton, 2010a). Due to the multi-disciplinary nature of the contributors (which had become an imperative in my own studies), I could further develop my case for the need to link with other disciplinary work.

The work of Riley, Tooke, Baker and van Doren is generally acknowledged as the first to publish in the field of movie-related tourism (Riley, 1994; Riley & van Doren, 1992; Riley *et al.*, 1998; Tooke & Baker, 1996). While they remain the first in the tourism literature, speculative thought was already being applied to this phenomenon by researchers in other disciplines. As a case in point, in 1979 psychologist Kindem (1979)discussed the difficulties of predicting a film's tourism potential through simply using economic factors, proposing that semiotics, ideology and psychology come into play and need to be considered. Kindem's proposal was not taken up nor even noticed in the tourism field, in part because he was 'before his time' in his musings, but also due to the initial need to justify movie-induced tourism (as it was initially termed) as an appropriate area of academic study. Riley and the others noted above primarily focused on locating evidence of a growth in visitor numbers post movie screening, arguing that movies and tourism require further research from a business and marketing perspective.

I developed the model in Figure 1.2 in order to illustrate how inquiry into film-induced tourism has progressed from early speculative work into what I have termed 'higher inquiry', which by its very nature is multi-disciplinary. Interestingly, it was quite easy to find a thematic pattern and chronological pathway, and while the development has not been solely linear, there has

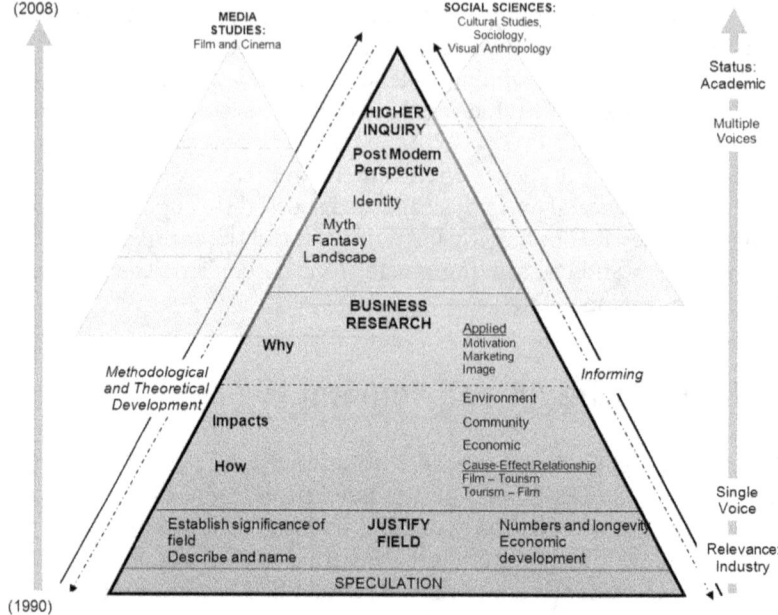

Figure 1.2 Model of film-induced tourism knowledge development
Source: Beeton (2010: 4).

been a clear progression over time that builds on earlier studies. It was also prompted by my discovery of film tourism based literature in other disciplines which had not engaged with the tourism literature. In particular, in a special issue on Tourism and the Moving Image of the journal *Tourist Studies* (2006), none of the authors referred to the body of tourism literature that related to film; however, they provided me with a good source of information from other disciplines, and expanded my own knowledge and thinking about film and tourism as well as supporting my burgeoning ideas and personal philosophy. Nevertheless, I was concerned that these authors were not accessing the extensive work already done in the tourism field. This led me to consider how and why these bodies of literature develop and also marked the beginning of my ongoing calls for cross-disciplinary research and knowledge sharing, which was also a driver for this book.

The various levels in this model (Figure 1.2) incorporate much of the tourism literature to date, commencing with Kindem's (1979) speculation as to how to predict a film's popularity in attracting tourists. As noted above, some 15 years later, tourism researchers began to look at this area, with a focus on justifying this little-studied phenomenon as one worthy of academic examination and research. This early work into film-induced tourism primarily centred on the numbers of people visiting the places featured in movies, aiming to provide empirical evidence of the significance of this new field of study. For example, Tooke and Baker (1996) cite the influence of the movie *Close Encounters of the Third Kind* (1977) on visitor numbers, with an increase to Devil's Tower National Monument (which features significantly in the movie) of 74% in the year following the movie's release. They also noted that, 11 years later, 20% of visitors to the monument had first heard of it via the movie. In a study of the small village of Goathland in the UK, where the TV series *Heartbeat* (1992–2009) was filmed, visitors increased from 200,000 to a staggering 1.3 million after the series aired (Beeton, 2005a).

Once the actual size of film-induced tourism had been established, research moved more into the business realm, particularly in terms of marketing, destination imaging and motivation. Popular media has been well documented as a form of image development and tourism marketing, with Crofts (1989) relating the success of *Crocodile Dundee* (1986) as the first movie to be used consciously and simultaneously to develop tourism to Australia. In fact, Paul Hogan was already known in the United States through contemporary Australian tourism advertisements, which commenced well before the movie. In New Zealand, Croy and Walker (2003) conducted research into the use of feature films by NZ regional tourism organisations, finding that a significant number saw the use of films to promote their destinations as important.

While Riley and Van Doren (1992) considered movies as a 'pull' factor in tourist motivation, Macionis (2004) combined Crompton's (1979) push-pull construct with Iso-Ahola's (1987) escape-seeking dichotomy, noting that 'the push and pull framework provides a simple and intuitive approach for explaining the motivations underlying film tourist behaviour' (Macionis, 2004: 89). In my 2005 publication, *Film-Induced Tourism*, I considered the complexity of film tourists' motivation to include their desire to re-live an experience (or even emotion) encountered in the film, to reinforce a myth, storytelling or fantasies, or for reasons of status (or celebrity) (Beeton, 2005a).

As the 20th century drew to a close, interest in the impacts of tourism increased, which is also mirrored in relation to film tourism, with researchers studying the host communities where TV series and movies are set and/or filmed (Beeton, 2000, 2001; Mordue, 1999, 2001). These were still primarily management issues, with a business focus, yet widened to include host communities rather than simply tourism operations. As the concept of corporate social responsibility (CSR) in tourism developed, I argued that film corporations need to take some responsibility for the potentially negative legacy they may leave once filming is completed, particularly in small, vulnerable communities (Beeton, 2007).

Once one moves beyond the business of film-induced tourism, postmodern epistemologies of inversion, authenticity, simulacra and play come into the equation, blurring the simplistic notions of film promoting tourism to places, which I have referred to in the model as 'Higher Inquiry'. This would include Urry's discussion of the tourist gaze in a postmodern context as well as Hirschman's (2000) consideration of the popularity and subsequent influence of film in terms of myth telling. Hirschman noted that 'the mythic impulse has always enthralled the human imagination' (Hirschman, 2000: 4), while Frost introduced the relationship of historic films to heritage tourism, stating that 'historic films may stimulate visitations to places that have little current visual relationship to what was viewed in the film' (Frost, 2006: 248). This is where those of us in the tourism field started to locate the research being done in other disciplines, such as visual anthropology, where the relationship between travelogues and tourism is demonstrated in the publication *Virtual Voyages: Cinema and Travel* (Ruoff, 2006b), and sociology, where Torchin (2002) added multiple perspectives (and voices) to the mix. Torchin's study looked at the film-induced tours of New York based operator, Manhattan TV Tours, in terms of the way the tour guides 'animate[d] local multiple locations in single sites: historical New York, New York's lived reality, the production history, and the fictive worlds' (Torchin, 2002: 259). The aforementioned special issue on Tourism and the Moving Image of the journal *Tourist Studies* (2006) presents a range of interesting work: Tzanelli on the construction of what she has termed the 'cinematic tourist' (via *The Lord of the Rings*); Iwashita on a relatively rare paper on Japanese tourists' imaging of the UK via the media (work which she is continuing via 'contents tourism' as discussed in Beeton *et al.*, 2013); Graml on the relationship between *The Sound of Music* (1965) tourism and Austria's national identity; Gibson on virtual mobility and the cinematic travel gaze (or glance); Sydney-Smith on crime film and tourism; as well as Pritchard and Morgan on fashion and exoticism as presented in the media (*Conde Nast Traveller*). This series of articles went some way to presenting tourism and film in the social sciences disciplines of sociology and anthropology, and in many ways connects back to the 'higher inquiry' aspects from the tourism field. Tzanelli followed up her work introduced in this journal with a book, *The Cinematic Tourist* (2007), where she discusses aspects of consumption, authenticity and the tourist gaze.

These disciplinary areas are presented in the model as separate pyramids with their own concomitant history of knowledge development, only partially intersecting with tourism studies. This is intentional, as it became clear that, while tourism researchers were broadening their base into other disciplines, it was (and remains) rare to see the reverse – little of the literature of film and tourism from other disciplines acknowledges the large body of tourism literature.

The pyramid structure of the model is not intended to preclude the earlier studies as, while it is important to introduce new research concepts, many earlier theories retain their relevance and application. Often, the later ('higher level') studies further inform the earlier work, providing further development in fields such as business-related research. The model enables us to see where we have gone, where we are going and where we still need to go in terms of knowledge development, both theoretical and practical. A primary goal of academic research should be theoretical development – academia is the place where the difficult questions need to be asked and concepts developed.

From the discussion so far we can see that the overall relationship between the moving image and tourism, coined in previous publications as film-induced tourism, cinematic tourism, movie-induced tourism, and so on, is extremely broad, personal and complex, which I have previously described as encompassing a range of forms, and have continued to develop as my own perspectives have developed, broadened and deepened, as outlined in Table 1.1.

Due to this diverse range of film tourism forms (and products), in this publication I have chosen to move away from a supply-driven description, such as the above, towards an exploration of the moving image and tourism in a far broader temporal and thematic sense. In order to address this in the work discussed in this publication, I move from the pre-cinema scenarios through to the internet age, embracing many aspects of the moving image.

In an earlier approach to what I termed *film-induced tourism*, I described the various different types of film tourism in relation to the tourist's motivation to visit a film site, be that primary, secondary or tertiary, which I referred to as incidental or even accidental (Beeton, 2005a). I have argued elsewhere that, while there has been a dominant approach to film (movies and TV) as a primary tourism motivator from the perspective of many general media stories and destination marketing organisations (DMOs) and from commentators such as Grihault (2003), it is more often the case that film has been incidental to the tourism experience (Beeton, 2005a, 2010b; NFO New Zealand, 2003). As noted in a previous article, 'this incidental nature of film related tourism is a significant aspect that has not been adequately explored or appropriately articulated in the current research' (Beeton, 2011: 51). By tracing the historical antecedents of film from a tourism perspective, we are able to examine the considerable role played by such media-based, non-primary and often unintentional tourism motivators.

Cultural change, moving images, tourism and travel

> *The only thing that is constant is change.*
> Heroditus, 5th century BC

As noted by Grünewald (2002: 1004), '[c]ulture change has been a concern in tourism anthropology studies ever since this field of research established itself ...'. He goes on to discuss various aspects of interest to anthropologists and sociologists regarding the host community under the aegis of 'cultural revival', finding that there are those who not only re-create an 'authentic' culture, but also invent certain traditions for commercial tourism consumption.

It is easy to accuse tourism of not simply preserving past cultures, but also creating one that may not have existed; furthermore, tourists' demands for such experiences can also force communities away from developing or modernising. These are common observations of the effect that tourism can have on a community, which at times can result in a certain cultural stagnation or even regression due to the tourists' desire to experience an imagined past.

Many years ago (shortly after I had enrolled in a graduate tourism programme), I attended a symposium on travel and tourism held by travel publisher *Lonely Planet*, where one of the speakers, travel essayist Pico Iyer, articulated what I was beginning to feel, but was too overwhelmed by the articulate, thoughtful audience to acknowledge. The discussion was about tourists' impacts on indigenous communities, in particular acculturation or even the demonstration effect where, by seeing us with our Western goods and behaviour, members of these communities develop a desire for them. Everyone was being very politically correct, discussing how they as travellers need to be aware of this and prevent it from happening. Then Pico took the microphone and said words to the effect of 'What right have WE to tell the Balinese woman that she can't use a food processor to prepare her temple offerings? Who are WE to say what they can and can't have?' I almost cheered at his inference that, instead of being sensitive travellers, we were actually replicating a form of cultural imperialism, where we knew what was best for them. His point was also that change will happen and can be for 'good'. I spoke to Pico about this many years later, and he remembered feeling very concerned about being so controversial, but to this day I hold his words close when I travel, as well as in my studies.

So, travel and tourism can change cultures, preserve them or even lock them into an imagined past, all of which present dramatic opportunities and challenges. Related to this, tourism can also work towards maintaining the status quo of the privileged visitor versus the exotic 'other'.

If we then look at the moving image, we can see where social change influences both the storyline and presentation of moving images such as films and TV, technologically as well as ideologically, while other films are used, both consciously and unconsciously, to instigate such change (such as the anti-war movies of the Vietnam era). However, films also provide escapism and entertainment, yet often work to maintain a status quo. The influence of Hollywood during WWI and WWII is a case in point, and is discussed in the following chapters.

Both film and tourism present us with a cornucopia of political and critical implications in terms of viewer and traveller attitudes and behaviour towards the places and communities which are presented, either in film or through travel and tourism. These elements are evident throughout this publication, and need to be kept in mind while reading it. While not a recent phenomenon, dating back to the 1920s (Bronner, 2011), the contemporary development of what has become known as 'Critical Studies' (or even the 'critical turn') in the social sciences goes some way towards providing us with the tools and perspectives from which to examine cultural change relating to tourism and, in this instance, film. As Bramwell and Lane (2014: 1) explain:

> In general, the new critical studies often seek to undertake theoretically and conceptually informed critical analysis, reveal power relations, understand different world views, develop political insights, and encourage progressive change and emancipation. (Bramwell & Lane, 2014: 1)

While not all of these elements are openly articulated in my own studies outlined in this book, many of the theoretical approaches I take are based on my attempts to tease many of them out. In particular, the reflexive nature of many of the autoethnographical cases in this book bring out elements of power relations and change, while also uncovering multiple subjective world views. Furthermore, my work here reflects the notion that there are no absolutes, but rather varying perspectives, as described by Bronner (2011).

Places of the imagination and the fans

One cannot consider film-induced tourism without either coming across, or even being a 'fan'. As Hills (2002) points out, we all 'know' what a fan is, but in order to be able to adequately analyse this phenomenon, he goes on to discuss academic definitions of fandom and the cult of the media, concluding that he does not find it possible to settle on single definitive definition. He ultimately arrives at the decision to use the term 'cult fan' for his work, as he believes that cult fandom implies a cultural identity, and one that I believe also can be associated with tourism. We can also find a link with travel and tourism in many of the examples he provides, such as *Casablanca* (1942), *Dr Who* (2005–), *The X-Files* (1993–2002) and *Coronation Street* (1960–), particularly when he notes that 'it is always performative' (Hills, 2002: iv) and can be seen today with the fans of *Game of Thrones* (2011). Many of those studying film tourists have also noted fandom behaviours, such as Graml (2006), Roesch (2007, 2009) and Buchman *et al.* (2010).

Hills also argues that fans are often not simply fans of one text (programme, movie, book or character), but rather that many are fans of numerous, seemingly unrelated texts or icons, and can be spatially mapped (Hills, 2002, 2005). In terms of these fans as tourists, we can consider this in relation to having quite distinct experiences based around travelling to numerous places that represent different texts, or even different sites within the same place. If we look at the personal examples that I use throughout this book, my own fan-based activities and experiences reflect this multi-modality.

Interestingly, Hills concludes his chapter, 'Cult geographies', by taking Horton and Wohl's (1956) work on PSI and introducing the notion of *paraspatial* interactions when considering the meaning and value that a fan may assign to specific places (Hills, 2002). This coalesces with my own use of the PSI of film audiences as tourists, outlined earlier. He sees the fan-tourist as directly valorising specific places that have been presented by the media text, rather than having it mediated through contemporary tourism practices. This supports the notions of the active role of these fans, from viewing through to experiencing a place or attending an event.

Locating imagination

In a most engaging publication, Reijnders refers to the relationship between film and tourism in terms of the 'symbolic contrast between imagination and reality' (Reijnders, 2011: 17). Based on ethnographic research and study, he proposes a model that I have found extremely interesting, in part reflecting my own interest in the way our imagination enriches our tourism experiences. He proposes a circular model of what he refers to as 'media tourism', where the creators are inspired by physical places in Phase 1, then through their imagination/s they construct the stories which are then transformed into imaginary places that become appropriated by fans who go in search of the actual (physical) places. As I moved through my research for this work, I found that this cyclical, iterative model got me thinking about how, if we think about it in relation to the 'typology of audience and tourist activity' shown in Table 1.2, we can develop (yet another) model to frame the work presented in this publication. However, I don't totally agree with Reijnder's model in terms of separating it along the lines of 'Imagination' and 'Perception', which I consider to be part of one another and not describing a delineation between imagined and physical places as he proposes.

Bringing it together: A model of audience and tourist activity

While there will be further theoretical developments regarding the process of travel and tourism and the moving image, after over 30 years of professional as well as academic exposure to film-induced tourism and the subsequent work of others, I have re-imagined and re-constructed my previously adapted Levy and Windahl model to more fully express my perceptions and understanding. So, Figure 1.3 re-presents the earlier model in an iterative style that currently frames my thinking by taking the audience themes introduced by Levy and Windahl, incorporating them with film touristic activities and emotions, illustrating the areas that cross over from before, during and after being exposed to a filmic experience (that is, watching and responding to a movie, TV series and other forms of the moving image and then participating in some form of remembering via tourist activities).

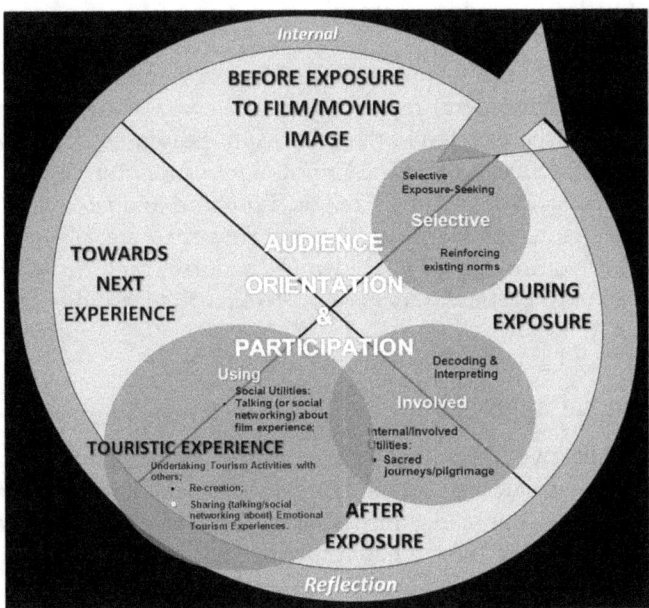

Figure 1.3 Modelling the relationship between audience and tourist activity

There is an overlap of the audience orientation and participation circle with those of 'Selective', 'Involved' and 'Using' as it connects both internally and externally with each individual. In the external realm we see the more public actions of the film tourist, which has been the basis of many previous publications. There is an element of *reflection* that is not easy to illustrate without confusing the model, which at its very best is a simplification of the process; nevertheless, I have attempted to do this by placing the 'Reflection' activity as part of the surrounding 'internal' arrow, which suggests that it is an overlayed aspect of this process.

In many ways, the stories and emotional representations present the viewer with a way in which to travel through similar places, either literally or figuratively.

Theoretical Framework

While the model above incorporates a range of theoretical perspectives, it is primarily about touristic and film 'activity'; the framework that forms the structure of the work in this book also encapsulates other theoretical approaches. The most relevant comprise the role of narrative and its link to travel and tourism, the place of imagination, the relevance of genre and fan theory.

Narrative as a research approach as well as communication is becoming more prominent in tourism research, often viewed as part of the 'critical turn' in tourism studies referred to earlier, and is discussed in some detail in the publication of that name (*The Critical Turn in Tourism Studies: Innovative Research Methodologies*) edited by Ateljvic, Pritchard and Morgan (2007). For example, the chapter by Harris *et al.* notes that they are 'playing with particular styles of communication (academic discourse combined with personal narrative) to send a particular message ... to a particular audience ...' (Harris *et al.*, 2007: 42).

Methodological approach

While qualitative researchers have criticised the overreliance on the positivist, quantitative paradigm in many fields of endeavour, it remains a dominant approach in many disciplines, including tourism. Holbrook finds himself 'often musing over what rampant lack of self-confidence would encourage a mechanical reliance on such self-imprisoning safeguards and such vision-restricting formulas' (Holbrook, 2005: 48). It can be argued that this is due to the fact that much of the tourism research is embedded within the cultures of many management or business based departments, along with the increasing reliance on measuring research 'quality' through quantitative assessments. This is also reflected in the previous model of knowledge development.

In the past, I have found participant-observation to be a powerful research method, especially when the researcher is immersed in the study. What is interesting, though, is that in many so-called participant-observation studies, the 'participatory' element is ignored, with the researcher referring more to what he/she observed, with very little about what he/she personally experienced, rendering many of these studies to be more of an outside observation than participant-observation. However, when the study is written from a deep level of immersion, the results can be very powerful. Such a deep level of immersion, where the personal experiences of the researcher are part of the study itself, leads us to consider the autoethnographic approach, which Noy (2007: 351) considers to be 'a critical and reflexive method of inquiry'.

Autoethnography

According to Jamal and Hollingshead (2005), notions of seeing, being, meaning, knowing and identity are central to the tourism experience, which in turns leads us into areas that are personal and even private. In order to research the more internal, deeply personal reactions and subsequent constructions, the process must be approached differently. One such approach may be autoethnography. However, tourism researchers from the interpretive paradigm are not immune to a reliance on using the same research methods again and again, with Westwood (2005) claiming that they are not necessarily open to the newer qualitative techniques in tourism research. This can limit attempts to uncover deeper, more personal issues that are not simple to uncover. As evidence of this occurring in other fields not dissimilar to tourism in terms of knowledge development, Holt (2003) relates his attempts to get an autoethnographic piece of research related to teaching (Holt, 2001) published in qualitative journals through presenting a further autoethnographic story.

As an educator, often when travelling I stand outside myself and examine my emotions and experiences as a tourist, bringing such reflections back to the classroom to illustrate a point as well as to develop an empathetic relationship with my students. Often my reflections revolve around the pervasive power of the popular culture I grew up in and live in, particularly in relation to television, cinema and music. Such a reflexive approach is also a valid form of academic research – one where the researcher becomes the researched. Supporting my personal musings, Mick (2005) sees self-observation as a valid *autoethnographic* research approach, with Denzin

Table 1.3 Forms and characteristics of tourism and the moving image

Form	Characteristic	Example
Motivation		
Film tourism as primary travel motivator	The film site (or studio) is an attraction in its own right – strong enough to motivate visitation	Disneyland
Film tourism as part of a holiday	Visiting film locations (or studios) as an activity within a larger holiday	Movie tours of numerous films in cities such as New York, New Orleans
On-location		
Film tourism pilgrimage	Visiting sites of films in order to 'pay homage' to the film. Possible re-enactments and potential primary motivator	Doune Castle (*Monty Python*) *Lord of the Rings* sites in New Zealand
Celebrity film tourism	Homes of celebrities Film locations that have taken on celebrity status	Hollywood homes
Nostalgic film tourism	Visiting film locations that represent another era	Mayberry: *Andy Griffith Show* (1950s era) Goathland: *Heartbeat* (1960s era)
Commercial		
Constructed film tourism attraction	An attraction constructed after the filming purely to attract/serve tourists	Heartbeat Experience (Whitby, UK)
Film/movie tours	Tours developed to various film locations	On Location Tours, The Movie Tours
Guided tours at specific on-location set	Tours of specific sites, often on private land	Hobbiton, New Zealand Coco Palms Resort, Hawaii
Mistaken identities		
Film tourism to places where the filming is only believed to have taken place	Movies and TV series that are filmed in one place that is created to look like another, often in other countries for financial reasons: known as 'runaway productions'	*Deliverance*, Clayburn County (movie filmed there, but set in Appalacha)

Table 1.3 (*Continued*)

Form	Characteristic	Example
Film tourism to places where the film is set, but not filmed	The films have raised interest in a particular country, region or place where the story is based, not where it was actually filmed	*Braveheart*, Scotland (movie filmed in Ireland)
Off-location		
Film studio tours	Industrial tours of working film studios, where the actual filming process can be viewed	Paramount Studios
Film studio theme park	Usually adjacent to a studio, specifically built for tourism with no actual filming or production taking place; many now create a place for animated/CGI films that do not have film destinations in the 'real' world.	The Wizarding World of Harry Potter, Universal Studios, Orlando, FL
One-off events		
Attending movie premieres	Especially those outside traditional sites such as Hollywood, but also at smaller, more specific sites	*Lord of the Rings: Return of the King* (Wellington, New Zealand); *The Man from Snowy River II* (Mansfield, Victoria); *Mission Impossible II* (Sydney)
Attending film festivals	Many cities hold large and small film festivals, attracting film buffs from around the world or country	Cannes; Venice; Italian Film Festival, Northcote, Melbourne
Participating in film conventions	More specialised and participatory than film festivals, attracting a passionate audience	Trekkie (*Star Trek*) conventions
Visiting museum/gallery exhibitions	Special feature exhibitions relating to film, filmmakers, actors, etc.	Tim Burton Exhibition (MOMA, New York; ACMI Melbourne)

(*Continued*)

Table 1.3 *(Continued)*

Form	Characteristic	Example
Armchair travels		
Watching TV travel shows	The successor to travel guidebooks, travelogues and travel lectures	*Getaway Pilot Guides*
Watching gastronomy programmes	Many cooking shows take the viewer to various places around the world	*Cook's Tour; The Hairy Bikers*
Watching reality shows	Competitive programmes set in exotic places	*Survivor, The Amazing Race*
Gaming	Some sets for computer games incorporate real places	*Grand Theft Auto*
Others		
Visiting permanent museum/gallery exhibitions	Museums and galleries set up to celebrate the story and history of film/moving images	Australian Centre for the Moving Image (ACMI) Melbourne

Source: Adapted from Beeton (2005: 10–11).

commenting that, by turning the ethnographic gaze inwards while maintaining an outward, critical perspective, we are able to understand 'the larger context where self experiences occur' (Denzin, 1997: 227). Furthermore, as Hackley notes, 'self-observation and reflexive accounts of experience cannot easily be disentangled, since, like sense and representation, they are mutually dependent' (Hackley, 2007: 102).

While it is not easy to differentiate this form of research from autobiography (or memoir), autobiographies tend to have a strong emphasis on literary style, whereas autoethnography focuses more on the self-reflexive content, often with the aim of exploring a singular aspect of the subject's life. As Hackley affirms, '[t]he notion of reflexivity... intrinsic to the interpretive approach, would seem to represent the point where style and substance coalesce' (Hackley, 2007: 102).

Despite the fact that this is a relatively underused approach in tourism research, there are those who have successfully applied autoethnography to tourism and support its inclusion into the tourism research mix, including Noy (2003, 2004, 2007), Westwood (2005), Miller (2008) and Beeton (2008). Noy nicely articulates the synergy between the autoethnographic approach and the tourist experience, noting that '[e]xploring tourists' experiences autoethnographically ... illuminates the fuzzy and liminal space that lies between tourism experiences and everyday experiences' (Noy, 2007: 352).

Autoethnography as personal narrative

At times the 'critical' aspect of autoethnography appears to be lacking in tourism studies, including some that I present in this publication; however, exposing oneself to the reader opens up various avenues of critical reflection. I take an autoethnographic approach in this book when relating many personal experiences, all with implicit as well as explicit critical reflection and exposure. The degree of explicit reflection is dependent upon the point being illustrated or studied. However, as Noy explains:

> autoethnography enables one to communicate experience and reconstruct it in vivid, lively and sometimes even painful ways, in ways that are not 'purely' academic or that result in an over-intellectualization of the sense of having an experience. (Noy, 2007: 350)

Certainly, self-reflexive, personal studies cannot be treated in the same way as the more positivist studies in terms of applying the results; however, they can provide insight into a complex area. By understanding how individuals respond to film, we are in a position to provide a stronger, more flexible and personal tourism experience for others.

Conclusion

This chapter provides the framework within which the work presented in this book is situated, with some background on tourism, the tourist gaze and moving picture audiences. It comes unashamedly from a travel and tourism perspective, while at the same time attempting to broaden this approach through acknowledging and incorporating the studies of complementary disciplines. While he is not referring directly to film or moving images and tourism, I take heart from Donald Horne's comment that '[t]he best writing on tourism is done by people who respect many of the landscapes and relics of material culture that are on the tourist schedules, but who can also contemplate the absurdities with which tourism can transform them' (Horne, 1992: x). When we consider a world where our travel experiences can be so influenced by the popular media, there are many absurdities to be enjoyed as the representation (movie, TV programme, video game) becomes a tourist attraction in its own right. And then the tourist takes a video or photograph of it to play back or view later with a public (YouTube) audience. . . .

As noted at the beginning of this chapter, the moving image has been (and remains) a powerful protagonist as well as a mirror of the culture of the time in which it exists, marking a time and place that is spatial, temporal and emotional. By studying the effects of film on the culture of the day, we can situate the tourist within this discussion through our understanding of the nature of the popular, 'mass' media of this period. The following chapter considers this in relation to the early era of the moving image and the emergence of a more democratised version of travel.

Note

(1) Definition of Mise-en-Scène:
- the arrangement of actors and scenery on a stage for a theatrical production *b*: stage setting;
- the physical setting of an action (as of a narrative or a motion picture) (Merriam-Webster Dictionary, 2011).

Part 1
From Static to Moving Images

> *Then came the film and burst this prison-world asunder by the dynamite of the tenth of a second, so that now, in the midst of its far flung ruins and debris, we calmly and adventurously go traveling.*
> Walter Benjamin, 1998[1936]

Cinematic film as a form of 'public' (able to be seen at the same time by more than one person) entertainment is considered to have its genesis in 1895, with the screening on 13 February that year of brothers Auguste and Louis Lumiere's film, *Sortie des Ouviers de l'usine Lumiere*, showing workers leaving their factory for lunch, followed in 1896 by their infamous *L'arrivée d'un train à La Ciotat (Arrival of a Train at La Ciotat)*, where popular myth has it that the audience ran from the theatre, believing that the train was 'real'. Gunning (1989) argues compellingly that that was unlikely to be the case, but nevertheless the new technology was awe inspiring and produced strong audience reactions.

This section begins by considering the antecedents of the moving image and its relationship with entertainment, travel and tourism, be that depicting scenes of places and cultures to visit, filming the tourists at these places, providing vicarious travel experiences, or simply using stories to create emotional images of places, travel and tourism. The magic and potential presented by the moving image has engaged humankind for some time, with the technological developments of the Industrial Revolution providing the means with which to truly imagine how we can move while being stationary, be that seated in a vehicle that moves or elsewhere where only the images move.

For some time now I have been particularly fascinated by the notion of 'phantom rides', which I heard about many years ago when I saw some footage of Edison's 1903 *Panorama of Gorge Railway*, but which I was unable to learn more about until my research uncovered more information on them in the past few years. Others have also shown us that the silent cinema was far from silent, with audiences actively engaging in the viewing experience. This 'discovery' became the genesis of this book, which I intend to explore them further as my skills in unearthing original material broaden.

The following chapters then move the story forward to the development of film during times of war as well as stories of war. While wartime itself and its themes are not congruent with 'travel for pleasure', storytelling (including propaganda), film techniques and their influence on audiences all developed. Finally, the move to Cold War, spies and espionage tales are discussed with the glamorous, globetrotting aspects of many of these stories linking directly to tourist dreams and desires.

However, it is not easy to present this as a linear themed discussion that seamlessly moves from war to war (and the same for all notions), so where relevant I occasionally digress to introduce other related elements, such as a broader understanding of the notion of celebrity, which is central to film-related tourism.

2 From Panoramas to Phantom Rides

> *I think cinema, movies and magic have always been closely associated. The very earliest people who made film were magicians.*
>
> Francis Ford Coppola

In the previous chapter, the concept of film audiences, travellers (and tourists) was introduced. As noted, one of the primary aims of this publication is to dispel the myth that film and tourism (or moving images and travel) is a recent phenomenon; consequently, in this chapter we go back to the early days of moving images and their relationship to travel. In an attempt to explore the premise that pictures (moving and still) have been closely aligned with various aspects of tourism since their inception, I have taken a broad approach to those early relationships in this chapter, relating to this as an historical narrative. The focus of early cinema on presenting audiences with sights of exotic places has clear tourism connotations, particularly in the way that they actually present such places, often directing the tourist as to how to engage with these places themselves. As a tourism scholar who came in to this field via a movie, I have always believed that this relationship is virtually innate, intricate, personal and powerful. Consequently, I agree with Strain who says that:

> It does, however, seem clear that a touristic position did exist within early cinema, even if a clear starting date cannot be established. (Strain, 2003: 123)

Gunning (1986) refers to the period from the acknowledged beginning of cinema in 1895 to around 1906–1909 as the *cinema of attractions*, where narrative was virtually non-existent, with the primary elements of cinema reflecting the desire of producers to show something 'new'. As with the Lumière brothers' early attempts, they consciously exhibited the technology, while the actors often connected with the audience by acknowledging them through the camera lens using vaudeville techniques such as gestures and asides. In relation to travel and tourism, many of these early representations were as much about the new technologies relating to the mass movement of people as about the picturesque scenery, providing limited, if any, storyline. Even though George Méliès' 1902 *Voyage dans la lune* (*A Trip to the Moon*) does tell a story about travel imbued with the sense that anything is possible in this modern age, it was primarily developed to demonstrate the magician's skill with the new technology. Gunning (1986) further argues that the concept of narrative in film did not become fully fledged until around 1906.

A further reason for this development of a *cinema of attractions* as opposed to narrative was that, due to the available technology of the time and screening of single-reel films, these early films were extremely short, initially running for only one minute. The focus on presenting panoramic views or scenes to audiences sat well within these restrictions, and has powerful travel and tourism connotations as discussed in the following section.

By understanding the development and use of images (static and moving) and their subject matter (the exotic, the foreign), we can begin to see the links between these forms of media and travel. What we can see is how often travel-related images and stories, literally and metaphorically, are used with moving images, and while there may not have been empirical research on travel and tourism undertaken in the 19th and early 20th centuries, we can see from certain travel narratives and journals that those who could were travelling, often in the footsteps of the stories experienced via various forms of popular media, including moving images. As noted in Chapter 1, the Grand Tour is a pertinent example of the influence of the media of art and culture on travel, and as the forms of media used to deliver such information developed, reaching beyond the traditional elite, so did the interest in travel. The late 19th century group tours organised by Thomas Cook are evidence of this interest, and in themselves celebrated aspects of the exotic and picturesque so often portrayed by the moving image. This chapter builds on this premise, considering the early phases and development of moving images, from panoramas and art to early virtual travel using moving images, the rise of the travel lecture and a discussion on the influence of silent cinema. While not 'moving images' per se, it is also pertinent to look briefly at the development of photography, which was concomitant with that of the moving image.

Panorama, Pictures and Travel

The term *panorama* has its roots in the Greek language, meaning *to view all*, and during the 18th and 19th centuries English, German and French audiences were able to view elaborate landscape scenes that often incorporated intricately drawn historical events. Battles in particular lent themselves to such a broad canvas, with antecedents seen in the frescos and immersive murals of antiquity (Grau, 1999). These scenes were painstakingly reproduced on long curved panels and canvases, usually viewed in a rotunda, where 'audiences would be barraged by 360 degrees of hyper-realistic imagery' (Mazow, 1992: 1). Those who participated in this highly popular form of entertainment found the immersive visual effect to be extremely dramatic and moving, and can be seen as a form of virtual reality. By the early 19th century the panorama had travelled to America, with over 100 million people visiting a panorama in America and Europe between 1870 and 1900 (Grau, 1999).

Such capture of the popular imagination is also reflected in the writings of the day, with the Romantic English poet, Wordsworth, describing the wonder of a manmade panorama in *The Prelude of 1805; Seventh Book: Residence in London*, as follows:

> Whether the Painter, fashioning a work
> To Nature's circumambient scenery,
> And with his greedy pencil taking in
> A whole horizon on all sides, with power,
> Like that of angels or commissioned spirits,
> Plant us upon some lofty pinnacle,
> Or in a ship on waters, with a world
> Of life, and life-like mockery, to east,
> To west, beneath, behind us, and before;
> Or more mechanic artist represent
> By scale exact, in model, wood or clay,
> From shading colours also borrowing help,
> Some miniature of famous spots and things, –
> Domestic or the boast of foreign realms;
> The Firth of Forth, and Edinburgh throned
> On crags, fit empress of that mountain land;
> St. Peter's Church; or, more aspiring aim,
> In microscopic vision, Rome itself;
> Or, else perhaps, some rural haunt, – the Falls
> Of Tivoli; and high upon that steep,
> The Temple of the Sibyl! every tree
> Through all the landscape, tuft, stone, scratch minute,
> And every cottage, lurking in the rocks –
> *All that the traveller sees when he is there.*
>   (Wordsworth, 1805: lines 257–281; own emphasis)

This selection from such a popular poet as Wordsworth illustrates not only the period's fascination with the mechanics and artistry of reproducing the picturesque, but also his own influence on his society's Romantic interest. He also pre-empts the discussion of the virtual gaze, along with the argument that one can experience travel virtually through modern technology, in line 281: '[a]ll that the traveller sees when he is there'. However, what we have seen is that such experiences tend to create a desire to experience these simulacra/virtual gazes for real, encouraging tourism rather than replacing it. In his history of 19th-century entertainments, historian Richard Altick notes that 'London's panoramas served as appetite-whetters for the real thing' (Altick, 1978: 478).

These panoramic scenes also reflect the period's notion of *picturesque*, which was a product of the aforementioned Romantic movement of the 18th and 19th centuries, as an 'ideology of landscape as pretty pictures for consumers to be enjoyed as a visual experience divorced from any concept of use value or human purpose except private enjoyment' (Seaton, 1998: 9). Wordsworth's allusion in the above poem to the panoramas created by painters (and dioramas by mechanical artists) reflects a desire to experience the picturesque and a rural idyll while residing in the city (London), and celebrates the artists' skill ('like that of angels') to facilitate such a phenomenon. As technology (and the desire to flaunt it) increased, oversized canvases were suspended between rollers and moved before the audience, further enabling a sense of travelling through a landscape and certainly instilling a passion (or desire) for travel in the general public.

The concept of the panorama per se is considered today to be more of an historical phenomenon, with the term being used to conjure the sensation of expansive yet at the same time immersive experiences. Nevertheless, echoes of this technology can be seen in our widescreen cinematic experiences, particularly IMAX and so-called '4-D'.

As the era of the painted panorama slipped into history, a new technology arose to cater to society's fascination with picturesque representations of 'reality', the exotic and travel – that of photography. While not being moving images in their own right, photos simulate mobility and have been used to create a sense of movement, as did the paintings in a panorama, deserving a note in this publication.

From paintings to pictures: The development of photography

> *They [photographs] provided simulated mobility experiences that brought the countryside, ancient times and exoticism to modern metropolises...*
> Urry and Larsen, 2011: 165

In terms of technological developments, one of the key leaps during the 19th century can be seen in the development of photography, which came to represent a certain, arguable 'reality' as opposed to the interpretive representations of artists. While photography has come to be more than a mere representation of reality, with what is left out of the frame often being as important as what is in it, for some time it was believed that 'the camera did not lie'.

The concept of photography had been foreshadowed in the 5th century BC by Chinese philosopher Mo-Ti, who noted the phenomenon where a concentrated pinhole of light could project an inverted image of its surroundings (Gernsheim & Gernsheim, 1969). This became popularised in the 17th century as the *camera obscura*, a box with a hole in one side where light from an external scene passes through the hole and strikes a surface inside the box, reproducing the scene. It could be projected onto paper and traced to produce a highly accurate representation (depending on the skill of the artist), or re-inverted via mirrors on to a larger screen for a more public viewing, and at this stage was primarily part of the fairground entertainment. However, others were experimenting to find ways to capture these images directly, without the need to hand-trace them.

After some 50 years of experimentation, in 1829 Joseph-Nicephore Niépce and French artist, Louis Daguerre, succeeded in achieving the reproduction of an image. By applying the discovery that an iodised silver mix darkens when exposed to light, and developing their pictures in the controlled environment of a darkroom, they were able to produce one-off prints on plates, becoming highly valued one-off productions (Benjamin, 1972). At the same time, others were making progress, such as Hercule Florence who had developed a similar process a few years earlier, calling it *photographie*. After Niépce's death in 1833, Daguerre continued to build on their work, naming the process the *daguerréotype* (Nelson, 1996). In fact, in 1839 Daguerre took the first ever photo of a person when a pedestrian stopped for a shoe shine in the street scene he was taking a daguerreotype of, inadvertently remaining there for the several minutes required for the long exposure. He was eventually required by the French government to make the technique publicly available in exchange for a much-needed pension. This enabled others to use and further develop the technology far more rapidly than those who patented their inventions, such as amateur English scientist, William Fox Talbot.

Even at this point, the connection with travel is evident, with Talbot claiming that 'to the traveller in distant lands ... this little invention may prove real service' (Talbot, 1839: 11, cited in Urry & Larsen, 2011: 165). By the 1840s, we see the coming together of a series of developments and events, including 'the means of collective travel, the desire for travel and the techniques of photographic production' (Urry & Larsen, 2011: 165).

After approximately a decade of use, the *daguerréotype* became superseded by other technological developments such as Talbot's paper negative process, and the era of the photograph was well on its way. Talbot's process took some time to gain acceptance over the 'free' *daguerréotype* technology; however, the convenience of paper-based photographic prints and processes eventually overcame this issue in the latter half of the 18th century (Nelson, 1996). In 1884, George Eastman, founder of the Kodak organisation, replaced the photographic plates with film, the forerunner of today's film cameras. In a 1885 advertisement for his new film, Eastman stated that 'shortly there will be introduced a new sensitive film which it is believed will prove an economical and convenient substitute for glass dry plates both for outdoor and studio work' (www.kodak.com). For over a century, Kodak was synonymous with travel, enabling people to bring back images and stories from their travels.

However, the practice of photography has not been without its critics, particularly in relation to photographing people, with early Christian church leaders proclaiming that only the 'divine artist, divinely inspired, may be allowed, in a moment of solemnity, at the higher call of his genius, to reproduce the divine-human features, but never by means of a mechanical aid!' (Benjamin, 1972: 6). This is similar to the reaction of other societies encountered by anthropologists, photographers and tourists, who were unfamiliar with the process, and considered that the photograph contained an essence of themselves. While our Western, developed cultures are familiar with the technology, I must admit to experiencing some consternation myself when I was staying in a cottage in the seaside village of Barwon Heads, Australia, made famous by a TV series (*Sea Change*; see Beeton, 2000, 2001, 2005a, 2007). Every time I looked out of the window or stepped out of the door, someone was taking a photograph of the cottage. While I knew they were not intentionally photographing me, I still felt slightly 'abused', and that something quite personal had been taken from me, eventually curtailing my stay.

With the development of digital technology and social networks, the pervasiveness of the photograph has become extreme, with Bell and Lyall (2005: 135) noting that 'relentless documentation accompanies every tourist experience'. These experiences must also be conveyed to others and usually include the protagonist (the tourist) in the photo, reinforcing the fact that *they were there*. I recall visiting the Louvre in Paris to see Da Vinci's *Mona Lisa*, of which you could not take any photographs, unlike in the rest of the gallery. I was standing there, taking in the experience, when a young man behind me commented to his companion, 'So, what are we supposed to do?

Look at it?' He was struggling to find a way to experience something without capturing it on film. This, along with my Barwon Heads story raises many issues regarding the role of photography and filming in tourism, which we consider further when we look at the development of the moving image in the more personal, amateur realm in Chapter 12.

Early three-dimensional experiences and moving images (stereoscopes and kinetoscopes)

Where the panoramas of the 18th and 19th centuries worked to physically surround the viewer with picturesque scenes, limiting any distractions that may enter the viewer's peripheral vision, creating a sense of 'being there', another technology appeared on the back of the nascent interest in photography that worked to 'trick the mind' even further by bringing the viewer's eye completely into the picture via the stereoscope.

Stereoscopy is a technique that creates the illusion of depth in an image by presenting two images simultaneously to the left and right eye of the viewer, with a minor deviation between them which combines in the brain to give the perception of three-dimensional (3D) depth. As it was important to have the image at the correct distance from the eyes, an individual goggle-like viewer was developed with magnifying lenses placed before the picture. The viewer had to adjust the distance between the picture and their eyes by sliding it in and out until the 3D effect was obtained. By magnifying the picture and focusing the viewer's eyes totally on to the scene, peripheral vision was limited, creating a similar, but more personal experience to the panorama. While the pictures were initially small sketches and paintings, it was the development of photographic cards around the 1850s that gave the stereoscope its true power and popularity, particularly in relation to depicting important events along with exotic people and places.

These small photographs (around 3 inches square) were inexpensive, costing a few pence each, and portable, subsequently attracting a wide audience who could not attend (or pay for) a panoramic experience (Strain, 2003). By creating affordable images that present a realistic sense of depth, stereoscopes soon became popular among all classes, not just the elite upper classes. An 1856 catalogue advertisement from the London Stereoscopic Company heralds the excitement of this technology by citing a quote from a London newspaper:

> Everything grand and beautiful in the world brought to our firesides. (*Morning Advertiser*, from the 15-page *Catalogue of Binocular Pictures*, the London Stereoscopic Company, in Brewster, 1856: 241)

While first developed in Europe, with popular versions being manufactured in Scotland including the pocket-sized *Lenticular Stereoscopes* (Brewster, 1856), the stereoscope gained traction in the United States with Oliver Wendell Holmes' 1861 hand-operated, hooded stereoscope which soon became a popular form of domestic middle-class entertainment. Supporting the pioneering role of the railways in relation to tourism, photographers were hired by railway companies to document the railway and the scenery through which it passed, with the stereographs being sold at the railway stations and on the trains throughout the Western world. By 1872 some five or six stereoscopic photographers had studios at Niagara Falls to cater to tourists' demand to purchase the images as souvenirs (Strain, 2003). British physicist, Sir David Brewster, noted in 1856 that:

> Photographers are now employed in every part of the globe ... among the ruins of Pompeii and Herculaneum – on the glaciers and in the valleys of Switzerland – among the public monuments in the Old and the New World – among the shipping of our commercial harbours – in the museums of ancient and modern life – in the sacred points of the domestic circle – and among those scenes of the picturesque and sublime. ... (Brewster, 1856: 36–37)

Initially, stereograph images were distributed individually, with no consciously articulated connection between the photos – one was able to view a picture of the *Banquet Hall, Kenilworth Castle*, followed directly by an image such as the *Bust of Ariadne by Bacon* or a *Carpenter, Porter and Boy* (*Catalogue of Binocular Pictures,* the London Stereoscopic Company, in Brewster, 1856: 246). As a response to a slowing of demand due to a growing fascination with the new technology of moving pictures, organised box sets of cards with lengthy notes were developed, often applying a tourism or geographic narrative to link each image, as many of the stereographs represented famous heritage sites, exotic locales and cultures often romanticised in the travel literature (Strain, 2003). Publishers Underwood and Underwood introduced the *Underwood Travel System*, comprising box sets on particular locales with companion books written by travel experts and academics, significantly slowing the stereograph's demise. After they ceased production in 1920, the Keystone View Company continued to produce their stereographic tours until 1939, after which they focused their card manufacture on optometry.

In a development pre-empting cinematic moving pictures, Thomas Edison filed a patent for the kinetoscope peep-hole viewer and kinetograph camera in 1891. A single person could watch a moving picture filmed for the first time on 18 mm film which ran horizontally between two spools. The device was both the viewer (kinetoscope) as well as the camera (kinetograph) (Robinson, 1996). By printing many of his frames onto paper as contact prints, some can still be seen today, including the first movie, *Dixon Greeting* (1891), of a gentleman doffing his hat and bowing and *Fred Ott's Sneeze* (1894), where Edison's assistant is filmed taking a pinch of snuff and then sneezing (which was the first motion picture to be copyrighted in the United States), through to more exotic, anthropological travel- or tourism-related titles such as *Imperial Japanese Dance* (1894) and *Sioux Ghost Dance* (1894).

The main issue with these early stereographs and kinetoscopes is that they could not be seen simultaneously by a mass audience (or even a small group), as one needed to be directly engaged with the viewing device; consequently the techniques became superseded by the cinema and challenged by the earlier magic-lantern slide shows as a form of mass entertainment or education, as in the travel lecture or travelogue. However, the technology remains in use, with Edison's filming and screening process being virtually the same today. The optical profession uses stereographic technology and, in relation to film, the process has developed further, with stereographic lenses being used in today's 3-D movies, with the audience wearing special individual glasses in a mass environment such as a cinema or theme park. This technology is being continually developed, with some 3-D films now able to be seen without glasses, yet we can still see the roots of these early inventions in today's technology.

Early screen projections (magic lanterns)

The magic lantern is an early type of image projector developed in Europe during the 17th century as a variant of the *camera obscura*. The magic lantern was a forerunner of the modern-day slide and film projectors, comprising a concave mirror that gathered light from a mechanical source, then projected it through a slide with an image painted on it, throwing an enlarged picture of the original image onto a screen (Barber, 1993). While the early light sources of candles or oil lamps were inefficient, producing weak projections, this improved over the next century, culminating in the invention of the electric arc lamp in the 1850s and incandescent electric lamps. Furthermore, by the late 1840s, the hand-painted slides began to be replaced by photographic slides, which in turn were often hand coloured or tinted.

The early magic-lantern shows were used by showmen presenting magic and phantasmagoria shows, where slides of so-called 'phantoms' were often projected onto smoke, allowing them to shimmer and move (Nelson, 2000). Also, many of the slides were animated, changing rapidly, as in a 'flip book', illustrating stories and comedies (Barber, 1993).

There is a logical link between magic-lantern slide shows and the developing technology of film, as they both required the same type of physical space, projecting images on to a screen and employed similar production methods (Barber, 1993). As other forms of projecting moving pictures engaged the popular imagination, the phantasmagorical and magic performances fell out of popularity, with showmen embracing the new technology for their performances. It is interesting to consider the role that the magicians and showmen played in the development of moving images – they were always the early adopters of such technology, bringing them into the public realm in creative ways designed to intrigue and entertain. However, the magic lantern continued to be used in the more 'educational' and informative events such as the public travel lecture (Borton, 2015), underlining its connection with travel.

Virtual (Vicarious) Travel of the Late 19th and Early 20th Centuries

The popularity of the stereograph box set was significant in terms of actual as well as virtual travel, with many of the descriptions on the cards or the accompanying books expressed in such a way as to put the viewer into the picture or the place of the photographer/observer. In 1901, Underwood and Underwood wrote to one of their expert authors, James Henry Breasted, requesting that he 'put what he has to say in the first person much as he would talk as if he could stand with a person in the presence of the actual places' (cited in Evans, 2003: 5–6). The boxes could then be purchased as a record of a trip (souvenir) or as a way to vicariously experience exotic and remote places and cultures.

Moving panoramas and phantom rides

By the second half of the 19th century the concept of *panorama* had shifted from the extensive, static, painted landscapes of the 18th century to refer to continuous passing scenes and an unbroken view, not unlike that viewed from a train. When travelling on a train, the windows frame the view which does not move; however, the train moves, which is the inverse of, but not opposite to, the concept of the 'moving image' which moves while the audience remains static. In fact, we see the first cinematic panoramas being a representation of a train journey, where the pseudo-traveller sits in a simulated 'carriage' while the scenery scrolls past them, viewed through the frame of the window.

Arguably the first film technique to present such moving panoramas to a mass audience was that of the *Phantom Ride*. While there is some doubt as to when and where the first of such films was shown, with some suggesting London, 1901, there is evidence of such a screening in 1898 (Fielding, 1970). A camera was attached to the front cowcatcher (or rear caboose) of a moving train (trolley or subway car), filming the panorama of the countryside through which the train travelled. Out of the 141 films on the topic of trains and other vehicles made between 1899 and 1906 that are in the records of the Library of Congress in the United States, over 50 are *Phantom Ride* films shot from the cowcatcher or rear of the train by the American Mutoscope and Biograph and Edison Companies (Niver, 1967). Some examples of the genre include *Havershaw Tunnel* (Biograph, 1897) and Edison's 1903 *Panorama of Gorge Railway* where the train traversed the landscape near Niagara Falls. While it has been argued that the term 'phantom' comes from the fact that the train is not visible (Strain, 2003), the *Phantom Rides* also contain no people, celebrating the cinematic technique of putting the viewer in the seat of the passenger or even driver of the vehicle. To become known as the *travelling shot*, the movement carried the viewer into the image to create a sense of being there (Gunning, 2006), and many became virtual tourism advertisements. As Beeton (2011: 53) explains, '[t]hey were not made to promote tourism per se, but in turn contributed to people's desire to visit and experience the sites shown on the screen as well as their sense of already "knowing" a place when they arrived'.

The development of early 20th-century cinematic film and its presentation further blurred the distinction of who (or what) was actually moving. A powerful example of such themed experiences comes from the United States, where a chain of up to 500 theatres known as *Hale's Tours* showed films of scenes taken from moving vehicles. The theatre was arranged to simulate the experience of being in the vehicle itself, with the audience sitting in a specially constructed 'carriage' on seats set so all could see, and open at the front where a movie that had been filmed from the front of a train was screened. These experiences were complete with effects simulating the 'clickety-clack' of a rail journey that could be sped up according to what was on the film, the train rocking and swaying, blasts of air and uniformed conductors taking tickets (Fielding, 1970). Some shows also included a lecturer who elaborated on the scenic points of interest as they were shown. Hale's Tours soon expanded from the United States to South Africa, South America, Mexico, Europe, the British Isles and Hong Kong. While initially highly successful, the novelty of Hale's Tours wore off after a few years, as it was not an experience that many people repeated; however, as Fielding explains:

> the influence of his little show on the emerging motion picture should not be underestimated. It served not only to introduce and popularize the early projected motion picture, but also acted as a bridge which

linked the primitive arcade peep shows and vaudeville presentations of the day with the makeshift motion picture theatres which spread across the United States between 1905 and 1910. (Fielding, 1970: 47)

The fact that travel-based notions of escape, picturesque, exotic experiences were being offered again ties the audience into the travel experience.

Today's 'phantom rides' and '(Hale's) Tours'

Knowledge of these early and dramatic forms of cinema appear to have fallen from popular memory; however, allusions to the Phantom Rides are reflected in many of today's IMAX films, often promoted as a 'new' approach. The travelogue format is the foundation of many IMAX films, with panning techniques similar to that of the Phantom Rides, placing the viewer in the driver's seat, such as in *NASCAR: The IMAX Experience* (2004) (Beeton, 2011). In an interesting turn and a nod to the debt IMAX owes the early proponents of the moving image, *Across the Sea of Time* (1996) is the story of a young Russian immigrating to New York in search of his aunt, with only pictures on a stereoscope and letters to aid him in his quest (Griffiths, 2006).

The 'Road Trip' genre, where the protagonists take a journey of discovery through a landscape, also owes a great deal to these predecessors, with many of them taking almost a Hale's Tour approach to the landscape which passes by as the film's central characters conduct their lives in or on their form of (usually motorised) transport. These movies also introduce the landscape as a central character, often incorporating phantom shots from the front, back and side windows of the vehicles. We consider this in more detail in Chapter 6, where I draw further parallels with the Road Trip and other genres.

Furthermore, the legacy of Hales' Tours and the Phantom Rides can be seen in today's film-based theme parks. The primarily American concept of the *theme park* grew from the entertainment palaces and amusements parks of the 19th century, such as Coney Island, with a number of movie studios constructing film-themed parks in the third quarter of the 20th century, including Disneyland, Warner Brothers and Universal Studios (Beeton, 2005a). While there is more discussion of this phenomenon and its development in Chapter 10, it is interesting to note the similarities with some of the movie themes rides of today and the Hales Tours. There are many movie-based theme park 'rides' that place the participant in a contained environment where images are screened surrounding them, complete with movements and sound simulating an experience from a movie or TV programme. For example, the *Back to the Future* ride at Universal Studios in Burbank, CA presents participants with the sensation of flying back through time, being buffeted by storms and other phenomena, without them moving at all spatially. When I experienced this 'ride' close to 15 years ago, I was immediately reminded of the Hales Tours, which I assume I had heard about some time during my youth, as I am certainly not old enough to have been there myself, and did not really travel back in time! Such simulated experiences of a simulation (movie) are truly postmodern representations of 'reality' which I find quite fascinating.

Disney even features old stereographs in Disneyland, Anaheim and Tokyo. On my visits to the US Disney theme parks, this was not an especially popular activity as they are relatively static experiences compared to the high levels of immersion and excitement now on offer at such destinations, as I discuss in Chapter 10. However, in Tokyo, the stereographs were crowded with young Japanese men, possibly reflecting their passion for the various Japanese mechanical games and Pachinko Parlours. Even as our technology develops, the ways in which we 'trick' the mind seem to remain very close to the magic shows, illusions, phantasmagoria and panoramas of the 19th century and earlier.

During the 18th and 19th centuries the public lecture developed as a popular form of education and entertainment, often being presented by educated amateurs and, in terms of lectures about foreign places, anthropologists. Anthropology is based upon fieldwork, usually undertaken by one person in a distant and foreign locale. The first-person reporting of their work via books, lectures and films implicitly states 'I was there', often to the extent of a picture of the anthropologist being printed on the cover of their publications, much as today's tourists place themselves in their own photos then publish them online (Strain, 2003). This privileged position of direct experience and engagement while (in theory) remaining objective is the foundation of the participant-observation research approach often used in tourism research, where the level of investigator immersion can result in differing perspectives illustrating the complex, subjective nature of the tourist experience (see Beeton, 2005b). Anthropological publications, slide shows, films and talks all share experiences with their audience, who gain a sense of 'being there', vicariously experiencing and travelling to places, and remain popular in all their forms today.

During the second half of the 19th century, live, illustrated lectures were an extremely popular form of travel-related entertainment, with the magic-lantern lectures playing to fascinated, well-dressed middle-class audiences in grand lecture halls (Beeton, 2011). The lectures and images of other places and cultures provided a respectable and edifying, yet highly evocative, form of entertainment. While those referring to themselves as anthropologists (both professional and amateur) continued to present lectures based on their experiences of the exotic, another group of individuals began to gain attention around the mid-19th century – the habitual/professional traveller who then presented his work in the form of a travel lecture, which tended to focus on less exotic places than the anthropologist, talking about places that the primarily middle-class audience may have the opportunity to visit.

While the travel lecture predates the magic-lantern shows (and moving pictures), by the late 19th century most lecturers were using the slides as a visual accompaniment, with purchased magic-lantern slides supplementing their own photographs (Strain, 2003). Subsequently, moving pictures also took their place as additions to the slide show in the lecture, as taken up by Burton Holmes – arguably one of the first to do so (Caldwell, 2006). As noted previously, this was not such a large leap, as the lighting, screens and other physical requirements for both the magic lantern and moving pictures were similar.

The most highly regarded travel lecturers had visited the places they were talking about, not using a script prepared by another, as some were apt to, and included Henry H. Ragan, James W. Black and Edward L. Wilson (Barber, 1993). These itinerant lecturers presented silent travelogues with live narration, with the filmmaker/lecturer's interpretive presence becoming the most important aspect of the experience. According to Ruoff (1998: 3) '[t]ravelogue lecturers are cultural brokers, translators and interpreters for American [sic] audiences'. American, John L. Stoddard has been acknowledged as the leader in this field during these early years, presenting some 3000 lectures to four million people over the years from 1870 to 1897 (Barber, 1993). Such popularity was due primarily to the entertaining and authoritative manner in which Stoddard presented his lectures. He was a charismatic performer who spoke only of places he had personally visited, illustrated with fine-quality, carefully selected slides. His 'exhibitions' attracted the higher classes as well as the aspirational middle classes and were meticulously planned and rehearsed.

Following Stoddard's retirement in 1897, he commended Elias Burton Holmes as a worthy successor, who in turn became the leading travel lecturer in America. Holmes first attended Stoddard's lectures as a nine year old and met him a number of times throughout the 1890s (Caldwell, 2006). He continued to develop the genre, coining the term *travelogue* in 1904 in an attempt to differentiate his work from that of the amateur anthropologist and those he considered to be less authentic travel lecturers (Lowell Thomas, 1958, in Beeton, 2011).

Burton Holmes and the travelogue

Boston-born Burton Holmes (1870–1958) was a great self-promoter, boldly stating that '[t]o travel is to possess the world' (Holmes, 1953, cited in Caldwell, 2006: 7). Consequently, sorting through his many oft-repeated claims can tend to obscure his influence on travel and the travelogue; however, over his 60-year career as a travel lecturer he provided Americans with a world view that most had previously not experienced. It is undoubted that he also encouraged others to travel and explore the world, being one of the early promoters of travel in the developing age of increasing traveller access and mass tourism.

Holmes' early ambition was, however, to become a stage magician, and as a boy he familiarised himself with the nature of the magic shows of the time by presenting them to his family and neighbours. He enlisted his friend George Ellery Hale (the future astronomer) to produce their own 'Theatre Magique' show based on the work and style of the leading magician of the time, Herman the Great (Caldwell, 2006). He also developed an interest in photography, purchasing his first camera at 13, a few short years before his first overseas travels with his mother and grandmother in 1886. He took his camera with him on the voyage, discovering a passion for travel photography. After a long trip to Europe in 1890, he produced lantern slides of his photographs and displayed them at the Chicago Camera Club, accompanied by tales of his travels which he presented as a seamless story, rather than simply a series of snapshots (Barber, 1993). This small beginning slowly developed into the travelogues for which he became famous. Considering himself to be primarily a photographer, Holmes saw his travel exhibitions as a natural extension of the magic shows of his childhood, applying his understanding of illusion to his photographs and lectures. Unlike Stoddard, where the lecturer was the focus of the show, Burton Holmes considered his images to be the primary element of his shows, foregoing the use of a spotlight and structured notes. He applied a more informal, yet carefully planned style aimed at keeping the audience's attention focused on the visual imagery. Burton claimed that he 'wanted the show to move smoothly to create the illusion of travel, not to be just an exhibition of lantern slides' (Caldwell, 2006: 11). However, the lecturer still dominated the public's perception of these shows as the font of all knowledge, and Holmes' name remained at the top of all the promotional material with the theme of the travelogue taking second billing (Altman, 2006).

Holmes introduced motion pictures into his show in late 1897, revitalising the travel lecture. Initially, as they did not always relate to his topic, the moving pictures were used almost as a novelty addendum to his lecture; however, he soon integrated more relevant films into his actual lectures.

Holmes and his collaborator, Oscar Bennett Depue, made many of the films shown, breaking new ground in the early days of the moving picture through filming in remote, exotic places, and being responsible for the first footage of many countries, including Korea, Japan and China (Caldwell, 2006). In fact, Holmes saw himself more as a film producer (and photographer) than a lecturer, but even so there were occasions when his lectures were supplemented with some commercial travel films.

During his 60-year career, Holmes visited most countries of the world during the North American summer, while he gave over 8000 lectures throughout the winters (Caldwell, 2006). As evidence of his fame and crowd-drawing potential, he regularly presented his travelogues to well-dressed 'opera crowds' at Carnegie Hall in New York, Symphony Hall in Boston and Orchestra Hall in Chicago, fuelling their desire to travel. The Burton Holmes audience certainly epitomises various stages of the model developed in Chapter 1, where at the very least, they move through the Before Exposure, During Exposure, towards the After Exposure activities as an audience and potentially as tourists.

The travel lecture today

While most historical narratives of film relegate the travel lecture to the era discussed above as a somewhat insignificant footnote to the development of film and cinema, it continues today as a viable genre in its own right. Ruoff (1998: 2) notes that '[t]ravel lectures take place at hundreds of venues across North America'. However, one of the problems in studying and acknowledging this genre is its ephemeral nature – as it involves a live performance, it is difficult to analyse it after the occurrence.

In an attempt to address this issue, Ruoff (1998, 2006a) has been undertaking research into the current state of the travel film or travelogue, attending many lectures 'live' across North America in a participant-observation role. He has found that this genre tends to appeal to an older, well-to-do audience who continue to dress formally for such occasions, much as audiences did in the Stoddard and Burton Holmes era. The lecturers also continue to often dress in tuxedos and reflect a similar age to their over 60-year-old audience. It remains a predominantly male genre, with only two out of the 48 filmmakers active in the late 20th century being female. Furthermore, as with early cinema discussed in the following sections, these modern travelogues do not have any 'stars', to the extent of often having no people in them, focusing on the scenic aspects of the place/s and relying on the lecturer to provide the human element. One can only speculate as to whether the travel lecture will continue once these older participants and creators pass on; yet we can experience similar lectures on many of today's cruise ships, often catering to a younger audience *'in situ'*, both before, during and after their travel experiences.

However, it is clear that moving pictures are an integral part of today's travel lectures, so we turn below to trace further developments of the moving image by returning to the earlier discussion of the panorama.

Short, Sweet and Silent: The Movies of the Early 20th Century

Thousands of films were released during the silent movie era (for our purposes here, being the period from the first film in 1895 to the first 'talkies' in 1927), but unfortunately the majority have been lost – either through poor storage conditions, the volatility of the acetate film (even burning it to film as fires in later movies), or simple disinterest. Consequently, it is problematic for those who wish to make any grand, sweeping statements regarding the genre. However, in terms of film and tourism, we can consider the remaining written records and reviews as well as those remaining films and draw some conclusions.

The earliest surviving American silent film with intertitles (title slides interspersed between the moving scenes in order to provide a narrative link) relates directly to travel and the Grand Tour. Edwin S. Porter's satirical comedy, *The European Rest Cure* (1904), tells the story of a male tourist who visits all of the main sites of a Grand Tour, with disastrous results. The tourist in the movie is depicted as an innocent abroad, falling foul of loose women and alcohol in Paris and taking many pratfalls off pyramids and mountains. Friedberg (1993) presents the storyline as an illustration of the similarities between the narrative conventions of early cinema and tourist operations, with a focus on the spectacle. Part of Friedberg's description of the film follows:

> The European Rest Cure is a thirteen-shot film that mixes actuality footage with acted fictional setups. It was a common trope for Porter to mix actuality footage with contrived narrative; of the film's thirteen shots, six are exterior (five introductory and one concluding shot), and seven are studio tableaux. The story is designed to dissuade the traveler from exotic locales; the natural beauty of home is presented in the photographic fluidity of the exterior shots of the harbor and pier. ...
>
> The tour itself is a series of claustrophobically circumscribed studio tableaux. Each shot is a stop on the 'grand tour' (Kissing the Blarney Stone, Doing Paris, Climbing the Alps, Hold Up in Italy, Climbing the

Pyramids of Egypt, The Mudbaths of Germany). The narrative is told as a series of 'foreign' spaces, each made static and confined. ... In each tableau, our tourist is thrown off balance, or falls off frame, or cowers at the center of the shot. For the spectator of the film the foreign is presented in very clumsy faux-virtual landscapes, coded in a set of familiar xenophobic clichés. Paradoxically, 'home' is represented with more realistic detail – actual footage of the harbor and port and with more camera mobility. As a film that professes an antitravel message, it asserts the beauty of cinematic spectatorship as a more spectacular and fluid form of virtual mobility. (Friedberg, 1993: 97–100)

In contradiction to Friedberg's analysis that the film had an 'antitravel message', after viewing the movie from a tourism disciplinary perspective, I would argue that its comedic and satirical nature presents the male tourist as an ingénue who is unable to appreciate the joys of travel. It would be just as easy to say that the movie *In Bruges* (2008), where one of the lead characters actively opposed being a tourist, did nothing for tourism to that city, but, in fact, not only has the movie encouraged tourism, but a movie map of the various sites featured is available from the Brugge tourism office.

In *The European Rest Cure* (1904), the women tourists are presented as sensible, continually rescuing the male tourist, and one may well assume that they benefited from their Grand Tour. Regardless of our differing opinions as to the main thrust of the film, current research into the relationship between the storyline of a film and its tourism effect suggests that such a story would be effective in encouraging tourism (see Beeton, 2011). Other extant examples of this comedic part location-based story include *Rube and Mandy at Coney Island* (1903), *A Romance of the Rails* (1903) and *A Policeman's Tour of the World* (1907), all of which 'showed fictional characters in films that also functioned as travelogues' (Grieveson & Kramer, 2003: 79) due to the practice of interspersing studio sets with 'actual' (location) footage.

Often the use of landscapes such as the New York skyline in the above movie (which was genuine footage, not a studio tableau), while integral to the story, also present inadvertent (or accidental) tourist images. The skyline referred to here, according to Friedberg, represented 'home'; however, many of those viewing the film would not have visited New York, and so this safe haven becomes an exotic tourism locale.

The not-so-silent cinema?

The earlier discussion on the travel lecture relates to the period of 'silent cinema', where it has been primarily the lecturer (or showman) providing the sound for the images shown. However, it was not only the 'expert' on the stage who broke the silence of those moving pictures without recorded sound, with others actively engaging in the experience, from musicians to the audience themselves.

It has become a 'given' that silent cinema was always accompanied by music and/or other sound effects, and many screenings of silent movies today are accompanied by live music, such as the work by the Australian band, *The Blue Grassy Knoll*, who, for the past 20 years, have been writing and performing musical scores to Buster Keaton's movies around the world. However, as with the travel lecture, actually studying the use of sound in silent films is difficult due to the ephemeral nature of these performances, and the lack of a sufficiently large body of surviving written accounts of the experience of the actual show, with many of the surviving reviews of silent films based on pre-release silent recordings (Altman, 1996).

Altman (1996) details the case presented by film historians that early cinema was *not* silent, but always accompanied by live music and sound effects, then goes on to argue that the assumption that silent films were never silent tends to be based on repeated or 'given' knowledge that he believes needs to be challenged (see Altman, 1996 for his detailed and thorough case). Altman's well-argued and challenging premise is that 'silence was one of a number of acceptable film exhibition approaches throughout the pre-1910 era' (Altman, 1996: 677). However, by the time of the feature film in the 1920s, musical accompaniment was the norm. Altman describes this development in the following manner:

> In 1908, theatres in the same block on the same day might well offer varying combinations of silence, sound effects, voices behind the screen, a lecturer, a synchronised sound-on-disk Cameraphone projection, a phonograph cylinder or disc, and live music.... [R]ecognising that they were losing control of the interpretation of their own products, film producers waged a series of campaigns to reduce the current cacophony to a set of standardized practices ... [culminating in] the negotiated settlement that not only brought silent film practices into line after approximately 1912 but also helped establish a durable social definition of cinema as a coherent audiovisual whole. (Altman, 1996: 690)

While it can be argued that this is not such an issue in terms of travel and tourism, the additional emotional layer provided by sound (especially music) may well have had some influence on the audience's emotional responses, indirectly affecting their feelings towards the places they discover through their filmic experience.

Non-commercial silent film

As the power of film to document activities became understood, a non-commercial, educative field of filming emerged, not unlike the more formalised work of anthropologists, with much of this film unedited and not intended for public consumption at the time. One of the most interesting extant collections of such work is that compiled by Frenchman, Albert Kahn, in the first decades of the 20th century. In a desire to document the modern world, Kahn (a philanthropic banker) commissioned a series of unedited, non-commercial, non-fiction films. The cameramen were instructed to produce views counter to the more narrative style of the commercial conventions of non-fiction film making, presenting us with an accumulation of visual 'facts'.

As opposed to the commercial travelogue, which has been described as 'a film that strings together ... a series of often mobile views of either foreign or local noteworthy sites in order to provide a form of vicarious tourism for Western spectators' (Amad, 2006: 107), the work commissioned by Kahn was raw and unedited footage. His aim was to document all of the world's events, from major events to simple domestic activities, and while his collection of 72,000 photographs, 4000 stereographic images and 183,000 m of film was not intended to document travel or tourism per se, a significant amount of the collection does just that (Amad, 2010). These un-authored fragments of visual information remain as a document for future generations to interpret and ostensibly gain an 'unmediated' understanding of the period.

From Talking Audiences to Talking Pictures

For decades, engineers such as Edison had been working on technology to combine moving pictures with sound. In 1923 an American inventor, Lee De Forest, successfully placed a soundtrack directly on a film strip, providing synchronised sound to a newsreel. However, the film industry itself was more concerned about the high cost of such technological advances. A new Hollywood studio, Warner Brothers, turned to sound as a way to differentiate themselves from the other larger studios, in 1926 releasing the film *Don Juan*, with a synchronised film score (Mintz & Roberts, 2010). However, it was the Warner Brothers movie *The Jazz Singer* (1927) that is generally accepted as marking the end-point for silent film. In an interesting development, the first accents heard on film were American and, while there were complaints from other countries such as the UK and Australia about the 'squawkies' (Collins, 1987), this in many ways assisted the growing dominance of Hollywood and the Americanisation of Western culture.

In spite of the complaints, the popularity of the 'talkies' soared, presenting a major change to the way in which audiences interacted with the films on the screen. No longer did they provide their own sound track, either as an arranged musical accompaniment or through their own comments, but had to quietly listen to the movie. It is this change that led some to see the movies as a passive form of entertainment, with the audience now sitting and absorbing what was on the screen. However, as argued throughout this book, audiences are not passive.

Conclusion: Active Audiences, Active Tourists

While there may have been no musical accompaniment to some early film, the audience was far from silent, often adding their own sound effects and engaging with the action. Gunning (1986) explains that, as early silent film related closely to vaudeville and spectacle, it was a noisy, interactive affair. He refers to Marinetti's comments that the variety theatre of vaudeville (and moving images) created 'a new spectator who contrasts with the "static", "stupid voyeur" of traditional theatre. The spectator ... joins in, singing along, heckling the comedians' (Gunning, 1986: 66). In other words, they participated in the production of meaning (Popple & Kember, 2004). While not always as vocal, today's cinema and television audiences are also far from passive, with many actively participating in the experience, not only at the time as with some of today's cult cinema screenings – such as *The Rocky Horror Picture Show* (1975), which continues to attract fans to late night screenings where they actively participate in the screening – but also afterwards by developing and sharing their own parodies, as discussed in Chapter 9.

As noted in Chapter 1, we can situate the tourist within this discussion based on our understanding of the nature of the visual, mass-media culture of the period. This recognition of the active and participatory nature of film viewing is also reflected in the nature of tourism during this period – tourists were not passive consumers as has been assumed by some, but rather active participants in their experiences. The tourists of this era (the late 19th and early 20th centuries), with the beginning of mass travel via trains and slow steamships, were also active participants in their travel, before, during and after their trip, often maintaining journals or other records reflecting their experiences. These journals would refer to the literature and art that informed their experiences, and also at times to travel lectures and films that they had seen. In 1900 a range of amateur film cameras and projectors was launched, including one that could record and project film within the home (Popple & Kember, 2004). As the 20th century moved into its third decade, we start to see the adoption of the more portable cine camera equipment by travellers, producing their own home movies, with their approaches toward storytelling often mimicking that of Burton Holmes and other travelogue producers as well as the popular travel literature (Nicholson, 2006). It is through these early home movies that we can trace some of the influence of the travel lecture on to the (albeit wealthy) traveller.

This presents an excellent example of the efficacy of the model illustrating the relationship between audience and tourist activity introduced in Chapter 1, where we are not only beginning to see the travellers themselves re-creating the style of the travel lecture or even phantom ride in their home movies, but also the narrative style of the films and lectures that so clearly influenced them to travel in the first instance.

From the earliest days, moving images also play a central role in times of civil unrest and war; as the technology developed, so did this relationship. The following chapters take up the challenge of linking this with travel and tourism, particularly from an emotional perspective. What particularly fascinates me is the way in which today's cinema (and other forms of moving images) remains travel focused, continuing to apply techniques and approaches pioneered over 150 years ago.

3 The Emotions of Motion 1: Travel, War and Unrest in the Era of the Moving Image

> *Apparently if there is a war, there is tourism.*
> Valene Smith, 1998: 206

The following chapters, under the aegis of 'The Emotion of Motion', consider the relationship between war or civil unrest, travel and the moving image, which we begin to see around the 1890s with details of wars such as the Anglo-Boer War (1899–1902) presented in the multimedia format of the travel lecture, often supported by film. This then brings us to the introduction of the newsreel, with its genesis sometime after 1910, but growing in sophistication and popularity with the introduction of synchronised sound in 1927. We then consider the impact of the two World Wars and their use of film as propaganda, with a focus on WWII and the eventual move to the era of the 'live' war on our TVs such as the Vietnam War, along with the Gulf War which was particularly dominated by the CNN network's 'embedded' reporters. Visual representations of civil unrest including the Tiananmen Square protests in China, the fall of the Berlin Wall and more recent uprisings in Egypt and the Middle East all play their part in creating images and emotional responses that encourage as well as discourage travel and tourism, often through a form of exoticisation of such places.

What we are looking at in this group of chapters is not so much factual information about such events, but rather indicators of the cultural environment of the time in which these films were made, not the time in which they were set, be that prior, during or even after the event. Recognising the cultural environment that the audiences lived in is critical when working to understand the links between film, audience and tourism through cinematic images and stories. Consequently, the connecting theme in much of this work involves journeying, a quest and travel. While my focus is on notions of movement and 'tourism', I do not mean to belittle the existence of hardship, deprivation, fear, torture, death and killing during these times. Yet, as Smith comments, 'despite the horrors and destruction (and also because of them), the memorabilia of warfare and allied products... constitutes the largest single category of tourist attractions in the world' (Smith, 1996: 248).

The various concepts of *the gaze* introduced in Chapter 1 play an important role here, particularly Friedberg's *mobilised virtual gaze*, which refers to perceptions (provided by the filmmakers) where the viewer 'travels in an imaginary *flâneurie*' (Friedberg, 1993: 2). The concept of the flâneur is discussed elsewhere in this book, but basically it relates to wandering, ambling or strolling with the purpose being simply to observe, or even gaze. What we find in this chapter are discussions on mediatised representations of places to which people travel (usually to engage in battle) in which the audience virtually participates. This gaze can ultimately be transferred to the *tourist gaze* through the films, eventually moving into the real experiences of the tourist. So, while war per se may be counter-productive towards tourism in the short term, it can, particularly when interpreted via moving images with a strong narrative, lead to future pleasure travel. Furthermore, war and civil unrest are powerful forces for cultural change, which can be reinforced by the visual images and narratives of film and, subsequently, travel.

As well as considering how war and unrest have been represented by the moving image and what that may mean for tourism, we also look at films that were made during such times to either distract us or propagandise along with the role of film, travel and tourism in postwar recovery. A significant element here is the way in which film makes places (as well as people) famous, at times creating sites of pilgrimage – from the very early days of moving images, people regarded the screen as a place where dreams and desires can be fulfilled. We look at this in this chapter in terms of the cult of celebrity as well as the theory behind Celebrity Worship Syndrome, which is described and discussed in Chapter 11.

If we regard the link between moving images, unrest and tourism in terms of the themes of journeying and quest, the relationship between civil or political unrest and travel does not end with the filmic representations. This enables us to consider other forms of moving images and battles, including computer games, science fiction and fantasy epics, all of which contain significant travel narratives alongside war.

A Typology of War Films

When we look at the range of films based on war they can be organised into a small number of categories in terms of their 'authenticity'. Using filmmaker R.W. Paul's range of early Anglo-Boer War films, Christie (2007) identified five types of early 'war' films (departures and arrivals, actuality, documentary, reproduction and allegories) that we can use as a framework for many of the war films discussed in this chapter, especially in relation to location-based narratives. This work, as well as other types of film referred to later in the chapter, informs the typology of war films in Table 3.1.

In R.W. Paul's oeuvre, he openly acknowledged his staged (or fake) films; however, not all filmmakers so clearly acknowledged their actions, adding other types of war film to the typology that have not been identified by Christie, namely those of the 'deceptive fake' as well as fictional narratives. For example, Stuart Blackton's *Battle of Santiago Bay* (1898) from the Spanish-American War was re-created in a bathtub (Collins, 1987). When viewing the footage today, it is hard to believe that the audience was not aware of the subterfuge, and they may well have been, yet were happy to use their imagination to re-create the emotion of the battle. Popple and Kember (2004: 60) agree, proposing that '[a]udiences became adept at distinguishing between scenarios that had been elaborately staged for the benefits of the camera and films that depicted real events'. This is a point I come back to time and again when looking at film and tourism, particularly later in the book when we look at animation and developing technologies. Furthermore, we see the rise of more escapist romantic fictions based around a war story, such as the famous and much loved classic, *Casablanca* (1942).

We can frame this in terms of the relationship between audience and tourist activity model introduced in Chapter 1 (Figure 1.3), representing the audience's orientation of selection, involvement and using the filmic experience. We can posit the case that each type of film outlined in Table 3.1 elicits a reaction from, or responds to a need of, the film audience. For example, an allegorical film may tend to create feelings of nostalgia and loss, with a potential touristic response along the lines of pilgrimage or sacred journey to a site of war, while a fictional narrative such as *Casablanca* engages notions of romance and sacrifice which may translate into touristic responses such as emotional re-creation at places such as Rick's Bar. Friedberg's (1993) *virtual gaze* as introduced in Chapter 1 can be seen here, with the audience receiving a mediated, emotionally laden perception of war, in effect also pre-empting and social organising a future *tourist gaze*, intertwining it with the consumption of media images, as noted by Jansson (2002).

Table 3.1 Typology of war films

Type of film	Description		Example
Actuality material	Following the established practice of filming topical items on location	Precursor to the newsreel	Footage of Anglo-Boer General Cronje in captivity (R.W. Paul)
	Dockside departures & arrivals	Pathos of seeing distant friends and relatives captured on the screen (precursor to the newsreel)	Numerous untitled and often uncredited examples
Documentary	Longer film encompassing a broader theme with its own narrative	Precursor to the modern documentary	*Army Life* (R.W. Paul) covered all aspects of induction and training
Reproduction of incidents	Dramatic narratives	Labelled as such and supervised by an official (army officer)	*A Camp Smithy* (1901), *Shooting the Spy* (1901) and *Bombardment of Mafeking* (1901) by R.W. Paul. Filmed near his UK studios
	Deceptive fakes (dramatic narratives presented as authentic)	Aimed to deceive – patronising approach to the audience	*Battle of Santiago Bay* (Stuart Blackton, 1898)
Allegorical films	Sentimental semi-fictional pieces, offering emotional engagement	Often using flashback narratives to link battlefield with home	*His Mother's Portrait*, *Britain's Welcome to her Sons* (R.W. Paul)
Fictional narratives	Escapist, sentimental, romanticised pieces	Featuring brave, self-sacrificing and good-looking men and women	*Casablanca* (1942)

While in this chapter my main goal is to tease out the relationship between film, war and postwar tourism, there are those who travel for war, apart from the actual combatants. This includes journalists, camera operators, artists and photographers, many of whom had official positions within the armies as recorders and reporters. While not examining this in depth, the work of Burton Holmes is discussed in this light as well as considering the (tourism) role that the news media and those associated with it have played in the more recent wars, particularly the 'embedding' of journalists with troops in the Gulf War.

War in the Age of the Moving Image: Travel Lectures, Newsreels, Movies and TV

While I defend my rationale for my interest in the way that travel and tourism relate to war, the connection between them is at times a little tenuous, particularly in this section, which primarily deals with the development of the presentation of war and the gaze of the filmmakers rather than that of the audience or tourist. However, such a dialogue is necessary in order to contextualise the ensuing discussion and allow us to consider how representations of war influence our images of and feelings about a place.

Once the realm of writers, artists and still photographers, the reporting and presentation of war began to change in favour of the filmmaker as soon as the technology was available. The ways in which war has been depicted in the age of the moving image, and the opportunity to present actual (or at times simulated) footage of people and battles in a 'moving' manner are related, building on the historical aspects of previous chapters. Being able to show ordinary as well as famous people actually travelling to places and undertaking the various activities related to war was no doubt a personally moving experience. It can also be seen that some of the technical developments such as mobile filming techniques, telephoto lenses, efficient viewfinders and editing skills were accelerated due to the need to get stories of the war out as quickly (and authentically) as possible. However, not all film was about presenting actual war footage and stories, but also in creating stories for entertainment, edification and even escape.

From wartime travel lectures to newsreels

The early presentations of 'war' were based around magic-lantern lectures, and included mixed entertainment such as animated slides, films and songs along with the personal narrative and connection of the lecturer to the story (Christie, 2007). For example, a filmed account of a prewar group tour to South Africa, *A Trip to the Transvaal*, gained the interest of the general public due to the Anglo-Boer War (1899–1902). This comprised a group of four films covering the group's departure, their arrival at Cape Town, the modernity of the town and finally a film of mounted policemen cantering down the street, which were contextualised by the lecturer in terms of the war by inserting a series of magic-lantern slides and references to a relative fighting there.

While it is not always easy to locate extant film from this period, there is further evidence of this rather opportunistic approach being taken by numerous filmmakers and entertainers in relation to the war in contemporary reviews and media reports. This can be found in an English music hall presentation from December 1899, which advertised 'animated photographs of ... War Scenes, Episodes and Incidents' (Christie, 2007: 84), yet only three of the 20 films that were presented in the travelogue-style narrative were of the war. This was deemed sufficient to give the 'war experience' top billing. As noted by Christie, both of these Anglo-Boer War examples from the early days of the moving image 'offer travelogue-style narratives that dwelt on picturesque aspects of South Africa, and, while war "motivated", touch only briefly on the war itself' (Christie, 2007: 84). Whether these travelogues were being used due to the issue of limited war footage, or if they were there to 'promote' tourism is open to conjecture; however, the connection between war, travel and tourism in film is certainly evident from this time. During his 1904–1905 lecture season, the famous travel lecturer Burton Holmes showed films presenting aspects of the Russo-Japanese War and the sinking of the Russian fleet in Manchuria; however, unusually for Holmes, these were not his own images, using photographs from war correspondents Joseph Rosenthal and James Ricalton (Caldwell, 2006).

Due to the popularity of documentary war film through the early mixed-media lectures such as those discussed above, as technology developed, the rise of the newsreel was a natural progression, and has become arguably the best known of the 'factual' films of the early era of the moving image. The newsreel exploited an item of current interest, which often related (although not exclusively) to stories of civil unrest or war, and was so popular that, as noted earlier, if the filmmakers did not have authentic footage, instead of presenting prewar footage as previously, they faked it.

However, not all footage was faked or reconstructed. Frustrated with his reliance on others for war footage, and recognising an opportunity to apply his film-making skills, Holmes decided to visit and film WWI on location. As a civilian, this was not possible, so in 1918 Holmes sailed out of New York as a uniformed war correspondent with the United States army. He filmed the battlefields of Belgium, France and Italy during WWI, in effect becoming one of the early 'embedded' reporters.

> My precious filmed pictures of the war as I had seen it – and recorded it – were safely with me and I began the making up of my most dramatic

programs of 'The Yanks in England' and the other four travelogues about the Yanks in Paris, in France, at the Front, and in Italy. (Holmes, 1953, cited in Caldwell, 2006: 136)

While Holmes' work was authentic on-location film, utilising the increasingly mobile technology of the period, dramatic re-creations and fake footage continued, primarily due to the dangers of travelling to war. Holmes himself says 'I kissed myself good-bye' as he headed across the Atlantic in a convoy comprising 23,000 soldiers of the American Expeditionary Force in 1918 (Holmes, 1953, cited in Caldwell, 2006: 131).

The rise of the newsreel from 1910 onwards saw the so-called documentary films of the late 19th and early 20th centuries move from the world of the live performance of the travel lecture into a product for general consumption through the growing network of commercial cinemas. Moving away from the travel lecture format, these became stand-alone productions, with the information previously provided by the lecturer presented by intertitles. As Altman summarises, '[t]ravel and war films had been severed from the live stage, turned instead into commodities expected to stand by themselves' (Altman, 2006: 76).

Being presented in cinemas prior to the main feature, or as part of a variety of filmed and performed entertainment as in the early decades of the 20th century, newsreels became an integral element of the cinematic experience, presenting a wider, more 'realistic' and tangible view of the world to cinema patrons. In Australia, by 1913 at least two newsreels had regular national screenings – one being Pathé's *Home Gazette*, presenting news 'from home' (that is, Britain) and the other being the *Australasian Gazette* – often referred to as 'living newspapers' (Collins, 1987: 38). Australian stories such as the opening of the first Federal Parliament in 1901 and the visit of the American naval fleet in 1908 were covered, as well as news of the wars affecting Britain. By 1919, '[t]he longstanding fascination of film audiences for newsworthy events was now fully exploited by Pathé, who inaugurated weekly newsreels' (Popple & Kember, 2004: 19). Audiences responded passionately to the newsreels; for example, in Australia when a film of the British dreadnought battleship (seen as the lynchpin of Australia's security) was shown, the cheering audience spontaneously rose to its feet singing *Rule Britannia* (Collins, 1987). Newsreels were also important throughout Europe, particularly as information and propaganda vehicles during the war years, which is looked at later in this chapter.

It is pertinent to note that, particularly during these early years of the 20th century, many of the industrialised nations had very low educational levels; consequently the newsreels became a powerful popular education medium. As Collins (1987: 43) explains, 'the factual film gave women and men new geographical and cultural contexts in which to locate themselves and their experiences'. Through comments such as this from Collins, we can consider the possibility of some connections with the desire of viewers to travel to the exotic locales and cultures depicted in these newsreels as they become more aware of the size and scope of the world. This marks a significant era of cultural change, where the general populace began to consider the possibility of travel to these exotic lands, while at the same time the technology began to be developed that would enable this.

Creating famous places

As noted at the beginning of this chapter, one of my primary propositions is that the media representations of war make places 'famous', taking on their own celebrity status that people love to 'brag' about, and which in turn can influence people's desire to travel there. Furthermore, the public display of travelogues to a broader audience than simply that of the travel lecture has similar potential. One example of this is Cape Town in South Africa during the aforementioned Anglo-Boer War, which created a great deal of public interest in the place itself. The use of earlier films of prewar tourists visiting Cape Town being screened due to this interest in the war was a way to provide contemporary footage in order to contextualise the ensuing battles. However, the region was also introduced to potential future tourists, and it can be argued that, if not for the Anglo-Boer War, the opportunity to view a travelogue on that region of South Africa may have remained in the realm of the educated elite, the traditional travel lecture audience.

That such emotional and often sorrowful occasions such as war and civil unrest contribute to people's fascination with a place may be seen as an indictment of human nature; however, it does happen, and while not condoning war, it has provided us with many inventions that we now use in peacetime, including travel and tourism. For example, WWI and II were instrumental in the development of the aircraft and communications that are central to today's travel.

In other publications, I have commented that many places seem to take on what we now see as 'celebrity status' from their exposure through film, and the desire for people to be able to say 'I was there' seems to be almost irresistible (Beeton, 2005a). While the notion of celebrity has come to dominate today's society, the belief that knowing someone (or somewhere) famous brings an added cachet to the individual is certainly not new, dating back to the early days of American cinema. As a result of public pressure to know who the actors in the films were, the 'star system' came into existence in the United States. In 1910, the first popular (previously anonymous) actress, Florence Lawrence, was named and publicised in order to promote the movies in which she appeared (Mintz & Roberts, 2010). The genie was out of the bottle, and actors' salaries and influence grew exponentially along with the public's passion for their films, details of their personal lives and a need for reflected glory through the collection of autographs, memorabilia, photos and shared experiences.

This led to places also taking on elements of celebrity. Today, we see places being promoted in relation to their proximity to a famous person ('where ... slept/ate/drank') as well as simply being in a film ('as seen in ...'). Where the location becomes a character in its own right, as in many western movies, these locations become even more famous, often forming strong emotional connections with the audience. As such, they are extremely attractive to tourists as discussed in detail in Chapter 5. Locations of battles depicted in a film also seem to have this famed status, attracting tourists and pilgrims alike in a form of tourism known as *battlefield* or even *dark* tourism. Taking this to the extreme are tourists who visit sites of war during actual conflict, often appropriating their own digital media technologies (cell phones, video recorders and so on) not only to record their adventure, but also to be able to demonstrate to others that 'I was there' (Bell & Lyall, 2005).

Secular pilgrimage sites and the film connection: An autoethnographic tale

While pilgrimage traditionally has religious connotations, today it has come to embrace a broader, more secular meaning. As Cousineau notes in his study of sacred travel and the pilgrimage, it is 'a powerful metaphor for *any* journey with the purpose of finding something that matters deeply to the traveler' (Cousineau, 1998: xxiii). Throughout his work he refers not only to sites based around history, religion and literature, but also movies, such as his reference to the 'secular sacred site' in Iowa from the movie *The Field of Dreams* (Cousineau, 1989: 18). He also talks about the way movies can create a desire for experience: 'Have you seen a movie like *Zorba the Greek* that makes you hunger to dance on a beach in Crete ...' (Cousineau, 1998: 52).

While many commemorative sites based around war (such as memorials, cemeteries and battlefields) are pilgrimage sites for many people from all sides of the conflict, which is often reinforced through filmic narratives, film itself can also create personal pilgrimage sites. The emotional experience can be very powerful, even at sites not directly connected to war or civil unrest. As Schramm notes, '[r]igid distinctions between (serious) pilgrims ... and playful tourists ... have become blurred' (Schramm, 2004: 134), which is evident in Dubisch's (2004) ethnographic research on a pilgrimage to the Vietnam Veterans' memorial in Washington, DC. She finds that the pilgrimage to this site not only brings back memories for the participants, but also reconstructs their personal memories.

In my first book on film and tourism, *Film-Induced Tourism*, I speak briefly about a 'pilgrimage' to Doune Castle, one of the locations of the filming of the Monty Python movie, *Monty Python and the Holy Grail* (1975). It is interesting to note that the movie's storyline is of a religious quest (albeit with tongue firmly planted in cheek), incorporating many fictional battles and sites of unrest, such as the castle manned by the English-hating French soldiers; however, it was not the storyline per se that made my journey a pilgrimage, but rather the cultural environment surrounding my actual viewing experience.

The movie was released at a time of personal change and growth in my life as I transitioned from school to university, where I became familiar with the humour of the likes of the Monty Python team. This was extremely important for me, as I felt part of an elite group who 'got it', as opposed to parents, youngsters and those 'less intellectual'(!) who did not. So, when I had the chance to visit one of the pivotal sites in the film in Scotland, I ventured out there. While not a particularly difficult journey to Doune Castle, as would be more common in traditional religious pilgrimages where hardship is part of the experience, I still felt that I was on a pilgrimage to a place where I could locate and revisit my powerful feelings from that time, fulfilling a nostalgic longing for those days – days when everything seemed possible and when I belonged to a group.

The site itself provided an additional treat for those 'in the know'. The castle is a ruin (one of my favourite types of places as they are so open to imagining and reflection), with a Visitors' Centre in one of the few remaining rooms in the keep. This was full of Monty Python memorabilia, but the clincher was one not publicised – if you went to the counter and asked for 'the coconuts', you would be given two hollow coconut shell halves. You were then able to use them to replicate and re-live scenes from the movie where the coconuts had been used to make the sound of a horse clip-clopping along by a servant following the king pretending to ride a horse (Figure 3.1). For a visitor with no knowledge of the movie, this is extremely bizarre behaviour, but such a ritual became part of my almost numinous and joyful experience. I also was taken to and shown some of the costumes not usually seen by others – providing a sense of being in an 'inner sanctum' of relics (costumes and props) and part of an exclusive group. These costumes were kept in plastic garbage bags, but were shown to me with great pride by the Visitors' Centre manager, who was clearly a Monty Python fan. While

Figure 3.1 Tourists with the coconuts at Doune Castle

initially shocked that such 'valuable' material was being treated in such a cavalier manner, I came to believe that this would be exactly how the Python team would like their work to be presented.

While not aware until writing this story and reflecting on my emotional responses, the desire to 'belong' drove much of this experience, both now when remembering, then when on the pilgrimage, and when I was younger actually experiencing the Monty Python oeuvre. I came away feeling emotionally fulfilled, but also curious to understand further why this was so significant for me. I continue to ponder this, especially when I visit other places that engender similar responses, as in some of the western movie landscapes. I confess that I do enjoy relating this experience to other fans, who are not only interested in and excited by my story, but also a little envious. Such 'bragging' is often part of the tourist experience, yet it is rarely openly admitted. I also agree with Torchin (2002), who notes that participants on film tours are often treated to 'backstage' experiences or knowledge that gives them a certain cachet with their friends and colleagues.

If we look at this from the perspective of a fan, these reactions become more understandable. As Hills explains, 'the "sacred" focal point of the cult fan's touristic pilgrimage … [is] … an affective-interpretive process with spills into and redefines material space' (Hills, 2002: 144). Hills also supports my use of this experience to illustrate the notion of secular pilgrimage.

While others may find the above story somewhat frivolous, this very personal, emotional (fan) experience reminds me of Cousineau's statement in relation to tourism, travel and pilgrimage that, '[t]he sacred, in its various guises as holy ground, art, or knowledge, evokes emotion *and* commotion' (Cousineau, 1998: xxvii). Furthermore, by examining this through an autoethnographic lens, certain personal elements can be identified and opened up for examination, including:

- emotional elements of pilgrimage and fandom;
- reflections on personal meaning;
- youthful, nostalgic emotions;
- belonging;
- pride and 'bragging rights';
- joy, laughter;
- reminder of a time of 'innocence' (when all was possible);
- fulfilment.

These, in turn, can be seen as potential drivers for deciding to visit certain sites of personal pilgrimage which have been developed entirely through film. In terms of relating to this autoethnographically, it is worth reiterating a pertinent quote from Noy used in Chapter 1:

> autoethnography enables one to communicate experience and reconstruct it in vivid, lively and sometimes even painful ways, in ways that are not 'purely' academic or that result in an over-intellectualization of the sense of having an experience. (Noy, 2007: 350)

The sites of famous battles, both victories and defeats, have become sites of another form of secular pilgrimage where visitors are motivated to visit by a wide range of reasons, and while they will talk about 'showing respect' for those who fought there, what is often occurring is a very personal, emotional, internal response to the place and what it represents for that individual. Many of the sites are touchstones that represent a wider struggle that can be simultaneously cultural and personal. That many of the famous battlegrounds have been represented in war movies contributes to this complex relationship. Such complexities are evident in a book on battlefield tourism edited by Chris Ryan (2007), where the notion of pilgrimage is almost taken as given, being referred to in a variety of contexts from 'hot war pilgrimage' to overseas visitors to Gettysburg and Culloden, along with virtual pilgrimage sites. Furthermore, sites such as that of the Battle of Gettysburg were made even more famous by movies (*Gettysburg*, 1993; see Riley *et al.*, 1998).

Two significant Australian movies that shaped a generation's views on war (and travel) and were based on early (Australian) war stories are the Boer War based *Breaker Morant* (1980) and the WWI movie *Gallipoli* (1981). While

I do not have a strong personal desire to take a pilgrimage to the sites of these movies, many others do. The town of Burra in South Australia where *Breaker Morant* was filmed continues to promote this connection, with a major celebration there for the 30th anniversary of filming the movie, presenting a more accessible site than South Africa for 'pilgrims' who may be film buffs, historians or simply interested tourists. This link to the movie and historical story is still used by South Australia Tourism as well as the South Australian Film Commission to promote the region to visitors and filmmakers.

Gallipoli (1981) was also filmed primarily in South Australia, apart from the exotic scenes of the Cairo bazaar which were filmed in Egypt. However, the South Australian beach in Coffin Bay on the Eyre Peninsula that was used to re-create Anzac Cove has been renamed Gallipoli Beach and its connection to the movie is heavily promoted. Illustrating the value of 'bragging rights' to the sites of both the movie and actual event, the 2011 travel blog of Mike and Trish states:

> To the north west of this beach is Gallipoli Beach, so named as it was a location where some of the famous Australian movie Gallipoli was filmed, Following a rocky dirt 4WD track for 4Klm we drove around a bend to see the most beautiful cove with turquoise waters below us, After actually visiting the real Gallipoli we could see the similarities and understand why the movie was made here. (https://www.travelblog.org/Oceania/Australia/South-Australia/Eyre-Peninsula/blog-662383.html)

In effect, this Australian beach has become a pseudo-pilgrimage site, where visitors can connect with the story, emotions and meaning of Gallipoli, both as presented in the movie and in 'reality', without travelling to Turkey. A number of beaches in Hawaii where war movies were filmed, such as *South Pacific* (1958) on the island of Kauai, have become sites of attraction and even pilgrimage, while *Pearl Harbor* (2001) film sites in California also developed a certain significance, alongside the real Pearl Harbor in Hawaii.

Conclusion

Wartime is a time of great cultural change, leaving all those connected to it, even if it is virtually (or imaginatively) through film, affected. In this chapter, I have provided some evidence of films creating an emotional link between the viewer and a place, as well as war providing sites of great personal (and cultural) meaning, particularly in terms of unrest and war. When these elements combine, the result can be extremely powerful. I have touched on the notion of pilgrimage and noted that such sites, while often historically situated (such as sites of famous battles – wins and losses) can also be created through the storytelling of film, where even the places of filming can become pseudo-pilgrimage sites. Furthermore, the early use of film in the travel lectures of Burton Holmes brought wartime places and stories to a predominantly domestic American audience.

In the next chapter, we take this discussion based in the eras of WWI and WWII to consider further the various roles that film plays in presenting propaganda, and the concomitant rise of what has been termed 'national cinema'.

4 The Emotions of Motion 2: War Propaganda, National Cinema and Travel

After the discussion on war, travel lectures and pilgrimage in the previous chapter, I continue to outline the development of moving images and travel related to times of civil unrest by looking at how cinema was used as a propaganda tool of war, not only in Hollywood but by all national powers, resulting in the rise of the concept of national cinemas. In order to trace these developments, understanding the ascendancy of Hollywood is a good place to start, especially in terms of my own cultural upbringing and awareness.

The Ascendancy of Hollywood

It was during the early 20th century that we began to see the rise of the dominance of Hollywood on the international film scene. Initially based in the theatrical centre of America, New York, filmmakers started moving west to California around 1908 to take advantage of cheap land and labour as well as a climate suitable for year-round outdoor filming. The European (primarily Jewish) immigrant entrepreneurs, who were less conservative than American-born producers and saw the film industry as a customer-based enterprise, were instrumental in the rise of Hollywood. By catering to what the audience wanted, movies coming from the Hollywood studios soon attracted a large and diverse audience. As one of the leading Hollywood moguls, Samuel Goldwyn stated, '[i]f the audience don't like a picture they have a good reason' (cited in Mintz & Roberts, 2010: 12).

From the 1920s Hollywood became widely acknowledged as the world's film capital, with many European audiences embracing the rawness and vitality of American movies. While other national cinemas also developed during this period, as discussed later in this chapter, the dominance of Hollywood (and the American accent and culture) cannot be denied. As an Australian growing up in the 1960s and 1970s, Hollywood's influence on my own life and travels permeates this book, particularly when we look at the role of westerns, film ranches and theme parks.

Further assisting the growth of cinema, in a somewhat perverse way, was the Great Depression (1929–1933). With the seeds of the Depression being sown shortly after the end of WWI, the general populace in the United States and other parts of the world embraced the cinema as a form of escapism; however, they also desired to share their fate with those on the screen with realist movies depicting the long labour lines, poverty, and so on. We look at the relationship between the Great Depression and film further in Chapter 5, regarding the rise of gangster movies during that period. The momentum gathered and enthusiasm for the movies rolled into the period of WWII (1939–1945), where the United States continued to produce films, while Europe's capacity became severely restricted due to the changes being wrought by war.

In relation to movies about WWI and II, and as a highly influential propaganda machine, Hollywood came into its own, particularly in WWII, which occurred after the introduction of the 'talkies' and eventually colour. While the aim of this publication is not to provide a complete history of the moving picture, the developments of sound and colour are important not only in terms of the growth of Hollywood, but also because of the significant effects they had on the representation of places, travel and tourism. As noted in Chapter 2, the silent cinema era finished around 1927 with the successful integration of a synchronised soundtrack with *The Jazz Singer* (1927). However, the acceptance of synchronised sound did not occur overnight, with many attempts being made over the previous decades to develop such technology, and even the commercial efforts of the 1920s needed some adjustment. As Charlie Chaplin stated:

> it was a terrible shock ... as the picture progressed the dialogue became funnier, but not as funny as the sound effects. When the handle of the boudoir door turned I thought someone had cranked up a farm tractor, and when the door closed it sounded like the collision of two lumber trucks. ... I came away from the theatre believing the days of sound were numbered. (Chaplin, 1964)

As with synchronised sound, there were many efforts being made to produce films in colour before it became accepted. Ultimately, it was the development of the three-colour *Technicolor* process that came to represent the beginning of serious moves into colour filming, with the first feature colour film being *Becky Sharp* (1935), based on Thackeray's popular novel, *Vanity Fair*. The first outdoor drama filmed in full colour was *The Trail of the Lonesome Pine* (1936). While expensive, the positive public response to sound and colour ensured their eventual uptake. The majority of the ensuing work discussed in this book refers to the era after the development of such initiatives.

The Role of Moving Images in Propaganda and Distraction

As the public's fascination with and demand for war news increased, we began to see not only re-creations of actual events, but also the development of 'action dramas' based on battle stories with acknowledged actors presenting stories with very specific messages. The Boxer Rebellion in China during the first few months of the 20th century presented such an opportunity, with James Williamson shooting the film, *Attack on a China Mission* (1900), at a house in Hove, England. The titles state that this was 'based on an incident from the Boxer Rebellion' with a list of credits of the actors playing the roles of the missionary, his wife and the officer (IMDb, n.d.). Viewing the extant fragments of the movie (one and a quarter minutes out of the original four minutes), it is clear that the Chinese were the disorganised, cruel enemy who were eventually overcome by the brave and organised British soldiers.

With the luxury of political, temporal and spatial distance, one may question this simplistic propaganda perspective today – the Boxer Rebellion was an attempt by a secret society to rid China of English foreigners and, in particular, missionaries, but the English perspective places the Chinese in the role of exotic and dangerous foreigners. So it can be argued that this was the first 'propagandised' film created to support the desire for English supremacy over the East. These 'factual' dramas remained popular and moved on to dramatise other famous victories as well as more fictional accounts of war. Such re-creations filmed in places other than where they are set have become known as 'runaway productions' and, while such deception has the potential to confuse tourists wishing to view and experience the actual place, there are numerous examples of the runaway, as well as 'real' destinations developing tourism based on such films (Beeton, 2010a; Frost, 2006).

At the outbreak of WWI in 1914, filmmakers rushed to produce feature 'real life' documentaries, including titles such as *On the Belgian Battlefield* (1914), *The War of the World* (1914), *Battles of a Nation* (1915), *The History of the World's Greatest War* (1915), *The Warring Millions* (1915), and so on. Still in its infancy, many of the films made by Hollywood during WWI were overtly propagandistic and most likely (at least in part) to be inaccurate, depicting unsubstantiated enemy atrocities, such as German soldiers ravishing innocent women. According to Koppes and Black, 'World War I offered two types of propaganda about the enemy that attracted the filmmakers ... – atrocity stories and hate pictures' (Koppes & Black, 1990: 248). However, it is worth noting that there are limited records of Hollywood's WWI oeuvre, and they certainly do not feature in any listings of 'classic' films, due in part to the aforementioned issues of lack of preservation.

While the United States did not enter the war until 1917, Universal Studios was prepared for this political move, immediately opening a special unit, Universal Preparedness Productions, which produced serials, short films and features including Rupert Julian's *The Kaiser, The Beast of Berlin* (1918) and a satire, *The Geezer of Berlin* (1918). It was reported that a man in Iowa fired at the screen during one showing of the satire. Also in 1918, American Pictures released *Berlin via America*, which was a convoluted spy story starring Francis Ford, forming the basis for many of the US WWII spy movies. However, most of the films made during WWI were simple propaganda-based profiles of the enemy rather than highly narrative.

While such movies did not overtly encourage travel, especially for pleasure, their representations of previously little-known exotic places and cultures set up an interest in witnessing such exotic sites and sights in the future. However, it was air travel that truly engaged the general public's romantic imagination, particularly as it was presented to them during wartime.

The romance of the air: From battles to passengers

From the beginning of WWI, aircraft were used for scouting, photography, directing artillery fire and patrolling the Front; however, when Fokker developed a way to synchronise the firing of a machine gun with the aircraft's propeller for the German army, aircraft truly became part of the battle. This innovation was also instrumental in the development of the 'cult of the air fighter' (Paris, 1995: 24). Removed from war on the ground, which was grim, dirty and filled with peril, the aircraft flew above this in clean air, fighting individual duels that were far easier for the propaganda machine to glamorise, being presented by all sides as chivalrous, honourable men. 'In newspapers, through morale-boosting tours of the homeland, on postcards and magazine covers, but above all *through the moving picture*, the image of the air fighter was promoted' (Paris, 1995: 26, own emphasis). The Germans produced the most famous of the ace fighters in the Red Baron (Manfred von

Richthofen) who was the focus of many stories and films made to promote the success of Germany.

As well as meeting the propaganda needs of all sides in the conflict, these romantic heroes and valiant villains played out beautifully on the screen, with the air films taking on the glamorous heroic roles of the ancient classics. They also represented and perpetuated a fascination with travel to exotic places by exotic means, in many ways marking the early days of the romance of air travel. As Paris so aptly explains:

> [i]n *With the RFC*, for example, the scene of the pilots of 60 Squadron lined up before their machines show us exuberant, cleanly dressed young officers laughing and joking. An almost identical scene is to be found in the German *War Fliers on the Western Front*. We ... cannot help but compare them with the grim faces of the trench fighters to be found even in such propagandist films and the *Battle of the Somme* (1916). (Paris, 1995: 33)

By 1916, the UK film industry had overcome the shortages of personnel and equipment brought on by the war, and was able to develop full-scale dramas, such as Smith's *The Strafer Strafed* (1916), a recreation of a famous defeat of a Zeppelin over London, which he reconstructed in his home using cotton wool, models and trick photography – another example of a 'deceptive fake'.

War movies in general fell out of popularity after the Armistice, but we see resurgence in interest in films about the air war in the late 1920s, with over 30 American films based on that theme. The best known and most commercially successful of these were *Wings* (1927) which won the first Academy Award for Best Picture of the Year in 1928, *Hell's Angels* (1930), and *Dawn Patrol* (1930) – often cited as an anti-war film but denied as such by its producer, Hawks. The success of these films ensured the place of the war flying film during peacetime, further exoticising and romanticising travel. As Paris (1995: 55) explains, '[m]any of those working in the industry saw the potential of the aeroplane as an exciting ingredient for fiction films, while others became interested in aviation as a revolutionary form of transportation'.

The period leading up to WWII saw a substantial increase from all sides of the conflict in stories and films that perpetuated the myth of the romantic, gallant air force pilot. For example, the Nazis used the image of aircraft and flying as a link between past and present, often representing the movement from a dark past to a bright future, as in *The Triumph of the Will* (1934). Along with the European and American fascination with aviation, chivalry and bravery, Japan also produced films that celebrated and perpetuated such ideals, such as *Soaring Passion* (1940) and *Nippon's Young Eagles* (1940), telling the stories of young men training to be pilots. Once WWII had been declared, the movie industries in all countries found a great deal of material in the stories of the heroes of the air, with countless movies made and stories told by all sides of the conflict. By the end of the war, the romance of flying was well established.

The development of aircraft and experienced pilots during both World Wars paved the way for the successful introduction of commercial passenger air travel, which is a cornerstone of today's travel industry. As Smith comments, 'the technological innovations which helped to win the war also spawned peace-time airborne international tourism and the awareness that freedom to travel is a human right' (Smith, 1998: 202). In spite of some of the more prosaic approaches of today's budget airlines, the romance of flying as first presented on film during the war remains prevalent for much of today's travel and tourism experiences. Even today, commercial pilots continue to wear military-inspired uniforms. Certainly, the romance of the fighter pilot is not dead, with movies such as *Top Gun* (1986) and even the Captain America series such as *Captain America: The Winter Soldier* (2014) perpetuating the exotic lifestyle, adventure and travel of the pilot.

The war and travel films from the Red Cross

During WWI, many of the national Red Cross organisations around the world were not only active in providing medical support to the troops, but also encouraged filming of their activities, realising the potential it presented in terms of showcasing their work. The American Red Cross was initially sceptical of commercial filming of their work, but as they soon needed to rapidly increase their level of financial support during wartime, they developed a highly effective advertising campaign based around many of their films (Veeder, 1990). In 1917, the American Red Cross formed The Red Cross Bureau of Pictures, which made more than 100 films between 1917 and 1921. In 2010, the movie, *Heroes All* (1920), featuring the activities of Red Cross staff as they assisted in the rehabilitation of returning WWI veterans, was one of the 25 films to be selected that year for inclusion in the US Library of Congress National Film Registry (American Red Cross, 2010).

Red Cross organisations continued to use film to assist in their fundraising and public relations efforts, with films being produced in Australia such as *Red Cross Activities During and After World War I* (1919), while the American Red Cross produced films such as *To the Aid of Poland* (1919) and *The Fall of Kiev* (1919) to assist their ongoing work (American Red Cross, 2005; National Film and Sound Archive, 2011).

Following its wartime success, the American Red Cross continued to film its work in the field after the end of the war. Filmmakers were given an enormous amount of licence and, as Veeder notes, 'they worked, without supervision and with very general directions, to photograph Red Cross activities and *interesting scenes of local people and their lifestyles*' (Veeder, 1990: 59; own emphasis). What they ended up with was significant scenic and cultural footage, which some in the organisation realised would appeal to the postwar cinema audience, so the Red Cross Travel Film Series was developed. This included movies such as Schoedsack's *Neath Poland's Harvest Skies* (1920) and *Shepherds of Tatra* (1921), which were upbeat, focusing on the 'quaint and exotic lives of the peasants in a devastated Europe' (Nacify, 2006: 118). While most of the films have not been preserved, making any comprehensive study of them difficult, we can consider other films in the series, including *Appleblossom Time in Normandy* (1920) and a range of films by LaVoy, including *Marie, Queen of Rumania, Children of the Sahara* and *Constantinople* and *Gateway to the Land of the Arabian Nights*, to present these exotic cultures to a world beginning to experience the democratisation of travel, particularly in the West. Veeder explains that:

> The structure and content of the travel films was different from the war films. Cameraman Edouart enthusiastically approved of what Waddell was doing with their footage. The films, he noted: '... commence with interesting European scenic stuff to attract and hold interest, then ease in a few snappy unposed and effective Red Cross scenes, then working into the scenic stuff again, they leave a very satisfactory and pleasing impression'. (Veeder, 1990: 60)

It appears that the Red Cross was not simply using films to promote their work, but also to make money, which is where one can assume the travel films sit. What is interesting here is how filming wartime activities seamlessly shifted into filming tourism-related scenes, providing us with an interesting link between war, film and tourism.

Europe's wartime cinema

In spite of severe deprivations of finance, equipment and expertise, European cinema was producing some remarkable work, particularly prior to America's entry into WWII. While many filmmakers were influenced and at times controlled by various propaganda and censorship regimes, it is worth looking at some of this work.

Due to the evacuation of many of the large studios from Moscow, in 1941 Russia was focusing on the production of short-story films that could be joined together to form new wartime programmes, known as *albums*.

However, not all filmmakers followed this path, with Eisenstein producing his final great films, *Ivan the Terrible Parts I and II* (released in 1944 and 1958) about Ivan IV (1530–1584) of Russia. The late release of Part II was due to disapproval from the Russian government of the portrayal of Ivan as less than a hero. The first major feature production of the war years was of the Russian civil war (1918), the Vasliev Brothers' *Defence of Tsaritsin* (1942), which portrayed Stalin in a positive light, presenting a positive story of past battles, with other features including Ivan Pyriev's *Russian Guerrillas* (1942) and Donskoi's adaptation of Ostrovsky's 1930 novel of the civil war, *How the Steel was Tempered* (1942) (Manvell, 1974). While there were feature films about the current war, much of the storytelling of that era was left to the albums; however, directors such as Roberto Rosselini worked on official films such as a feature-length documentary on a hospital ship, *La Nave Bianca* (1941), and *L'Uomo della Croce* (*Man of the Cross*, 1943), set on the Russian front during the summer of 1942. Somewhat surprisingly, in light of his earlier films, Rossellini went on to become the great protagonist of the Italian Resistance, with movies such as what became known as his postwar neo-realism trilogy, *Rome, Open City* (1945), *Paisà* (1946) and *Germany Year Zero* (1948), along with *Viagio In Italia* (1954), one of numerous Rossellini films starring Ingrid Bergman (IMDb, n.d.). Rossellini's fascist-era stories seem now to be an embarrassing prelude to this later work, and are often ignored or even forgotten (Manvell, 1974).

The propaganda films of the Germans initially reflected a mood of elation and triumph, making feature-length documentaries including *Feuertaufe* (*Baptism of Fire*) (1940) and *Sieg im Westen* (*Victory in the West*) (1941), which were filmed on the Front Line, and were not reconstructions. In fact, newsreels often overtook the 'feature film' in German cinemas as they were often up to 40 minutes long. According to Manvell (1974: 93) 'every effort was made to ensure that the maximum number possible in the population saw the feature-documentaries'. Moving away from the newsreel documentaries, the most celebrated anti-British film was *Ohm Kruger* (*Uncle Kruger*) (1941), based on a Resistance story from the Boer War, with Queen Victoria being portrayed as a cunning old witch addicted to whisky and an obese and lecherous Prince of Wales, and so on. Anti-Polish films also appeared in 1941, with the most virulent propaganda film expressing an anti-Semitic sentiments.

Italian filmmakers had been severely censored during the Mussolini era, yet towards the end of its dominance the status quo was famously challenged by Luchino Visconti through the development of films such as *Ossessione* (*Obsession*) (1941). Based in part on Cain's *The Postman Always Rings Twice*, *Ossessione* presented a 'realistic' view of Italy not desired by the fascists or the Church, and was banned for some time (Manvell, 1974).

While its role during this transitional era has become distorted into legend, it certainly encouraged the emergence of other neo-realist directors once Italy was liberated.

During the early period of the WWII, cinema patronage in Britain was around 20 million, increasing to 30 million by 1945. Interestingly, the feature film industry in Britain was not hampered by any sort of national propaganda policy, with the government (even Churchill) leaving it to create what propaganda it liked, which tended to be rather simplistic and damning of the Nazis – a stance the British government seemed loath to take, yet did not try to prevent (Manvell, 1974). As well as basic battle movies, thriller stories were conceived with the Nazis as the enemy, such as Summer's *Traitor Spy* (1939), Powell's *Contraband* (1940) and Reed's *Gestapo* (1940).

Hollywood's WWII

What came to be seen later as the golden age of British cinema from around the 1930s to the 1940s saw war films such as Noel Coward's *In Which We Serve* (1942) being produced. However, by around 1943, as the severity of WWII increasingly hit the UK, the supply of British films diminished, assisting in the growth of Hollywood.

Possibly as a reaction to Hollywood's overt efforts to promote public support for WWI, and concern from the Jewish immigrants who were worried about anti-Semitic sentiment, throughout much of Hitler's rise to power during the 1930s after WWI, the now dominant Hollywood studios seemed reluctant to produce films about the European political situation. For example, when Charlie Chaplin first proposed his first talking picture, a 'burlesque of Hitler' in 1938, he was reprimanded for applying his talent to a film that would have negative repercussions on the Jews in Germany (Koppes & Black, 1990). The film was ultimately produced and screened in 1940 as the satirical *The Great Dictator*, becoming an enormous success and cinematic classic.

However, as the mood in the US moved towards supporting those nations that opposed Hitler, the temper of many movies also seems to have changed. Starting with *Confessions of a Nazi Spy* (1939), Hollywood presented a number of movies that had overtly anti-German and pro-British themes. Other examples include *Foreign Correspondent* (1940) and *A Yank in the RAF* (1941), which alarmed those opposed to US involvement in European affairs, as the United States was not yet officially involved in the war (Moser, 2001). In 1941 Senator Burton K. Wheeler, who felt that the eight largest movie studios were taking advantage of their position to influence people via their films, appointed a subcommittee to investigate alleged war propaganda in Hollywood movies. One of the committee members, Senator Gerald Nye, accused Hollywood of producing many pictures 'designed to drug the reason of the American people, set aflame their emotions, turn their hatred into a blaze ...' (cited in Mintz & Roberts, 2010: 18). However, in actual fact, the movies were generally balanced in terms of presenting some 'good Germans', inferring that not everyone is evil. This is different from much of propaganda of the earlier wars, and certainly from German propaganda films.

While there seems to be little doubt as to the nature of the selected films noted above, there are varying interpretations as to the role the movies and the investigation played in Americans' attitude towards the war and the country's eventual involvement in WWII. Suffice to say that, after the Japanese attack on Pearl Harbor in Hawaii, America found it had little choice but to join the war, and the investigation was discontinued. What is of interest here is the belief of the power of the moving image to influence people's attitudes, beliefs and desires, which continues today.

Once committed to the war, the movies rolled out of the studios, with Hollywood's greatest contribution being that of encouraging (or even developing) morale, with combat films emphasising 'patriotism, group effort and the value of individual sacrifices for a larger cause' (Mintz & Roberts, 2010: 19). Many also operated as allegories of a democratic nation at war, reinforcing the American philosophic ideal. During the war years, some 90 million Americans went to the movies every week, seeking information, news and escape, where they could participate in virtual travel experiences.

War in the Pacific

While the Germans, in spite of being 'horrible and deadly', received a relatively nuanced treatment by Hollywood, the Japanese fell victim to the notion that such exotic Easterners were subhuman and repulsive, as in the English portrayal of the Chinese rebels in the Boxer Revolution. While the Chinese came to be seen by Americans in a positive light, after Pearl Harbor the Japanese became the focus of general hatred by the Allies. They were presented in film 'primarily as the beast in the jungle' (Koppes & Black, 1990: 248). Frank Capra's *Know Your Enemy – Japan* (1945) affirmed the general prejudice that the Japanese were a race, not of individuals (some good, some bad), but as one with a herd instinct that unquestionably followed their emperor. In virtually all of the war movies about the Pacific, the Japanese remained faceless, nameless and usually speechless, rendering them less than human. One of the most vicious anti-Japanese films, *Objective Burma* (1945) starring Errol Flynn, was about American paratroopers fighting in Burma, where they never actually landed; however, such details were unimportant in the desire to portray the Americans as good and the Japanese as evil.

During the war, Japanese war successes were celebrated in a number of Japanese feature films, such as Kajiro Yamamoto's *The War at Sea from Hawaii to Malaya* (1942), which was released on the anniversary of Pearl Harbor, and Tetsu Taguchi's *Generals, Staff and Soldiers* (1942), filmed in North China under strict Japanese military control. Numerous Japanese anti-espionage films showed the failure of English and American attempts to use spies, such as Kimisaburo Yoshimura's *The Spy is Not Dead Yet* (*Kancho Mada Shisezu*) (1942). However, the Japanese did not parallel the extreme type of anti-Oriental caricature favoured in the British and American films, with the propaganda focusing more on the historical perspective of the British as intruders into Asia (Manvell, 1974).

According to Seaton (2007), at least 235 Japanese war films set in the years of WWII were given public screening, with the greatest number produced in the 1950s and 1960s. Those films produced shortly after the war were more nostalgic, working to glorify the military, and many were produced to a predictable formula, becoming the cash crops of the Japanese cinema. As the postwar years progressed, the Japanese developed ways in which to present their war memories in a commercially successful fashion, often by presenting them within conceptual frameworks that included presenting the Japanese as innocent victims, or victim-heroes, requiring a moral central character (Seaton, 2007). Seaton points out that the 1980s were 'arguably the golden age of Japanese war cinema' (Seaton, 2007: 157), which included a number of atomic bomb related films, such as *Black Rain* (*Kuroi ame*) (1989) and the highly acclaimed, hard-hitting *Merry Christmas Mr Lawrence* (*Senjo no meri kurisumasu*) (1983) about the treatment of Allied POWs. The latter movie and other award-winning movies such as *The Emperor's Naked Army Marches On* (*Yuki yukite shingun*) (1987) that related a former Japanese soldier's campaign to force confessions of atrocities out of other ex-soldiers, winning an award at the Berlin Film Festival, can be seen to reflect the country's attempts to come to terms with their actions in WWII.

While it is not easy to quantify the relationship these films had to tourism, we can assume that the aim of most propaganda-based films was as far from travel and tourism as one can get. However, vilifying a culture while valorising another can, at times, lead to a later, peacetime fascination and desire to learn more about the reality by visiting their home countries. Also, as noted previously, many of the famous battle sites (from film and in reality) are based in these countries and have become pilgrimage sites. Today the Japanese are the primary international visitors to Hawaii, with many making their own pilgrimage to Pearl Harbor, while those most damaged by the Japanese, the Koreans, are one of their major tourist-generating regions.

The Rise of National Cinemas (1914–1926)

During and after WWI, we see the rise of what has become known as 'national cinema', where the desire for nations to reinforce their individuality (and superiority) after such tragedy is reflected in potent symbols of nationalism and creativity. National cinemas played a central role in constructing national identity during WWI, an example of which can be seen in Australia, where the war functioned as a form of initiation for the Australian nation, taking on mythical proportions through the feature films of the time.

There was also a reaction to the rising domination of Hollywood, which comprised over 90% of the cinema available in Europe and Australia, with filmmakers from other countries attempting to differentiate their work from Hollywood. Consequently, national cinemas initially focused on their domestic context, followed by the international environment. Simply put, national cinema referred to the cinema of nations other than Hollywood, and is used to differentiate them from the its dominance.

The antecedents of a national cinema can be seen in some of the movies of the silent era, with the marketing of the settings and landscapes of the silent films focusing on national differences, particularly as perceived by those for whom the cinema was being made, which was primarily the domestic audience (Moody, 2007). It was clearly in the interests of the production company to portray a coherent national ideology that would appeal to a wide audience.

However, the notion of 'national cinema' remains somewhat nebulous, being a local as well as an international form of cinema (and TV) with a close relationship to the state, often receiving some sort of government financial support. As O'Regan (1996) explains, national cinemas:

> are an aesthetic and production movement, a critical technology, a civic project of state, an industrial strategy and an international project formed in response to the dominant international cinemas (particularly but not exclusively Hollywood cinema). Australian cinema is formed as a relation to Hollywood and other national cinemas. (O'Regan, 1996: 45)

War Movies, Escapism and Tourism

The central theme of this book is about the various emotional responses and actions of audiences, travellers and tourists. What I trust I have demonstrated in these two chapters is that, particularly in the early days of the moving image, war provided the opportunity to show films about travel (and tourism) to those places, including those made previously. It also presents the world with images of 'other' foreign places, at times couched in the romance and bravery of battle as well as a compelling, beautiful counterpoint to the savagery of war.

Furthermore, war makes places famous, while the movies themselves developed the cult of celebrity, further increasing the currency of the notion of fame and tourism that I have noted elsewhere (Beeton, 2005a). From a cultural perspective, war movies tell us about the audiences/people of the time in which the movies were screened (not set), which is often also part of the quest of a traveller of that particular time, while others may use this as a way to understand a place's past.

Postwar tourism owes a great deal to the images and ideals presented in the war movies – we see tourists visiting sites not only made 'famous' during wartime, often becoming sites of pilgrimage, but also those made famous through their (often emotional) exposure in popular war movies. One classic case is the romantic war espionage melodrama, *Casablanca* (1942). Not actually filmed in Casablanca, Morocco, due in part no doubt to the ongoing war, the movie nevertheless continues to generate interest in the town in which it was set, with tours today still using material from the movie to promote Casablanca. For example, the company Journey Beyond Travel offers a movie tour of Casablanca, Morocco, and while acknowledging the 'runaway' production status of *Casablanca*, its introductory paragraph uses it as an entrée to the tour:

> Morocco is a land of mountains, deserts, medieval cities, roman ruins and famous film sets. Thinking about Morocco and film undoubtedly conjures up images of Humphrey Bogart and Ingrid Bergman in the 1942 American classic, *Casablanca*. Ironically none of *Casablanca* was filmed in Morocco, but many classics were, such as *Lawrence of Arabia* and Alfred Hitchcock's *The Man Who Knew Too Much* as well as recent hits like *The Mummy*, *Gladiator* and *Sex and the City 2*. (journeybeyondtravel.com)

Other movies during wartime were produced to provide 'replenishment and release' for 'war-tired civilians' (Collins, 1987: 202–203) with cinema goers often preferring to watch comedies and musicals after the stark 'reality' of the newsreels which began every session. Musical comedy was particularly popular, with this period seeing the rise of stars who remained popular for decades to come, and the songs in these films frequently topping the popular music charts. Musicals such as *Yankee Doodle Dandy* (1942) were fun to watch and provided strong morale boosters during wartime, while Judy Garland in *Meet Me in St Louis* (1944) and Rodgers and Hammerstein's only big screen musical *State Fair* (1945) presented reassuring slices of American life. These movies were subsequently shown on TV, contributing significantly to my own image of America, even though I saw them many years after the war.

Exotic locations such as Singapore, Morocco and Hong Kong were popular in the early 1940s *Road* series of genial musical comedies starring Bob Hope, Bing Crosby and Dorothy Lamour, while the song and dance movie, *Holiday Inn* (1942), produced the enormous Crosby hit 'White Christmas'.

Romance also played an important role in the movies, not only in the musical comedies. While based during wartime (the American Civil War, 1861–1865) and released prior to America's participation in WWII, *Gone With the Wind* (1939) provided audiences with escapism to an earlier, heroic time of wealth, grace, bravery and romance. This epic romance overrode the war elements of the movie, and has influenced tourism to the southern states of America, with tourists wishing to experience the opulence of the old South. On visiting Louisiana a few years ago with a friend, she insisted on visiting a typical Southern mansion, dreaming of sitting on the porch sipping a mint julep. Interestingly, many of the bartenders we spoke to informed us that, while tourists wish to drink a mint julep and emotionally connect with Scarlett O'Hara from the movie, many do not enjoy the bourbon whiskey based cocktail. Recently, when visiting Little Rock, Arkansas, I was shown the old mill that was filmed for the opening credits of the movie (Figure 4.1), prompting me to return home, purchase and watch the whole epic movie again.

Figure 4.1 Photo of the *Gone with the Wind* mill and signage noting the connection with the movie

As with movies such as *Gone with the Wind*, which was made in 1939 yet set during the Civil War of 1861–1865, there are movies I have included here that were made well after the World Wars yet were set in those times, often presenting a very different perspective from that of the time in which they were set. However, what I am interested in is not so much a discussion of the full representation of any particular war, but its contemporaneous representations of place and how that may have affected people's interest in foreign places and their desire to visit them. Certainly, it is not possible from the perspective of the 21st century to quantify such a response, nor fully appreciate the influence that film had at the time, except to concur with the statement that 'the cinema did have remarkable persuasive power' (Collins, 1987: 199).

Conclusion

As discussed in the previous chapter, pilgrimages to sites connected with war is a significant aspect of travel, and certainly we can see that many movies not only reinforced them, but also provided new emotional sites and places for pilgrims to visit. It is also worth reiterating the quote from Smith cited early in the previous chapter, that 'despite the horrors and destruction (and also because of them), the memorabilia of warfare and allied products ... constitutes the largest single category of tourist attractions in the world' (Smith, 1996: 248). If we consider this in terms of the model of the relationship between movie audience and tourist activity introduced in Chapter 1 (Figure 1.3), the audience's position certainly moves around the circle, with a strong emphasis on the 'involved' aspects of the sacred and possible re-creation from the tourists.

Just as cinematic technology developed, so the world moved on – yet war is never far away, from the Cold War of the 1950s and 1960s to the terrorism of the 21st century. The next chapter brings us towards modern times and examines the ways in which the moving image presents war and travel.

5 Travel in the Era of Modern Warfare and Moving Images

> *It's the movies that have really been running things in America ever since they were invented.*
> *They show you what to do, how to do it, when to do it, how to feel about it, and how to look how you feel about it.*
> Andy Warhol

While we have looked at the role of visual representations of war, both during and after, and its relationship with the early days of cinematic film making, and anthropological notions of the exotic and travel, no consideration of the role of the moving image, tourism and war can ignore its place in modern warfare, from the Cold War through to today's era of terrorism and civil unrest. While moving pictures often present such negative times in a somewhat depressive light, they continue to present us with places and stories of fascination, often exoticising the mundane. The term 'exotic' does not necessarily denote beauty, but rather the difference and 'strangeness' of others (or 'Otherness') as considered from a more anthropological perspective – in order to assess and valorise our own cultures and lifestyles, we desire to experience such differences.

Often fictional stories (movies and TV series in particular) present a romanticised or exoticised version of reality, which can also be in the form of a disaster or tragedy, where our emotional responses are extremely powerful, creating a strong personal reaction in the reader/viewer. This type of audience engagement can in itself lead to pilgrimage-style travel desires and experiences, particularly in relation to war and unrest as discussed in the previous chapter. A further case in point is a personal response I had when visiting Cambodia as a tourist, which is presented autoethnographically in the section, *Uncivil War*.

Due to the less obvious touristic nature of much of the discussion in this chapter, in order to appropriately to contextualise this, it is timely to revisit the relationship between audience and tourist activity model introduced in Chapter 1 (Figure 1.3) and re-presented here as Figure 5.1 in order to facilitate the discussion.

This iterative model reminds us that audiences often actively, emotionally engage with what they witness on the screen (large and small) and argues that, as tourists, we tend to re-live some (if not all) of these emotions, at times expanding these emotions through this additional experience. This can be witnessed through the more obvious touristic activities of picture taking and re-enacting, but can also manifest itself in their stories and personal emotions communicated directly or via various social networks. So, while reading this chapter (as well as the whole book), it is important to keep this typology in mind as a means within which to frame our understanding. As with all things involving people, tourist experiences and motivation are extremely complex, as is an audience member's response to film, giving us a great deal to consider and study.

In this chapter, we take the elements of war, film, travel and tourism introduced the previous chapter and move on through time and place, looking at espionage and the Cold War, aspects of modern-day war and

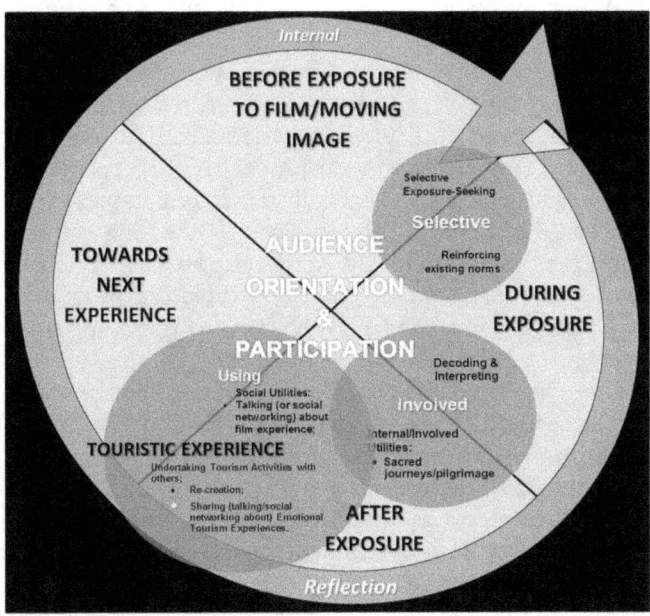

Figure 5.1 Modelling the relationship between audience and tourist activity

civil unrest, anti-war movements, postwar recovery and 'unreal' unrest in the form of battle-themed video games. In this chapter, the appeal of the exotic along with the desire to experience it is central to much of the discussion.

The Spy Movies of the Cold War (circa 1947–1991)

While fictional spy stories have been popular since the 1890s, and numerous propaganda-based anti-German spy movies began to appear out of Hollywood from 1915 onwards, as well as anti-espionage Japanese film (as noted in Chapter 4), it was the pervasive 'force' of the post-WWII Cold War that grabbed the imaginations of many filmmakers and storytellers. It can be argued that this was also the time that people were again beginning to imagine travel for pleasure/leisure, after the restrictions of WWII, and began to view the locations of these films through a different lens from that used previously.

After the end of WWII, a period of philosophical disagreement between the socialist/communist nations and the proponents of democracy, represented respectively by previous allies the USSR (Russia) and America, came to the fore. While not going to war directly against each other, the era was marked by extensive aid to politically and economically vulnerable states that included Russia's support of Cuba, proxy wars such as in Korea and Vietnam, and technological competitions such as the nuclear arms and space races, along with extensive media-driven propaganda and, finally, espionage.

While such circumstances provided a wealth of storytelling opportunities, during the 1950s Hollywood became hamstrung in presenting anything but the most banal or jingoistic stories due to the rising dominance of the House Committee on Un-American Activities (HCUAA). The work of the HCUAA resulted in prominent screenwriters, directors, producers and actors being banned from work in the film industry due to having supposed communist sentiments (Booth, 1991). As explained by the International Spy Museum, 'some spies were uncovered in the process, but history has shown that most of the accused were innocent, their lives and reputations destroyed by the Communist witch-hunt' (Earnest, 2010: 295). While not all those named were 'innocent', neither were they all guilty, and the blow to free speech and artistic expression in the United States was keenly felt, with the majority of films of that time avoiding any overt political commentary.

The spy stories that were presented demonstrated the 'accepted' propagandistic requirements, such as the 1950s TV series, *The FBI Story* (1959), which has been criticised as 'pure Bureau self-congratulatory propaganda, edited to Bureau Director J. Edgar Hoover's liking' (Johnson, 2008: 23). The synopsis from the Internet Movie Database confirms this: 'a dedicated FBI agent recalls the agency's battles against the Klan, organized crime and Communist spies' (IMDb, n.d.). This could also have contributed to the dominance of the western at the time, with its various metaphorical references and notions of *Manifest Destiny* as discussed in the next chapter on the US settlement of the West and the associated narratives.

When again able to express a range of opinions in the 1960s, the film industries produced a plethora of espionage-related stories, developing thrillers, adventures, satires and comedies all set in the Cold War period, with a particular fascination with espionage, spies and the secret service. However, Hollywood seemed to remain somewhat nervous about presenting certain aspects of the Cold War, with the mainstay of the genre being developed in the UK. These stories often featured double agents, romance and sexual entrapment from the *femmes fatales* double agents, with output and storylines dominated by the British film industry (Booth, 1991), most notably the James Bond series.

The UK-produced James Bond movies were first screened during this time, beginning with *Dr. No* (1962), which was set in Jamaica. With their beautiful women, open sexual encounters, striking locations and innovative technological gadgets and tricks, the world of the international spy is seen as an exotic place, inhabited by the trappings of wealth and leading-edge concepts. Even today, while the plots and fears of many Cold War movies appear dated, the Bond movies remain popular, marked by tongue-in-cheek humour and exotic, romantic locations with action scenes and thrilling car chases. Bond movies revel in showcasing exotic locations, many of which are, or have become, major tourist destinations. For example, *Quantum of Solace* (2008) was filmed on location in Tuscany, Craco, Matera and Basilicata (Italy), England, Chile, Panama, Madrid (Spain) and Austria, and *Skyfall* (2012) in Japan, Spain, Scotland and England, while even earlier movies such as *From Russia with Love* (1963) were filmed in Italy (Venice), Turkey, Scotland, Ireland and England (IMDb, n.d.). This focus on location filming, rather than a reliance on studio sets and computer-generated images, is a trademark of the Bond movies and has had an enormous influence on our image of, and response to, these places, often exoticising previously unknown sites. My personal favourite, *Live and Let Die* (1973) was not because of the plot, but more about the New Orleans music and was my first introduction to the concept of the Jazz funeral, which many years later I was able to participate in. Again, many of the relevant scenes were shot in New Orleans (as well as in Jamaica, New York, and so on . . .).

This series of movies has also survived many changes of actors playing the role of James Bond, from Sean Connery to George Lazenby, Roger Moore,

Timothy Dalton, Pierce Brosnan and Daniel Craig, demonstrating that it is the format, including the destinations, not the star that attracts (as long as he has some sort of 'sex appeal').

A further indication of Bond's pervasiveness in terms of exoticness and imaging (of place, culture and experience), was amply demonstrated at the Opening Ceremony of the 2012 London Olympics, where the fictional James Bond collected the real Queen Elizabeth II from Buckingham Palace, transporting her to the Games via helicopter. They supposedly parachuted into the stadium with 'traditional' James Bond UK flag parachutes. Apart from presenting the 'real' Queen alongside a fictional movie character (and current Bond actor, Daniel Craig), we witnessed the powerful link that movies have in relation to tourism – where a fictional character from the movies (the stories from the original novels ran out many iterations ago), interacts with one of the most symbolically powerful people in the Western world at one of the greatest tourist events in the world.

Bond can also be credited with developing the profile of casinos as luxurious, exciting places, not simply seedy gambling dens. I still cannot think of Monaco without seeing Bond in a tuxedo at a gaming table with wealthy men and women, or driving around the coastline at breakneck speed in his Aston Martin. However, Bond did not create this image, with casinos and gambling already possessing some sense of 'glamour' attached to them through many of the gangster movies and TV programmes, as looked at in Chapter 9.

The spy/espionage genre has also translated extremely well to TV, with contemporary series being aired on TV during the Cold War era such as the MGM studio-based *The Man from U.N.C.L.E* (1964–1968), the UK-produced *The Avengers* (1961–1969) and Paramount Pictures' *Mission: Impossible* (1966–1973; 1988–1990). In particular, the UK ITV series, *The Saint* (1962–1969), played on the popularity of the Bond movies, with glamour, high-class exotic locations and gadgets.

The themes of the older spy stories have not been erased from the public consciousness, with the screening of American series such as *The Burn Notice* (2007–2013), which pays homage to *James Bond* via its impossible storylines, tongue-in-cheek style and glamour. *Mission: Impossible* was later reinvented as a series of movies starring Tom Cruise and released in 1996, 2000, 2006 and 2011 (at the time of writing, the fifth movie in this 'series' was in production), as have numerous popular spy TV series (with varying degrees of success), including *The Avengers* (1998) which boasted a stellar list of spy-related stars including Sean Connery, Uma Thurman and Ralph Fiennes as well as *The Saint* (1997). Even the TV comedy series, *Get Smart* (1965–1970), which remains in popular re-runs today, reinforces the luxurious, globetrotting image of espionage, again released as a movie in 2008 with location filming in Russia, Canada (representing numerous 'exotic' locations) and California. Today, we still see series such as the modern-day UK espionage series, *Spooks* (2002–2011), attracting strong numbers of viewers.

In 2002, I attended a preview tour of the soon-to-be-opened International Spy Museum in Washington, DC, which has become one of the most popular attractions in the city. Radosh (2010: 287) argues that this popularity 'has a great deal to do with how espionage has been portrayed in the popular culture, especially in the movies' – particularly how it has been portrayed in English film and television. The museum features the first James Bond Aston Martin, plus many of the gadgets featured in these movies. Notwithstanding its private ownership, such a museum in the capital city of the United States lends itself to being accused of presenting a certain amount of American propaganda, representing the worst aspects of Soviet espionage. While it does illustrate the extremes of the German and Soviet espionage activities, the museum also includes the stories of some of the more infamous US double agents and illuminates some of the Western misconceptions regarding the various roles and activities undertaken by all sides.

Such attempts at balance and acknowledging humankind's own duplicity have also been criticised as pandering to political correctness (see Radosh, 2010); however, as more of the classified papers from the Cold War era become available, we are learning more about our own countries' roles in the Cold War, shedding some light on the no-so-nice elements of Allied spying. This is also reflected in the stories we are beginning to see in series such as *Spooks* (2008–current). Today, the International Spy Museum has exhibitions devoted to: 'Covers and Legends', where visitors are given a secret persona and the opportunity to role play throughout their visit; 'School for Spies', where they learn about various traditional spying techniques; the 'Secret History of History', tracing the use of spying throughout the ages; the 'War of the Spies', where neighbours in the Soviet Union spied on each other; plus information on cyberterrorism and spying in an exhibit known as 'Weapons of Mass Disruption'. One particularly interesting (and relevant) exhibit is the 'Spies Among Us', which has the following information posted on the museum's website:

> Ingenious deceptions. Double-crossed agents. Code-breaking masterminds. *It's the stuff movies*, and wars, are made of. Learn about the German and Russian spy rings operating under America's nose before WWII. Explore the unheeded intelligence that warned of Pearl Harbor. .... Then there are the celebrity spies, who traded on easy access and provided

invaluable intelligence, such luminaries as chanteuse Josephine Baker, *Oscar-winning director John Ford*, and pro ballplayer Moe Berg. And meet the relatively unknown agents, who risked everything to work behind enemy lines, and who paid the ultimate price. (http://www.spymuseum.org/exhibits; own emphasis)

The Museum also runs a series of podcasts (Spycasts) on topics that run the gamut of spying, from talks on the role of Mossad in Israel to the early years of Russian revolution, spying in the Middle East, discussions on defectors and traitors from all sides, and so on. There are also special events, podcasts, discussions and exhibits relating specifically to the fictional James Bond and other 'Spies on Screen'.

As with most of the movies we look at in this publication, the Cold War movies do not necessarily provide in-depth knowledge of the key historical players or events, but rather the beliefs and values characterised by the very culture of the times in which they were produced. This is particularly evident in the differences seen between the US and UK approaches towards spy films of the 1950s and early 1960s, and their legacy continues today. In addition, many of today's espionage movies and TV series tend to revolve more around the modern concepts of terrorism and uncertainty, with agents travelling the world to 'new' exotic places to combat hidden cells and shadowy characters. A few popular examples include the CBS franchise *NCIS* (2003–current) with Naval Intelligence, FBI/CIA-based plotlines, an ex-Mossad (Israeli Intelligence Agency) officer on the team and South American cartel connections in exotic, remote locations, as well as the US series *24* (2001–2010) and British spy series such as the aforementioned *Spooks* (2008–current).

A modern movie version of John le Carré's 1974 novel *Tinker, Tailor, Soldier, Spy* (2011) illustrates the resilience and appeal of the traditional British Cold War genre, and while the plotlines are mentally stimulating (and at times extremely convoluted), the locations, globetrotting and exotic lifestyles feature, even in this grim tale. Again, at the time of writing, yet another more recent le Carré story, reflecting a shift towards 'terrorism as espionage' with the plotline focused on terrorism (published in 2008), *Wanted Man,* is in movie pre-production (IMDb, n.d.).

Interestingly, many tourism promotions reflect this romantic, exotic nature of the spy stories, even when not a traditional location for such stories. For example, the Australian state of Victoria used images and music that highly referenced the Bond genre in an advertising campaign in 2001 with the tagline 'Romantic Melbourne'. The advertisements were in black and white, featuring an Uma Thurman-like woman being pursued by two 'agents' through the city's theatres, laneways, shops, cafes and heritage buildings, only to escape with a stylish, good-looking man via a Bond-era luxury motor boat or Aston Martin driving along the state's coast.

Representations of Asia via the spy movie

This chapter has primarily focused on the film and television industries of the US and the UK, particularly this section on spy movies and TV series. Apart from being part of my own (albeit Australian) culture, the cinemas of these two nations have influenced the world, particularly Asia. While we now recognise the significant cinema of India, including Bollywood, China and Japan as well as Korea, Malaysia and Singapore, many of them have been heavily influenced by the pervasiveness of Hollywood.

Consequently, in terms of the spy movie genre, many of the representations of Asia came to us via Hollywood, depicting 'inscrutable' Chinese and very sneaky Japanese spies. The James Bond movie, *Tomorrow Never Dies* (1997), is based around his efforts to prevent a media mogul's plan to induce war between China and the UK. It is filmed in England, the US, Germany, France and Thailand, with the usual exotic scenes, especially the Asian ones. Even the parody of *The Pink Panther* series (commencing in 1963) had an Asian sidekick, reinforcing the notion of Asian exoticness in detective and spy stories. The Australian–Hong Kong co-production, *The Man from Hong Kong* (1975) was set and filmed in Australia, bringing Asian 'exoticness' to this Western country based in the Asian region (or Asia-Pacific). This was not a great film, but contained the humour seen in many of other Asian-based Hollywood-style movies, such as many of those starring Jackie Chan.

There were spy stories being made and told by the local Asian film studios; however, many were more likely attempts to replicate Hollywood, rather than true indigenous cinematic tales. Examples include Philippine producer Bobby Suarez's series of spy movies based around INTERPOL characters such as Cleopatra Wong in *They Call Her Cleopatra Wong* (1981) and Franco Guerrero in *The One Armed Executioner* (1983), featuring the exoticised Eastern locations of Manila, Singapore and Hong Kong. Today, they are seen more as parodies of the genre than legitimate 'Asian' films. Yet, they still present the region as attractive and exotic, especially to Western eyes. These and other Asian spy movies contained a significant number of martial arts action scenes, contributing to the West's perspective, and acceptance, of Asian adventure movies.

Furthermore, the genre remains popular in Asia, with modern spy films coming out of Asia such as well-known South Korean director Seung-wan Ryoo's spoof *Dachimawa Lee* (2008), where a Korean super-spy hunts for a stolen national treasure. Seung-wan had a more serious spy thriller, *The Berlin File* (2013), about North Korean spies running from North and South Korean operatives in Berlin. Even though this movie is being shot in Latvia and Germany (with some studio work in South Korea), it certainly contributes to people's emotional responses and 'images' of Korea.

Furthermore, intra-Asian travel is significant in the region, with many visitors being attracted primarily by film and television. A classic example of this is the Japanese fascination with the popular culture of Korea, in particular that presented in the TV series, *Winter Sonata* (2002), while the historical series *Dae Jang Geum* (2003–2004) has been extremely popular in China.

Modern Warfare, Film and Travel

By the 1960s, television news had replaced the cinematic newsreels of the World Wars, with footage of conflict such as the Vietnam War being shown nightly to people in their living rooms. Even though it was highly edited, the influence of viewers seeing actual, timely footage of the war had a powerful effect on much of the civilian population. Strong anti-war sentiment grew during that period in the democratic nations. Interestingly, the major Hollywood studios made few Vietnam War films while it was happening, apart from *The Green Berets* (1968) starring John Wayne which presented the crack American team as heroes. The promotional taglines for the movie clearly illustrate the desired message:

> *They had to be the toughest fighting force on earth – and the men who led them had to be just a little bit tougher!*
> *A special force in a special kind of hell!*
> *So you don't believe in glory. And heroes are out of style. And they don't blow bugles anymore. So take another look at the special forces in a special kind of hell!*
> *First screen adventure of today's warfare.* (IMDb, n.d.)

However, it seems that this is one of the few pro-war propaganda films of the era. Was this due to an overall public aversion to the war, or simply reflecting the ownership of the major Hollywood studios, many of whom were Jewish immigrants with a direct interest in the World Wars, but not so much in this particular conflict, which in hindsight seems to have been more about an anti-communist ideology than an immediate threat. Certainly, many of the critical responses to *The Green Berets* were far from positive and 'provoked a violent left-wing critical response' (Roberts & Welky, 2010: 289) from influential publications including *The New York Times* and *Cinema*

Magazine, in effect discouraging others without '[John] Wayne's clout' from making Vietnam War films. Furthermore, it is generally accepted that, as a consequence of strong anti-Vietnam sentiment, the returning soldiers to countries such as the United States and Australia were abused and shunned by their contemporaries, struggling to be recognised in a society that so reviled this war.

As a reaction to the extremely negative consequences of connecting individual soldiers personally to the political ideologies of the government of the day as with the Vietnam War, when the United States became involved in current conflicts such as the Gulf War the government was careful to present the soldiers as 'doing the job asked of them'. In a controversial propaganda move, reporters from the US television channel CNN were sent to the front, becoming 'embedded' with the troops and reporting directly from the action, reminiscent of Burton Holmes' work almost 100 years earlier. This, and the rise of 24-hour news services, brought the war into our homes even more than the broadcasting of the Vietnam War, but it can be argued that it was even more carefully orchestrated to present the soldiers themselves in a positive light, supported by the limited criticism or political comment of the actual war on many of the US and allied news channels. However, as we have seen, the use of popular media for propaganda purposes is not new or isolated to one country or culture.

The broadcast images also include some more touristic views of sites of antiquity in this region – at times they were reported as being destroyed by the 'evil' enemy, but it has also made people in the West aware of the significant heritage in this part of the world. An example was the destruction of Persian archaeological sites in Iran and the ensuing outcry. This in turn contributes to implanting a touristic desire to visit, with a small group of 'adventurers' already travelling to the region for non-political, non-professional, recreational experiences. So, we can see some audience members responding 'actively' via tourism to what they experience through 'factual', and at times horrific, film and television reporting of a major conflict.

Fictional movies and TV programmes set around the conflict in the Gulf are relatively rare, often focusing on the duality of war in relation to notions of honour and bravery, such as *Courage Under Fire* (1996) starring Denzel Washington. It was critically acclaimed, but of more interest I understand that the US Department of Defense withdrew its cooperation with the film; I can only assume their rationale for so doing. In an interesting tourism development, for obvious reasons the Iraqi battle scenes were not filmed on the actual location, but rather in Texas at the Indian Cliffs Ranch where many of the props remained, creating an additional attraction for tourists to the ranch, which continues to be used for location filming. Unfortunately, many of the sets have become damaged by natural events including a tornado and sandstorm. Some other well-known Gulf War movies include *Jarhead* (2005) and *Green Zone* (2010). In 2002, HBO produced a TV movie *Live from Baghdad*, which focused on the story of CNN's efforts to be the 'first on the scene' in 1991, presenting an early perspective on what became the embedded (CNN) war correspondents in 2003.

Civil unrest

As noted at the beginning of this chapter, visual representations of civil unrest also play a role in creating and presenting us with images of exotic places in flux, which can affect not only our personal responses to that place, but also influence travel and tourism patterns. From the Cold War era and the fall of the Berlin Wall to the Tiananmen Square protests and the subsequent massacre in 1989, along with the more recent uprisings in Egypt and the Middle East, local people are presented to the West through the news media, demanding that they have a say in their lives, often becoming martyrs to the cause. This sits very well with the culture of the tourist-generating regions of Western democracies. While the tourism industry is keen to note the emerging generating markets of China, India and South America, countries such as the UK, US, Australia and New Zealand remain significant tourism markets. Also, as a member of a Western democratic society, my own perspective is influenced by my cultural background, consequently influencing my representation of this situation, as well as other aspects of this chapter.

The news items and subsequent TV programmes and movies set in these periods of unrest not only valorise the people fighting for their freedom, but also the places in which they live. The adventurous tourist (or 'traveller') soon follows, as can be seen in the growth of tourism to the Eastern European countries that were part of the previous Eastern Bloc of Soviet countries, such as Hungary and Croatia.

However, as other places of civil unrest were already tourist destinations, such as China and Egypt, most political uprisings have short-term negative effects on tourism, as once they are considered relatively safe to travel to, they recover quickly and often more strongly due, in part, to this added attraction. Sites such as Tiananmen Square have become imbued with a different, contemporary meaning for Western tourists who witnessed the 1989 events virtually 'first hand' via the media, unlike the country's classic history, and have become mediatised pilgrimage sites. *Lonely Planet*, the eponymous travellers' guide, now has publications on Iran and Afghanistan as well as a chapter on North Korea being included in its Korea guide.

Un-civil war: Travelling to Cambodia and *The Killing Fields* (1984)

As a first-year university student in 1976, I met a young man from Cambodia (known at the time as Kampuchea). He wanted to be friends, but I found that his experiences were so foreign and unimaginable to me that, to my constant shame and sorrow, I did not know how to be his friend. We had just started to hear about some of the Pol Pot initiated atrocities in Cambodia, and I recall him telling me that, as soon as he left Kampuchea, his parents destroyed all records of his existence so that he would be safe. However, this meant he would most likely never see them again. While we did not remain friends, I thought of him often, and was starkly reminded of his family's plight when the movie *The Killing Fields* came out in 1984. It was this movie that started me on a very slow journey to Cambodia, both literally and emotionally.

When I eventually visited Cambodia in 2004 as a tourist, one of the first things I did was go to the Killing Fields and the Genocide Museum set in a Pol Pot, Khmer Rouge prison, which had initially been a primary school. This remains one of the most harrowing experiences of my very sheltered and privileged life, and even now I struggle to talk about it. Seeing the photos of all those interred at the prison and hearing some of their stories confronted me with a powerful emotional reality I was not expecting. Walking over the bones of innocent people embedded in the paths and surrounding ground of the Killing Fields was harrowing, indescribable and almost too much for me to think about. The only way that I can even hope to express some of the horror is to let movies such as *The Killing Fields* (1984) speak for me, even though it is nowhere near as horror filled as even the small reality I experienced.

In many ways, although I had my university experience (and guilt) regarding my Cambodian friend to introduce me to the country, it was that movie that really sparked my interest by presenting an exotic, yet dangerous, country, ultimately leading me to visit Cambodia and consequently learn a great deal about myself and the 'human condition' – that we can be so evil, yet that in the end goodness can survive and even conquer. I cannot tell my 'friend' from Cambodia of this, but instead I work to assist some others in very small, but what I believe to be constructive ways. I went as a film-related tourist, but returned somehow changed. Would I have gone if not for the movie? Possibly, but it is unlikely that I would have visited the Killing Fields – hence the influence of the movie on my touristic experience was powerful.

The point here is that film tourism is rarely a frivolous, meaningless activity (as it is considered by many), particularly when related to wars and civil unrest, and can be extremely emotionally powerful and life changing. I cannot forget what I experienced and take with me the knowledge that such atrocities are not simply the realm of 'madmen', but that we are all capable and culpable.

Anti-War Films

Almost as soon as the pro-war propaganda-style film began to be produced, we see its opposite, the anti-war film. While some today may consider anti-war movements and films to be relatively recent, one of the most celebrated movies of that genre, *All Quiet on the Western Front*, was released by Universal in 1930 and set in WWI. The film is based on Remarque's famous novel of the same name, following the 'fortunes' of young volunteer recruits as they have their patriotic illusions shattered by the reality of battle (Wetta & Curley, 1992). The image of the hand of a young man stretching out to touch a butterfly, and being shot dead, is one of the most famous, poignant anti-war moments in cinema. As the primary focus of the film is anti all war, with little cultural perspective of where the war was actually based, there is no specific travel- or tourism-related element here. However, it represented a growing interwar repulsion against the role of war, which reverted dramatically with the commencement of WWII, only to rise again in the 1960s on the back of the Vietnam War (1962–1975).

Moving forward many decades to the Vietnam War, we see another damning portrayal of war in the black comedy movie *MASH* (1970), set during the Korean War (1950–1953), but clearly directed towards the current situation in Vietnam. It was later made into an extremely popular TV series that was not as black, but still with a strong anti-war agenda. While being severely critical of war, the movie and even more so the later TV series presents the local community and countryside in a rather more interesting role than other war movies of the era, where the locals and their culture tend to be backgrounded. The places staff visited in Asia for R&R (rest and recreation), such as Seoul, Korea, were presented in a favourable, interesting and desirable fashion as exotic places of entertainment and relative luxury. What is of particular interest here is that the spin-off TV series remains on television today, potentially making this series one of the most influential of the modern anti-war genre.

Other movies made that were based on the Vietnam War such as *Coming Home* (1978), *Apocalypse Now* (1979) and *Uncommon Valour* (1983) tended to reflect the anti-war mood of the West during that time and after, usually by looking at the fate/s of the returned soldiers. There were certainly fewer pro-war propagandistic movies being made during the 1970s, especially about a war which 'most filmmakers have shown as immoral and futile' (Paris, 1995: 193).

Emotional and Economic Recovery via Film and Travel

Post WWII was characterised by a strong sense of change and rebuilding, in part incorporating forced migration, as well as support from the wealthy nations who had been relatively unaffected by the War such as the United States and Australia.

When looking at notions of travel, Amad (2006) conceptualises them in three ways: 'travel as the burden of forced migration or expulsion resulting in the condition of permanent exile; travel as the mobilisation of expansionist and exploitative economic impulses; and travel as the condition of a humanist world-citizen outlook' (Amad, 2006: 102). So, we can consider the war migrant story as one where those who were forced to travel are moving on to become part of the 'world-citizen outlook'. One common aspect of war is the displacement of local communities, with many migrating permanently to other parts of the world. The post-WWII migration to the 'new countries' of Australia, New Zealand and the US have defined these countries. For example, Melbourne, Australia has a high level of Greek and Italian postwar migrants, with the city having the highest number of Greek residents outside Greece. These migrants often travel back to their home countries to visit their friends and relatives, and to introduce their children to their heritage. Their stories are told in documentaries, movies and TV programmes, both factual and fictional.

While the movies set in WWII may lead us to believe that the United States lost many fighters, in actual fact they sustained 202,131 wartime military deaths, compared with 3.5 million in Germany, 7.5 million in the USSR and 1.2 million in Japan, with an estimated 45 million European and Asian civilians dying (Smith, 1998). The postwar euphoria in countries such as the US, England and Australia as well as continental Europe in turn supported a sense of the potential of postwar rebuilding, growth and development, with tourism seen as playing a significant role.

In America, entrepreneurs saw an opportunity in this developing international travel market, establishing overseas hotel chains to support the recovery and meet the desire for postwar travel, particularly of Americans who came to dominate much of the European travel market in the postwar era (Smith, 1998). These entrepreneurs were also supported by various government initiatives to encourage postwar travel, seen both as an economic growth and recovery supporting mechanism. For example, in order to encourage American travel to France, the US and French governments subsidised transatlantic air and sea travel and supported hotel construction, as well as providing tourists in France with special access to the limited reserves of gasoline and food in the immediate postwar years (Endy, 2004).

Moving images supported such positive emotional recovery, with a high percentage of the postwar films presenting their stars as ordinary people overcoming extraordinary situations. In terms of encouraging Americans to travel to France, between 1951 and 1965 Hollywood produced some 25 films featuring Americans living or travelling in France. Endy (2004) relates one small-town Ohio woman's story regarding her desire to visit France as being motivated by the movie *Sabrina* (1954), where an American chauffeur's daughter goes to Paris and returns as 'glamorous, wonderful and sophisticated' (Endy, 2004: 130). Hollywood was also making films on location in France, such as Hitchcock's *To Catch a Thief* (1955), which featured the soon-to-be-classic aerial shots of car chases in exotic places, in this instance the French Riviera and Monaco. Hitchcock's exposure of tourist sites to his audience begins with the film's opening credits superimposed onto a close-up of a travel agent's window display featuring France, finally zooming in on a poster that says 'If you love life, you'll love France'.

Also, many of the postwar movies tended to look forward to a bright future, celebrating the general technological advances of the times as well as actually applying them to the film-making processes, many of which were developed during the war. People did not simply want a return to the stability of the past, but also had an increased desire to travel as a pilgrimage or to pay homage to others as well as simply for rest and recreation.

While fascinated by the Cold War, as discussed earlier, Hollywood was, in effect, hamstrung by the HCUAA as to what stories could be told in the 1950s and early 1960s; consequently the movies of that era tended to focus on celebrating politically 'safe' topics such as various technological and social developments including the growth in aviation, with Warner Bros producing the first major movie about the development of jet flight, *Chain Lightning* (1950) starring Humphrey Bogart and Raymond Massey. Aggrandising US ingenuity and individualism, this movie not only resonated with a postwar audience looking for positive stories, but again presents them with the notion of exotic places (even though it was filmed entirely at the Warner Bros Burbank studio) and reinforced the romance of flight, the handsome rugged pilot and the future potential of such travel. It is no coincidence that the commercial airline pilots of today wear air force style uniforms.

In addition, people became interested in travelling to learn, re-live and re-connect with wartime places and friendships. This desire was also fuelled by and reflected in the cinematic movies of this time, along with the new medium of television.

'Unreal Unrest'

While there is further discussion relating to computer games and science fiction movies and TV series in future chapters, in the interests of comprehensiveness and inclusivity a brief mention of their place in relation to battles, war and tourism is necessary. Smith (1998) comments on the role that the TV series, *Star Trek* (1966–1969), played in preparing the public for the notion of the Star Wars programme of the Cold War. It can also be argued that such 'exotic' travel adventures, struggles and battles also encouraged people to see tourism as a legitimate form of exploration, even into space.

However, an aspect of the moving image that has not been considered in relation to tourism is that of the genre of computer games. If we look at the development of these games over the past 45 years, many of them relate to battles and wars, both real and imagined. Released in 1984, the popular game *1942* was set in the Pacific during WWII with the Japanese clearly represented as the enemy to be destroyed. While most games shied away from specific scenarios as portrayed in *1942* and in making any commentary on war, the ironic social commentary of *Cannon Fodder* (1983), with its tagline 'War has never been so much fun', outraged many (Newman & Simons, 2007). These moves away from battling mythical creatures to be vanquished and princesses to be saved towards a (rather fictionalised and generally poorly realised) representation of an actual battle created a great deal of controversy, which continues today. Most of these early video games did not present them graphically in real (or even simulated) locations but, as the video technology improved, so did the visual rendering of places.

As battle games became more place specific and realistic in the 21st century, they incorporated cultural as well as physical elements of these places, creating or reinforcing their fame ('place in history'), and/or the emotional imagery and potential desire for engagement with these real places. The *Kuma War* series controversially replicates 'real events' from various wars, including the recent 'War on Terror'. According to their website, '[n]early 100 playable missions bring our soldiers' heroic stories to life, and you can get them all right now, for free. Stop watching the news and get in the game' (http://www.kumawar.com).

Reflecting the movie, *Sands of Iwo Jima* (1949), starring John Wayne, as well as the famous battle from WWII, the video game the *Battle of Iwo Jima* (2007) from Kuma Games is presented as one of three battles featured in the Pacific theatre. All three games perpetuate the story of the brave American soldier, undaunted by being severely outnumbered. Both are based on a real battle, but glamorise the victory, with the game's description telling us that:

> [a]s a Marine warrior your task is to single-handedly take out the enemies on Iwo Jima armed with one devastating weapon – a nasty modification of an m1919 called the 'Stinger'. With comrades to save along the way you'll rise against the enemy and against all odds inside the true story of one of the bloodiest ground battles in history! (http://www.kumagames.com/pacific/battles/iwojima.html)

As with much of the discussion on war and tourism in this book, the link can at times be rather tenuous; however, there are clear relationships between these games, their emotional content and tourism, especially in terms of exoticisation, imaging, fame, and desire to experience or re-create an emotional experience, as we summarise in the following conclusion.

Conclusion: Travel, Warfare and Moving Images

Modern war, film and travel have contributed significantly to the 'growing economic and cultural exchanges now associated with globalization' (Endy, 2004: 3), to which travel and tourism contribute.

The main themes we see coming out of this chapter relating to espionage and the representation of modern warfare on film (including computer games) revolve around the exoticisation of these themes and places, not only contributing to our imagery but also our interest in and desire to visit or, at the very least, it informs our responses to travel experiences. They do not need to be primary or sole travel motivations but, as seen in my Cambodia case, such exposure can contribute significantly to the overall experience, along with our personal responses.

While many of the spy movies and TV series are presented in more stylised and exotic ways, they represent a world that is far removed from our day-to-day lives, which is often what we wish to experience when on holiday. Furthermore, sites of commemoration, museums and exhibitions all become tourist attractions in their own right, especially when they have been informed by the powerful emotional narratives of film.

Part 2

Travelling In, On and Through the Landscape: Voyeur or Flâneur?

Nineteenth-century French poet, Charles Baudelaire coined the term, *flâneur*, when referring to a person strolling around a place in order to experience it – in principle, a form of conscious meandering by an impassioned observer, often a painter or poet. In his words:

> To the perfect spectator, the impassioned observer, it is an immense joy to make his domicile amongst numbers, amidst fluctuation and movement, amidst the fugitive and infinite ... to be away from home, and yet to feel at home; to behold the world, to be in the midst of the world and yet remain hidden from the world. (Baudelaire, 1986[1863]: 34)

Baudelaire, being a product of the 19th century, saw this as a particularly male-centric activity, yet as the century moved on women became freer to stroll alone, and did so in a mindful manner in order to experience places as well, so the term also came to be applied in its feminine form, *flâneuse*.

While Baudelaire saw his flâneur as one who uses art (as in poetry) to express his experiences, he did not embrace the 'new' form of artistic expression of photography. Nevertheless, modern-day thinkers such as Urry (2002) acknowledge that there is not only a link between the flâneur and photographer, but also the tourist who photographs the environment through which he/she is strolling. Flâneurie has also been tied to the cinema, with flâneurie and movie-going growing together in a period where new art forms and experiences relating to the virtual gaze were becoming apparent (Friedberg, 1993).

From the early days of the moving image, landscape has played a significant role, often in terms of the picturesque and panorama outlined in Chapter 2 but also through more emotionally charged landscapes. When considering the role of the rural landscape in British film and TV, Hutchings (2004) argues that landscape represents a nation's heritage and identity, particularly the notion of a *good* rural idyll that opposes the degradation of urban places. We can see examples of this in many films, both current and in the past.

As well as strolling through the urban landscapes, flâneurie can exist in landscapes where we often stroll, tramp, hike and walk in order to experience that land. In this way, the role of the landscape is often far more than simply a backdrop to our action, and when we consider this in relation to film and television, we can see many instances where audiences respond intensely to the landscape so that it becomes a protagonist in its own right. As film developed more varied narrative-based stories, the landscape came to represent a distinct character, which is particularly evident in genres where such landscapes are integral to the narrative. In many of the western movies (and TV series) as well as road trip films, and even in the Australian bushranger stories, the natural landscape is often presented as 'a haunting or brooding presence, that dominates and shapes the actions ...' (Britton, 2010: 182).

Over 10 years ago, the Australian Department of Communication, Information Technology and the Arts acknowledged the link between film, landscape and tourism, stating that not only can 'the film industry ... help tourism promotion ..., [but] Australian film and television is the most readily accessible and effective medium for providing an insight into Australia's landscape, lifestyle and political, social and cultural environments' (DCITA, 2003: 24). Unfortunately, this acknowledged link between film and tourism has not resulted in closer collaborations between the film and tourism sectors in Australia, as subsequent Australian national tourism marketing organisations have only occasionally actively used landscape-based films to promote tourism. This may be simply due to both sectors being so involved in their own areas that they have neglected these linkages, even though they have been acknowledged.

Other parts of the world such as some US states have, at times, achieved closer collaborations between their respective film and tourism commissions, yet the process remains patchy and primarily reliant on local political decisions. For example, the Hawaii State Government recently closed its film bureau, which was physically situated with Hawaii Tourism, as a response to cost-cutting measures following the global financial crisis. When we consider the popularity of movies as a strong image-creative mechanism and tourism drawcard to the State of Hawaii from the days of Elvis right through to the TV series *Lost* (2004–2010) and the current resurgence of *Hawaii Five-0* (2010–), this move appears short-sighted. I trust that by the time you are reading this, the situation has been reversed.

In this part we consider landscape-based stories primarily from my own cultural perspective, such as those in westerns, road trips and Australian bushranger tales, which leads to a discussion of the role of landscape and place in film and tourism. In many instances, I have strolled as a flâneuse through these landscapes, both literally and figuratively, providing a series of personal, autoethnographic reflections. As Horne (1992: x) states, 'the best writing on tourism is done by people who respect many of the landscapes and relics of material culture ... [and] who can also contemplate the absurdities with which tourism can transform them'. While my work may not necessarily live up to this statement, I trust that my comments are considered within this context. Certainly, the relationship between tourism and film provides many absurdities, which are amply illustrated by my own western experiences as an exemplar of the entire premise of this book.

One such absurdity is the touristic appeal of negative storylines, which tend to dominate many of the genres I discuss in this section, along with the previous chapters on war and civil unrest. In particular, the gangster films and post-1960s road movies, as well as many westerns and bushranger stories present what at times are unpleasant stories of crime and personal danger. While not wishing to trivialise the power (and negative emotions) of some of these stories, often as tourists we seem to get a vicarious pleasure from being close to danger without really being *in* danger. So, driving through America with a female companion may remind me of aspects of the story of *Thelma and Louise* (1991), and while our road trip is a safe experience, it has a slightly edgy undertone! Many have criticised tourists and tourism for belittling and commodifying what are significant cultural rituals and events, and in some ways this can also be argued when looking at these movies and TV series (as well as some of the war movies). While I accept much of this argument, I do not aim to discuss this in detail in this part; instead I trust that the reader will take this debate on board and consider it in light of what I present. In fact, this is an ongoing, underlying theme of the entire book, and one that I hope that you, the reader, will engage with as you ponder the various premises and forms that I present.

While not set in the natural environment, we can also see a link here between the urban landscapes and stories of the gangster movies, many of which could not exist outside that environment. We explore this further towards the end of this part, as well as a discussion on the development of simulated sites, sets and the experiences of film-based theme parks.

So, are moving image viewers and tourists simply voyeuristic watchers of filmic landscapes or are they consciously meandering and observing in an active, flâneuristic manner? If my primary premise of this book that audiences and tourists engage actively with their experiences holds true, then surely we are more of an impassioned flâneur than opportunistic voyeur.

6 Badlands and Beauty: Landscape, Travel and Place in the Western

For over half a century the western genre dominated US cinema as well as television, with more than one-fifth of the movies filmed between 1910 and 1960 being westerns. Generally, the 'western era' refers to stories set between the end of the American Civil War and the 1890s; however, at times Civil War movies express western sensibilities, such as *Dances with Wolves* (1990), while numerous spaghetti westerns and TV series including *Rawhide* (1959–1965) had a Civil War component. Despite the fact that the first acknowledged western movie, *The Great Train Robbery* (1903), was filmed in a studio rather than on location as subsequent westerns were, this represents an early example of a fully developed journey-based narrative, which was only beginning to be seen in this era of the 'cinema of attractions', as discussed in Chapter 2.

The first 'wave' of westerns comprised those filmed from around 1910 until the beginning of the US involvement in WWII (1940), when the genre was superseded for a few years by war movies with western stars such as John Wayne assuming heroic roles based around war. However, the western did not die, regaining its ascendency after the war in the form of what Bazin refers to as the 'superwestern', which he describes as 'a western that would be ashamed to be just itself, and looks for some additional interest to justify its existence – ... some quality extrinsic to the genre and which is supposed to enrich it' (Bazin, 1971: 151). This is represented by successful movies such as *High Noon* (1952) and *Shane* (1953), along with *Fort Apache* (1948), with its social rehabilitation of the hitherto despised (or ignored) Indian.

The body of work of the western is large, with over 7000 titles, and while many were formulaic matinee series and B-grade movies reminiscent of the cheap dime novels of the late 19th century, there remains a strong oeuvre of

A-grade movies, providing a breadth and depth to the western genre that casual observers may not appreciate (Buscombe, 2006). However, regardless of the quality, they were extremely popular throughout the world as well as in America, with many people growing up with the stories, adventures, actors and powerful landscape. As French film critic and theorist André Bazin notes, 'the western does not age' and has an almost universal popularity. He wonders:

> [w]hat can there possibly be to interest Arabs, Hindus, Latins, Germans, or Anglo-Saxons, among whom the western has had an uninterrupted success, about evocations of the birth of the United States of America, the struggle between Buffalo Bill and the Indians, the laying down of the railroad, or the Civil War! (Bazin, 1971: 141)

Laing and Frost (2012) explore the popularity of western books (fact and fiction), concluding that, as well as presenting stories that tap into a universal myth, they also fulfil a 'popular urban yearning for an escape to the frontier' (Laing & Frost, 2012: 90). Certainly, the era of the western books (from the late 19th century) and movies (from the early 20th century) coincided with increasing degrees of urbanisation, and while the books presented narratives supporting Frost's contention, it was the movies that were able to fully express and exploit the attraction of the non-urban landscape of the wild west. Furthermore, Bazin (1971) notes that, without the grandeur and scope of the cinema, the western stories would have remained minor American tales with limited international appeal. The expansive landscapes are more than backdrops, with the cinema providing the vehicle in which to present such epic, universal stories. Clearly, Bazin sees the audiences' responses to western movies as an active, emotional response to the power of the presentation on the screen.

Another theme that presents itself is that of a belief that it was America's divine mission to expand westward, which became known as *Manifest Destiny*, as coined by John L. O'Sullivan, editor of the *Democratic Review*. This perspective is evident in many of the pioneering-based movies, often presented as a romantic notion to 'go West, young man!' Related to this is the notion of the 'hero's journey', described by Joseph Campbell as having a series of phases or stages which incorporates a departure encompassing aspects of the call to adventure, the refusal of the call, the acceptance of the call, initiation (trials and temptation), and the return which culminates in the freedom to live (Campbell, 1949).

Table 6.1 presents examples of the universal themes, storylines and examples found in the western genre, where, with little extrapolation, we can also find a desire to travel to witness these places where such universal themes played out.

Table 6.1 Western themes and styles

Universal themes	Western storylines	Film/TV examples
Pioneering and settling ('Manifest Destiny')	Trail blazing	*The Big Trail* (1930)
	Civilising the west	*How the West was Won* (1962)
	Railroad bringing prosperity, civilisation and connection	*The Iron Horse* (1924)
Conflict	Cattlemen versus settlers ('dirt farmers')	*Shane* (1953)
	Criminals versus lawmakers	*The Man Who Shot Liberty Valance* (1962)
Morality of the underclass	Superior moral qualities of those disdained by respectable society	*Stagecoach* (1939)
Hero's journey	The hero's departure, initiation and return	*North to Alaska* (1960)
Revenge and redemption	Innocent victim is avenged by lover, relative. At times the protagonist or criminal is also redeemed	*Pale Rider* (1985)
Greed	Robberies of stage coaches and banks reflect the shallow nature of 'greed'. Bounty hunters motivated by greed	*The Good, The Bad and the Ugly* (1966)
Battle	Civil war	*Shenandoah* (1965)
	Indian as enemy	*Stagecoach* (1939)
	Cavalry as saviour	*Fort Apache* (1948)
Reconciliation	Indian as positive force of nature	*Dances with Wolves* (1990)
	Indian as colonialist refugee	*Fort Apache* (1948)
	North and South understanding (post-Civil War)	*Rawhide* (1959–1965)
Styles		
Musicals	Many were also stage shows	*Annie Get Your Gun* (1950)
Singing cowboys	Singing star, often Gene Autry, Roy Rogers	*Oh, Susannah!* (1936)
Road trips	Travel, journey	*The Big Trail* (1930)

Landscapes, Moviescapes and Mythscapes

Westerns are epic stories with superhuman heroes undertaking feats of valour reminiscent of the knights-in-arms of the classics. This is evident in the genre's underlying morality, which is even more dramatically displayed through the set-up of shots of 'vast horizons, all-encompassing shots that constantly bring to mind the conflict between man and nature' (Bazin, 1971: 147). Bazin was certainly not immune to the potential for the western landscape to overwhelm and emotionally move mankind:

> These immense stretches of prairie. Of deserts, of rocks to which the little wooden town clings precariously (a primitive amoeba of a civilization), are exposed to all manner of possible things. (Bazin, 1971: 145)

Directed by John Ford and starring John Wayne (both of whom became synonymous with the western), *Stagecoach* (1939) was the first movie to be filmed in the vast, evocative landscape of Monument Valley on the Utah and Arizona border, with its towering sandstone buttes and open spaces. This movie is seen by many as the pinnacle of the genre, where Ford 'struck an ideal balance between social myth, historical reconstruction, psychological truth, and the traditional theme of the western *mise-en-scène* [landscape]' (Bazin, 1971: 149). Other Ford movies filmed at Monument Valley and starring John Wayne include *Fort Apache* (1948), *She Wore a Yellow Ribbon* (1940) and *The Searchers* (1956), while Henry Fonda starred in Ford's *My Darling Clementine* (1946), also set in that location. In a clear reference to Ford's westerns, Italian filmmaker Sergio Leone set and filmed crucial establishing scenes in Monument Valley for his famous (and final) spaghetti western, *Once Upon a Time in the West* (1968). Other popular filming sites, apart from the film ranches discussed later in this chapter, include Death Valley and Lone Pine in California, with movies such as *Yellow Sky* (1948) and *Comanche Station* (1960) filmed there. Today, tourists visit the site known as 'Ford Point' (after John Ford) to participate in their own western dream (Figure 6.1).

While it has been argued that westerns can only be set in America due to their inevitable link to the country's history and heritage, this has not prevented filmmakers from shooting 'runaway' productions (movies set in one place but filmed elsewhere) in other parts of the world, while still depicting the United States. Today, numerous western movies and TV series have been filmed in Canada, including *Unforgiven* (1992), *Legends of the Fall* (1994) and *Brokeback Mountain* (2005). This is due in part to the availability of 'unspoiled' landscapes as well as financial imperatives along with the ease of filming in these regions (Anderson, 2009).

Figure 6.1 Tourists at Ford Point, Monument Valley

Reflecting the international fascination with the genre, filmmakers from outside the United States also made their own versions of the western movie, from Germany and France to the 'spaghetti' westerns of numerous Italian producers, the most famous being Sergio Leone. While Leone produced only five westerns, their success and quality brought the spaghetti western into mainstream cinema, ensuring their longevity. The spaghetti westerns generally lacked the Protestant morality of the US-produced westerns, focusing more on self-interest, lust, revenge or greed, and were at times extremely violent. However, directors such as Leone clearly loved the genre, often referencing other US westerns in their own movies. This was particularly evident in *Once Upon a Time in the West* (1968), which Buscombe (2006: 142) notes 'was more about other Western movies than it is about the west itself'. The movie referenced and paid homage to many of the American westerns, including *High Noon* (1952) and *Shane* (1953), as well as using famous western actors such as Charles Bronson, Henry Fonda, Woody Strode and Jack Elam, and was the only Leone movie shot (in part) in John Ford's iconic Monument Valley. Leone also imbued his movies with a sardonic sense of humour not unlike the Coen Brothers today, introducing long sequences featuring close-ups of the protagonists' faces and eyes, spinning out gunfights and dramatically using the wide screen and vast, panoramic landscapes. A feature of Leone's films was the overwhelming power of the landscape, from the New Mexico badlands and Monument Valley to sites in the Almeria valley in Spain and evocative, expansive graveyards, as in *The Good, the Bad and the Ugly* (1966) and *Once Upon a Time in the West* (1968). By combining his super close-ups of the human face with the vastness of the landscape, Leone elicited powerful emotions from the audience.

Apart from Leone's nod to John Ford depicting filming key scenes in Monument Valley for *Once Upon a Time in the West* (1968), these movies were not made on location in America, becoming classic examples of the aforementioned 'runaway movies'. Furthermore, his landscapes always resonate with the traditional 'western' characteristics, remaining a powerful drawcard for those of us looking for the emotion of the American western landscape. However, Leone's runaway sets have also become tourist attractions in their own right, in particular at what has become known as Mini-Hollywood in Almeria, Spain, which is a popular tourist destination comprising three separate sites or theme parks, not unlike the film ranches of California as discussed later in this chapter. Unlike many of the American western sets, which have burnt down or been overtaken by development, the Spanish set remains today.

While I tend to focus on the visual aspects of the moving image in this book, the role of music is also critical, and the western demonstrates a most powerful application which at times I find impossible to separate. It tells us what to feel, what to expect and whether this is a good, bad or ugly moment, from the drawn-out strains of the spaghetti western to the heroic music of cavalry-based films and even those of the singing westerns of artists including Gene Autry with *Oh, Susannah!* (1936) and his successor, Roy Rogers (*Don't Fence Me In*, 1945). Every subgenre of the western has an endemic style of music that is instantly recognisable. Along with others, Ennio Morricone's sparse, sonically based score from the spaghetti western, *The Good, the Bad and the Ugly* (1966), defines the subgenre and has become internationally recognisable, even to those who have not seen the movie. Morricone's use of particular themes for each of the characters creates an almost operatic feel in the various spaghetti westerns he has scored.

In 2004 a group of Australian musicians formed *The Ennio Morricone Experience*, now known as *The Spaghetti Western Orchestra*, performing their musical tribute to Ennio Morricone around the world. Between 2008 and 2014 they performed in Australia, Hong Kong, Macau, Finland, London, Edinburgh, France, Athens, Belgium and the Netherlands, along with a tour of North America, as well as numerous tours in the UK including the Royal Albert Hall during the 2011 Proms season. They also have performed their work in Italy, the home of the spaghetti western. Furthermore, in 2012 the 84-year-old Ennio Morricone presented his famous musical scores live in Australia at the Adelaide Festival to a sold-out audience, and while he has written many other film and TV soundtracks, the success of the collaboration between Leone and Morricone is internationally recognised and cherished, with these pieces being particularly well received.

On a personal note, while I believed that I had seen *The Good, the Bad and the Ugly* (1996) many times, it was not until 2011 that I watched it in full, realising that, while I was extremely familiar with the music and iconic scenes, I had never actually viewed the entire movie. Even in 2011, I found it engaging and fascinating and thoroughly enjoyed its droll humour, and have now viewed it numerous times. Along with the music, the landscape was one of the stars for me in this film, as with all of the spaghetti westerns, even if they were not all filmed in America. However, it is Leone's final western, *Once Upon a Time in the West* (1968), that for me presents the most powerful experience, particularly when the Mittens of Monument Valley come into view. When Morricone presented his music from the movie in Adelaide (which I had travelled to as a tourist solely motivated by this event) I was profoundly moved, along with the rest of the audience.

The Japanese connection with the western

While western movies were filmed in other countries, a number of the themes of honour and violent sacrifice noted at the beginning of this chapter also sit within Japanese cinematic traditions. In fact, Leone's *A Fistful of Dollars* (1964) is based on Japanese director Akira Kurosawa's movie *Yojimbo* (1961); however, this was not acknowledged, resulting in a court case over breach of copyright. Another Kurosawa film, *The Seven Samurai* (1954), was also used as the inspiration for John Sturges' *The Magnificent Seven* (1960); however, this time the connection was accredited. This was not a one-way influence, with Japanese westerns also being made, such as Takashi Miike's *Sukiyaki Western Django* (2007), clearly influenced by Corbucci's famous spaghetti western, *Django* (1966), as well as *A Fistful of Dollars* (1964) and *Yojimbo* (1961).

Unlike the spaghetti westerns that were filmed in Spain, Italy, Mexico and occasionally America, but set in America, *Sukiyaki Western Django* (2007) was set and filmed in Japan, but performed entirely in English, using many of the classic western colloquialisms. However, while the language contrasts with the artistic, almost elegiac Japanese sets, it is ultimately a Japanese (western) movie. Yet the storyline is classical spaghetti western, where a

> revolver-wielding stranger crosses paths with two warring clans who are both on the hunt for a hidden treasure in a remote western town. Knowing his services are valuable to either side, he offers himself to the clan who will offer up the largest share of the wealth. (IMDb; http://www.imdb.com/title/tt0906665/)

The movie references many of the Leone spaghetti westerns through its imagery and soundtracks, and also includes a cameo from American director Quentin Tarantino. The original *Django* (1996) was not released in the UK for some time due to its levels of violence, yet the Japanese version is even more graphic, verging on parodying the genre. A further example of Asia's interest in the western (or spaghetti western) genre is that of the Korean film, *The Good, the Bad, the Weird* (2008), which is based closely on Leone's *The Good, the Bad and the Ugly* (1966).

These cultural inversion interests also tie in to travel, in that the fascination of the West with exotic Eastern cultures (and vice versa) are played out in these movies, further enhancing the travel experience.

The Power of the Small Screen: TV Westerns

While the western movie is important, the role that TV series play in our lives and in shaping our cultural and touristic emotions and images is enormously powerful. Many B-grade movies were spun off to the smaller screen to feed the growing demand for this new form of entertainment. By 1959, 21 western series were being shown on prime-time TV in the US, with many exported internationally (Simpson, 2002). The characters and places in which they live are welcomed into our homes every night or week, where we interact with them in our own personal space. The human complexities of the characters could also be developed over the longer format of a TV series, as compared with a few hours in a movie, presenting the viewer with more realistic and complex characters that many formed a type of relationship with. We touched on this powerful relationship in Chapter 1 with the discussion of Horton and Wohl's theory of para-social relationships between actors and audience. It is interesting that they developed this theory in 1956 around the time of the broader introduction of TV around the world. This relationship between TV and tourism is further examined in Chapter 12.

Due to the powerful on-location aspects of western movies, from the early days of the TV westerns locations were used. For example, the series *Wagon Train* (1957–1965) featured the impressive landscapes of the western movies, including the iconic Monument Valley, so closely identified with John Ford and John Wayne. Interestingly, Wayne starred in his only TV role in *Wagon Train* in the episode directed by Ford, *The Colter Craven Story* (1960), even though he did introduce the first episode of *Gunsmoke* (1955), informing the audiences that 'I think it is the best thing of its kind to come along ... I predict he [James Arness] will be a big star'.

The earliest and one of the longest running TV westerns, *Gunsmoke* (1955–1975), set in Dodge City, Kansas, was initially written and directed by Charles Marquis Warren, with some episodes written and (others) directed by the famous western filmmaker, Sam Peckinpah. While much of the series was filmed on a Hollywood backlot set, it was also filmed at a range of Californian movie ranches including Bell Ranch, Big Sky Ranch and Corriganville, which also became tourist attractions (as discussed in Chapter 7), along with outdoor, on-location filming in Bronson Canyon, California and Coronado National Forest in Arizona. This provided even such an early TV series with a range of dramatic landscapes in which the stories of law, lawlessness and order were presented. For many young people around the world, this programme was among their first experiences of television, playing a significant role in developing notions of the power of such landscapes and their cultural relationship with them.

Another early TV western series also produced by Charles Marquis Warren, *Rawhide* (1959–1966), starred newcomer, Clint Eastwood, ultimately bringing him to the attention of Sergio Leone as his 'man with no name' for his early spaghetti westerns. Warren applied the format he had used in *Gunsmoke* of utilising a variety of establishing shots with a voice-over from the lead character to great effect, providing the viewer with an insight into the 'message' of the upcoming story. However, *Rawhide* is interesting not only for its use of varied establishing scenes but, along with *Wagon Train* (1958–1962), as an early 'road and buddy' series. The cattle are ostensibly being driven from Texas along the Sedalia Trail to Missouri, encountering different characters and situations in each episode, giving the opportunity for many cameo performances along with the coming and going of various cast members. While filmed primarily on a movie ranch and at MGM Studios in Culver City, with many scenes being repetitively used, it conveyed a sense of the West and travel – 'head 'em up, move 'em out' has become part of our vernacular, and is still today often used in relation to touring. Furthermore, hit movies such as *The Blues Brothers* (1980) and *Shrek 2* (2004) feature the theme song from the series, and even the format of the naming of each episode ('Incident at ...') is reflected in modern TV series such as *Friends* (1994–2004), who use the title format of 'The one with/where ...'.

Marginalised groups and ethnic minorities also found a place (albeit a little contrived, patronising and often trite, depending upon the contemporary cultural climate) in TV series, such as the fictionalisation of legendary Wild West sharpshooter, *Annie Oakley* (1954–1956), *Cheyenne* (1955–1963) about a half-breed Indian returning from the Civil War, and the first TV series ever filmed in colour, *The Cisco Kid* (1950–1956), with his Mexican sidekick, Pancho.

It was in the television series where we see the horse at times taking a central role, with the heroes' horses often having names and being included in the credits, establishing shots and theme songs. Famous man and horse duos include the Lone Ranger and his horse Silver, Hopalong Cassidy and

Topper, Gene Autry and Champion, Roy Rogers and Trigger, Zorro and Tornado or Phantom. These partnerships were celebrated, with the horse being more than an expendable mode of transport. There were even western TV series named after the animal star. Long before the popular 1990s' Austrian TV series, *Inspector Rex* (1994–2004), the cavalry-themed series set at Fort Apache (in the Corriganville Movie Ranch), *The Adventures of Rin Tin Tin* (1954–1959), was named after its leading character, a dog. While the Austrian *Inspector Rex* (1994–2004) is not a western, both series are about 'law and order', starring a German shepherd dog who has an uncanny understanding of the human world.

Due to the pervasive nature of the broadcasting of these prime time TV series, often repeating them for new audiences as the use of television spread, I suspect that my own fascination with the western genre and Monument Valley began from watching these TV series (usually as re-runs!) even more so than the movies.

An autoethnographic western landscapes story

Landscapes such as those described above are integral to many tourist experiences, and where an emotional link to the land is produced through exposure to powerful stories, the experience can be immense, merging on the numinous. As a case in point, the following story autoethnographically discusses my personal experiences with the western genre, landscape and tourism.

Growing up in the 1960s when many western movies were shown on TV as well as the made-for-TV series, I watched them avidly to see the beautiful horses (a fascination which has not diminished), not the stories or landscape. However, I soon engaged with the stories of good versus evil, and began to see the landscape as a protagonist where often men (and horses) were left to die, in the process receiving either redemption or their just deserts. While in actual fact there were not many stories where specific, named horses died, their fate was one that stayed with me longer than the human characters, such as Blackie in *True Grit* (1969, 2010) who died saving his mistress. Even today, when I think about the western, I see a horse and rider in a vast, magnificent landscape that towers over all, simultaneously threatening, promising, and even cathartic and cleansing with what can only be expressed as numinous emotions.

As a somewhat cynical and sceptical academic researcher, I should not confess to such simplistic and somewhat incongruous emotions regarding a genre such as the western which is (nearly) always violent, and often sexist and racist. But, there you have it – these emotions are authentic and remain with me in spite of my education and academic vocation. I tend to believe that it is the epic, mythical nature of the western that Bazin (1971) refers to that engages me so, along with the opportunity to stroll through these stories, themes and landscapes.

When, in my early 40s, I first visited the United States to attend a conference in Arizona, I took the opportunity to take a 'road trip' with a friend through Arizona and New Mexico. As I did not organise this aspect of the trip, I was not even aware that we would be travelling through the iconic movie site and landscape of Monument Valley. As we drove up to the entrance of the park down an unprepossessing unmade road, I was confronted by the powerful sight of the place I knew well, but had never 'seen' before.

To my delight, we hired some horses and headed off with our Navajo guide, whose entire interpretation of the valley was to recite which movies had been filmed where. I did not mind this at all, as I soon found out why I felt so attached to a place I had never been to before. I was able to head off on my own for a while and was amused when I started to pretend to be John Wayne in a western movie – here was an Australian girl pretending to be an American man acting the role of a tough cowboy! However, no matter how 'amused' I was at my reaction, it was an extremely strong and memorable emotion – one of freedom, pride and self-sufficiency (until I returned to my friend and our guide). I continue to re-live this emotion through my memories and the photos we took while there (Figure 6.2), as well as the movies set in that location that I now regularly revisit, each time becoming more, not less, powerful.

This sense of place goes beyond simply passively gazing at the scenery, and can be seen in terms of a numinous experience. The term 'numinous' refers to a highly spiritual experience where a spirit is believed to preside over

Figure 6.2 My Monument Valley moment

a place or inhabit certain natural phenomena or objects – a belief initially held by animists (Houghton Mifflin, 2000). It has been argued that tourists can experience such strong emotions, particularly at heritage sites. For me, certain landscapes have produced such strong emotions that I reach a euphoric and deeply emotional state that can last for a fleeting moment or remain for some time. I particularly experienced this when riding alone through Monument Valley.

What is interesting is that even though my 'numinous moment' occurred at a specific moment while riding in Monument Valley, I continue to experience it through viewing many of the western movies, including spaghetti westerns, even though most of them were not shot anywhere near Monument Valley. Even as I write this, a powerful sense of warmth and emotion floods my body.

After our horse-riding experience, my friend and I continued driving through the valley, stopping for lunch on the top of a promontory with spectacular views of the valley. Also there was a 'lone' Indian on his horse, posing for photos at the end of the promontory. Initially, we were the only people there, so he spent much of the time yarning with members of his family who had a native craft stall and the younger boys played with his horse. Just as I was about to ask the boys if I could photograph them with the horse, a group of Japanese tourists arrived. The Indian promptly resumed his position on the Bluff and the tourists paid a dollar each to have their photo taken either on the horse or standing next to it with him (their preferred position!). Even those totally staged photos that I ended up taking bring back powerful memories and reflect the image of the Indian and the land portrayed via the westerns. I later learnt that this is known as Ford Point, as the place from which John Ford would film his epic landscape scenes such as in his cavalry movies, *Fort Apache* (1948) and *She Wore a Yellow Ribbon* (1949) (Hughes, 2008).

I also have a further 'insider's' perspective here when I see photos in travel articles in the media featuring that same Indian in that same place. As noted earlier, the simple fact that these photos are continually used by the travel media illustrates their ongoing universal appeal and power.

On returning to Australia, I hired videos of *Stagecoach, Fort Apache* and other Ford/Wayne westerns and watched them avidly, experiencing great joy and deep (numinous?) emotion when Monument Valley's 'special character' was shown. I was a little disappointed to see that the same backdrop was used in many scenes, but I also felt pleased that I now had insider knowledge that enabled me to see this ruse and extend my vision beyond the edge of the screen, or outside the frame of the film. Since then, I have seen many of the westerns filmed in Monument Valley at least once, including *The Searchers* (1956) and even *Back to the Future III* (1989), and the fascination as well as my smug sense of being an insider continues. I also take great delight in 'bragging' to friends, colleagues and acquaintances about my close experience with this landscape, many of whom are fascinated to learn that these sites are authentic, giving me additional insider credence. But, for me, this experience was even more than another travel story. . . .

Prior to that first visit to the US, I was unaware of the influence American film and TV had on my images of the country, but even more so, I did not expect the emotional responses I experienced, particularly in Monument Valley. Gaining such an understanding of this influence has changed my relationship with, and opinion of, the United States. I can now see how many of the elements of the western film shaped my early ideas and form the basis of many of my underlying attitudes and beliefs.

It does not mean that I uncritically accept all things American, but I now have further insight into why I behave in certain ways and respond to particular aspects, such as those coming from the mid-west. Also, I now realise from where much of my own longing for a 'simpler time' and the dream of 'small town America' as well as frontier imaginings and even pioneering notions of *Manifest Destiny* have come, even if today I question some of these elements. Of course, it can be argued that such desires were there first and were simply reinforced by the western, but as I was experiencing them from such an early age (I would estimate from around eight years old), I suspect that they played a strong part in my personal development.

This experience has led me to wonder if this is how others feel when they visit and experience a place from a film that has had some meaning or resonance for them. From witnessing people re-enacting scenes from movies and TV series at various locations and discussing this at every opportunity, I believe that I am not alone.

Conclusion: Some Practical Implications for Tourism

We need to consider such influences not only in our studies of travel, tourism and the media, but also when planning the experience for visitors or even promoting a destination. There are some very interesting travel guidebooks being written by film buffs for travellers, taking a different approach from the standard 'where to go and how to get there' travel book. As Alain de Botton (2002: 9) notes, 'we hear little of *why* and *how* we should go'. Publications such as the 'curated' Museyon Guides (Museyon, 2008, 2009) series on film and travel illustrate an attempt to address this by having the entries written by 'curators' with extensive film industry experience and knowledge. By coming from the film rather than travel perspective, the books present the reader with a different way of travelling.

Concurrent to the development of the western movies and TV series is the establishment of movie ranches as places for filming and flâneurie, as discussed in the next chapter, along with the continued use of the western genre as a reference point for US and other Western culture.

7 Simply a Story? The Cultural Pervasiveness of the Western

If we look at the various storylines and universal themes of the western summarised in Table 6.1 in the previous chapter, it becomes clear that the western cannot be reduced to any one simple formula or archetypal tale. Where the previous chapter primarily focused on the western in terms of flâneurie and landscape, this chapter takes a stroll through the constructed spaces of the movie ranches, while considering the persistence and pervasiveness of the western genre. Here we also consider the western's influence on storytelling in other parts of the world such as Australia, along with its influence on tourism, as well as being a cultural marker and reference point for artists, commentators and viewers. Consequently, the story of the western (and its touristic relationships) is not simple.

Movie Ranches

While many of the TV series and movies of the 1930s, 1940s and 1950s were filmed on the backlots of the major film studios such as Universal and MGM, the establishing shots, credit scenes and other key scenes could not always be filmed in such constrained spaces. Nor was the technology of 'green screens' sufficiently developed to successfully superimpose the actors on to a previously filmed location scene. Yet financial constraints and punishing production schedules meant that it was not always possible to film on locations such as Monument Valley in Utah, which were far from the Hollywood studios. So a solution was found in the development of film ranches, some of which went on to become major tourist attractions, well before the development of movie-influenced theme parks such as Disneyland and Universal, which are looked at in Chapter 10.

As noted in the previous chapter, a few years after the production of the studio-based western, *The Great Train Robbery* (1903), western movies moved from the studio to location-based and filmed movies with great success. The landscape was such a powerful character in the stories that fully studio-based filming was problematic, with audiences demanding a higher level of authenticity. In spite of their higher budgets and longer lead times, the costs of location shooting affected movies as well as TV series. Furthermore, many of the places where the stories were set lacked the facilities required to support filming, such as accommodation, technical sites and skilled staff. So in the 1930s, movie or film ranches were developed in the San Fernando Valley and surrounds near Hollywood as the sets of western towns as an economical means to provide location-based filming without moving too far from the major studios. Certainly, the landscapes of the valley were such that they could offer appropriate backdrops, as well as the facilities to construct semi-permanent buildings of homesteads, towns and forts.

Another motivator for establishing these ranches close to Hollywood was more pragmatic. A workers' union agreement, where film staff were paid an additional load if they worked more than 30 miles out of town, had been established. The region within that 30-mile radius became known as the 'studio zone' and the nearby Simi Hills housed many movie ranches before the urban sprawl and freeways of Los Angeles encroached. While much of the land has been subsequently sold off for development, a small number of the ranches remain in use as filming sites, while some others have been incorporated into state historical parks. However, most of these have lost their set constructions, either through neglect, fire or both.

All of the major studios had a film ranch, including Walt Disney Golden Oak Ranch, Paramount Movie Ranch, Columbia Ranch (later Warner Brothers Ranch) and the RKO Encino Ranch. However, Metro-Goldwyn-Mayer (MGM) did not acquire land for its own movie ranch until a purchase of 2000 acres in 1967, much later than the other studios. A fort gate was erected on the property and the *Hondo* (1967) TV series used the site; however, its true value was never realised due to a series of financial setbacks and it was sold to a property developer in 1978 and subdivided.

Other ranches were owned independently, such as the Iverson Movie Ranch, where the Iverson family first agreed in 1912 for their property to be used for a Cecil B. DeMille movie, *The Squaw Man* (1914), marking the beginning of a long association with Hollywood, hosting over 3000 movies, including episodes of the TV westerns, *Bonanza* (1955) and *Gunsmoke* (1959). The Famous Players-Lasky Movie Ranch was developed in 1914, and has been the site for many major movies, including *Gone with the Wind* (1939) and

They Died with their Boots On (1940). According to the journal of the film industry of the day, *The Moving Picture World*:

> The Lasky company has acquired a 4,000-acre ranch in the great San Fernando valley on which they have built a large two-story Spanish casa which is to be used in 'The Rose of the Rancho' which has just been started. The new ground is to be used for big scenes and where a large location is needed. A stock farm is to be maintained on the ranch. It is planned to use 500 people in the story. There will be 150 people transported through Southern California for the mission scenes. The studio will be used for the largest scene ever set up, the whole stage and ground space being utilized. (Irvine, 1914: 198)

Originally owned by J. Paul Getty, the Big Sky Movie Ranch claims to be one of the oldest and largest movie ranches still in operation. It was used extensively to film western productions, particularly TV series including *Rawhide* (1959–1966), *Gunsmoke* (1955–1975), *Bonanza* (1959–1973) and *Little House on the Prairie* (1974–1983), with more recent credits including *Transformers* (2007) and *A Gunfighter's Pledge* (2008). Unfortunately, as with many other movie ranches, most of the constructed sets have been destroyed by fire. Yet touristic fans still visit and film their experiences, re-imagining the places, sites and stories, many placing them on YouTube for all to experience.

Gene Autry purchased the Monogram Ranch in 1953, which had been used for filming since the 1920s, renaming it Melody Ranch, from where he broadcast a CBS radio programme; however, many of the film sets were destroyed in a 1962 brushfire. Autry sold the final 22 acres of the ranch after his famous horse Champion, who lived there in retirement, died in 1990. It was purchased privately by the Veluzat brothers with the aim of recreating an active movie ranch for location shooting, and is now known as Melody Ranch Studios, boasting a range of sound stages and outdoor sets, and was used to film parts of Tarantino's *Django Unchained* (2013). In addition to this, the Veluzat brothers also own a large 750-acre ranch known as the Veluzat Motion Picture Ranch, just within the Studio Zone to the north of Los Angeles. This site includes a Spanish town, a 1950s town (with diner and gas station) and boasts the natural assets of desert, pine forest, open mesa and a lake.

So, movie ranches dominated western filming for most of the 20th century, with many of the constructed sets settling into the subconsciousness of viewers and fans alike. While the notion of film fandom seems fairly recent, it is not, starting with the development of the 'star' in the 1920s, as discussed in Chapter 2.

Tourism at the movie ranch

Responding to public interest in the movies, and many people's desire to actively participate in the storylines, a number of these working movie ranches also developed film-based tourist attractions. The first documented movie ranch open to the general public was the Jack Ingram Motion Picture Ranch, opened every Sunday from 1947, primarily providing souvenirs and snacks.

Among the most famous and successful ranches to open to the general public was the Corriganville Movie Ranch (established in 1937 by stuntman Ray 'Crash' Corrigan), which opened to tourists in 1949. One of the drivers here was to diversify the income of the ranch, and at its peak in the 1950s it attracted up to 20,000 visitors at weekends (Rothel, 1990; Schneider, 2007). For example, an estimated 10,000 people attended the opening day of the 1953 season (Moorpark-Simi Enterprise, cited in Schneider, 2007: 64). While Corriganville was not the first or only movie ranch open to the public, with others including Monogram Ranch and the aforementioned Jack Ingram Motion Picture Ranch, it was certainly the most elaborate. As well as the extensive facades and buildings of forts such as the famous Fort Apache and towns including Vendetta Village and Silvertown for filming, Corrigan provided not only re-enactments and photo opportunities with actors and animals for fans, but also arena-style shows, rodeos, concerts, dances and charity events, and eventually camp-style accommodation at this famous 1600-acre ranch.

Due to its proximity to the city of Los Angeles, urban development began to encroach on Corriganville. In the 1960s, the Simi Valley Freeway cut across the property, significantly reducing its footprint. Corriganville was subsequently purchased in 1965 by Bob Hope, becoming known as Hopetown and, while he promised to keep it operational, it generally fell out of use as a film ranch after a damaging fire in 1970, with the final blow coming when all the remaining buildings were destroyed by another blaze in 1979. Without the sets, even fans struggled to be attracted to the site, yet there are those 'cult fans' (see Hills, 2002) who still visit the area today. One such fan, David Rothel, recounts his pilgrimages to a range of western sites, including the movie ranches, recounting the stories and photographing rocks and trees where the buildings once stood (Rothel, 1990).

The remaining land of Corriganvile/Hopetown is again open to the public as the Corriganville Regional Park within the Rancho-Simi Recreation Park and, while nothing remains of the sets, fans continue to visit, seeking out their own very personal experiences. One of those who worked at Corriganville during the 1960s, Steve Gillum, formed the Corriganville Preservation Committee in 1988 with the aim of re-creating the town of Corriganville. While this has not eventuated, the committee's work resulted in a more 'natural' feel to a park that is surrounded by urban recreational facilities.

While many of the film ranches no longer exist, some are again being developed, while others remain as operating filming sites. They are also more likely to be open to the public, at least in part. Melody Ranch Studios has a museum of movie memorabilia that is open to visitors; however, the film sets and stages are only open one weekend a year for the Cowboy Poetry and Music Festival, which continues to draw western movie fans from around the world, since its inception in 1994 (http://cowboyfestival.org/).

When we think of Disney today, the theme parks of Disneyland and Disneyworld come to mind; however, Disney also had a movie ranch, the Golden Oak Ranch, north of Los Angeles in Placerita Canyon, also within the Studio Zone. While this was not purchased until 1959 (being Republic Pictures' Ranch prior to that), some time after the most famous movie ranches, and at a time many were being sold off for urban development, Walt Disney recognised his own need for a large site close to his studios (Rothel, 1990). He initially leased the ranch to film one of the segments of *The Mickey Mouse Club* (1955–1959), going on to film parts of the TV programme *Zorro* (1957–1959) and many of the exterior scenes of *Old Yeller* (1957), and culminating in its purchase in 1959. In more recent times, the ranch was used not only for Disney productions, but was also leased out as the site for Don Draper's childhood home in the first season of the TV series, *Mad Men* (2007), among others. At the time of writing, the site had increased its set offerings to include an urban business district and modern residential streets as well as the traditional, rustic western towns and natural settings (Disney Studio Services, 2011). The development of the Disney theme parks and the touristic link between such theme parks and film ranches is not being ignored, as it is discussed in Chapter 10.

The astute reader will have noted that at times I have stated that the same movie or TV series was filmed at differing movie ranches and locations. This was necessary to provide a variety of sites required by the stories, particularly for the TV series which could run for hundreds of episodes. For example, while much of *Gunsmoke* (1955) was filmed at the Big Sky Ranch, it was also filmed at Bell Ranch, Corriganville, Iverson Ranch, Kanab Movie Ranch, Melody Ranch, Old Tucson, and various canyons and parks including Bronson Canyon, and finally at CBS Studios, among others (IMDb, n.d.). This creates an interesting challenge for fans and many opportunities for these places to align themselves touristically with such a series.

As noted in the discussion on spaghetti westerns, Sergio Leone's spaghetti western sets in Spain have become popular tourist attractions in a region now known as 'Mini-Hollywood' in the spectacular Tabernas Desert in southern Spain. The region comprises three independently operated sites that present us with many similarities to the American movie ranches. While primarily constructed around Leone's second spaghetti western, *For a Few Dollars More* (1965), and being used for many subsequent movies, filming still occurs from time to time today, and all of the sites are open for visitors, offering a 'western experience'. They include the Oasys Theme Park (the largest of the three sites with 30 acres hosting a western town, safari park/zoo and pool area), Fort Bravo, and Western Leone which is still being used as a filming location. According to the promotional website of the Oasys Theme Park:

> ... you will experience a gunfight in the town square that ends (you'll actually hear the spectators sigh of relief) with an outlaw hanged next to Sheriff's Office, all this accompanied by Ennio Morricone's music.
>
> This Western town takes you back to the spaghetti western movies we have all seen on TV and cinema.
>
> You may also enjoy a real **Cancan dancing show** performed by Cancan girls in the **Yellow Rose Saloon** ... (Unique Almeria; http://www.unique-almeria.com/oasys-theme-park.html#ixzz1XQTODi9D)

Creating a further attraction for tourists and fans, the region hosted what they claim to be the first European-based festival of the western, the Almeria Western Film Festival, in 2011, with special screenings of spaghetti westerns being held in the evenings at Fort Bravo. Also, the sets were used for Rosefeldt's creative installation, *American Night*, as outlined in the section, 'The Western as a Reference Point'. I could even take a four-day horseback tour of the region and the sets! The thought that it may be possible to experience these places from my childhood (and later!) excites and moves me, and the continued interest of visitors to these sites and regions illustrates that I am not alone.

Movie ranches were not only used for filming westerns, with many of them used to shoot aspects of film and TV series that required large-scale vistas, including *Gone With the Wind* (1939) at Players-Lasky Movie Ranch and the *Hunchback of Notre Dame* (1939) at RKO Encino Ranch, along with the movie and subsequent TV series, *M*A*S*H* (1970, 1972–1983) and *The Towering Inferno* (1974) at the 20th Century Fox Movie Ranch.

In a direct link between the Australian pioneering stories and the American western, in the 1990s a modern-day film ranch was constructed in Australia near the Victorian town of Daylesford, less than two hours from Melbourne, known as Kattemingga. It was used to film an Australian television series based on the iconic Banjo Paterson poem, 'The Man from Snowy River', as opposed to the highly popular movie (of the same name as the poem) which was filmed on location in the Victorian High Country. Released in Australia as *Banjo Paterson's The Man from Snowy River*, the series was subsequently released in the US and UK as *Snowy River: The McGregor Saga*. The television series concentrated on the adventures of Matt McGregor (Andrew Clarke) and his family, as a successful farmer, set 25 years after the famous ride depicted in the poem and successful movie. As illustrated in Figure 7.1, the site was constructed in such a way as to be able to transform into a western set, with different aspects of the building having different finishes, such as logs for a western and paling for Australian settings. Consequently, the set was used to film a prequel series to the legendary US TV series *Bonanza* (1959–1973), known as *Ponderosa* (2001–2002).

Unfortunately, the terrorist crisis of 9/11 halted all American international filming and the film crew did not return to Australia to continue filming the series. The site is now run down; even though people want to visit and use the site for low-budget films it is not possible due to the condition of the site and related public safety issues. To return it to a usable state would be costly and, according to the owners of Kattemingga, such TV period dramas have gone out of popularity due primarily to the high costs of producing such dramas. However, it is used occasionally by students and independent filmmakers.

Completing the 'western' circle from America to Australia via Spain, Kattemingga has been used as a runaway western set for a short movie, *Gundown* (2004). This homage to the spaghetti western, written and directed by New Zealand based filmmaker, Andrew McKenzie, was shot at Kattemingga. The movie is silent, applying a Morricone-style musical soundtrack typical of the genre, with a lot of 'space'. The storyline is traditional, with a settler losing his wife and children to a bandit and then revenging them in a street shoot-out. Strong, metaphorical spaghetti western images are used, including a series of

Figure 7.1 The Movie Ranch, Kattemingga, Australia

tense facial close-ups along with the challenge being presented to the bandit through dropping a bullet into his outstretched hand (in close-up of course). McKenzie has also produced a short spaghetti western animation, *A Bullet Waits for You* (2006), specifically for downloading to mobile video.

Did it Really Go Away? The Resurgence of the Western

Although the western movie fell out of mainstream fashion during the late 20th and early 21st centuries, many of today's tourists were influenced by them in their youth and bring the images of the 'badlands' and the pioneering tales with them to the American 'west'. Travel guidebooks and news stories continue to refer to the movies of John Ford when writing about Monument Valley (woe betide the journalist/writer who fails to mention him!) and the other westerns that have shaped the American west, representing not only the on-location sites of filming, but also the constructed studios, towns and extant film ranches. While the western is unashamedly formulaic and predominantly sexist and racist, as a young horsewoman I identified strongly with the independence of the male protagonists and the landscape, and still (almost surreptitiously and at times conflicted) gain much from their particular type of morality and epic mythology. This important aspect of my personal relationship with the western movies and tourism is further described in a later section. Furthermore, many movies, TV programmes, advertisements and other popular media constructs, including Rosefeldt's controversial installation, continue to reference the genre.

In addition, we are now seeing a revisiting of the western by directors, including John Hillcoat's production of *The Proposition* (2005) with its powerful soundtrack from Australian musician Nick Cave, the Coen Brothers with the award-winning remake/reinterpretation of *True Grit* (2010), and the TV series *Deadwood* (2004–2006) and *Hell on Wheels* (2011–), among others. We are also able to view re-runs of western movies and TV series on free-to-air TV and the internet as well as cable television and DVDs. And, as noted previously, the interest in the Spaghetti Western Orchestra from such a wide range of people in Australia as well as Europe is further evidence of the enduring nature of the western along with its current resurgence.

In a review of the Coen Brothers' *True Grit* (2010), Andrew O'Hehir refers to it as a western in the John Ford style, being 'formed by the American ideology of Manifest Destiny and Protestant conceptions of morality and justice' (O'Hehir, 2011). While the Coen Brothers' approach tends to be partly ironic (as were certain elements of the original), it is also respectful of the western genre and true to the book on which the movie is based. Some of the western themes and myths have also informed other work and, one could argue, the sensibilities of numerous aspects of Coen films. O'Hehir supports this, noting that the brothers 'dive into a specific conception of genre and go all out, striving to make it their own without violating its terms and conventions' (O'Hehir, 2011). As discussed earlier, the forms and conventions of the western genre include loss and revenge, which dominate this movie, along with violent shoot-outs and knight-at arms battles, mythical bravado, death and, possibly, redemption. Underlining the landscape's central role, as the movie develops, the characters become 'figures in a bleached-out, majestic landscape' (O'Hehir, 2011), rendered as minor players in the monumental struggle between man and nature, life and death.

In 2013, Quentin Tarantino released his definitive western movie, *Django Unchained* (2013), which he wrote and directed (and had a small cameo in as an Australian). As with Sergio Leone's work, this movie references many iconic moments, places and themes of past westerns. Tarantino is particularly enamoured of the spaghetti western and uses much of Ennio Morricone's music in this film, including pieces from *Two Mules for Sister Sara* (1970) and *I crudeli* (1967), as well as pieces from *Django* (1966), the movie for which this one is named. The movie was filmed at various famous western locations, including Lone Pine, as well as Los Angeles movie ranches Melody Ranch and Ahmanson Ranch, reinforcing their iconic status on the fan and tourist circuit.

Again, what is of particular interest in these newer versions is the role that the land continues to play in the western – it is rarely merely a backdrop to the action, but rather an active protagonist in many movies and TV series, where the pioneers battle against its harshness and struggle to impose their superiority on it, while the native Indians seamlessly integrate with this landscape, as a 'force of nature' (Buscombe, 2006: 193). Bazin (1971) sees the Indians portrayed in the westerns as a race who could not impose their will on the land, consequently living *in* it and identifying with it through a form of pagan savagery, whereas the white Christian settler imposes (or attempts to impose) his moral and technical order onto the land.

The Western as a Reference Point

As evidence of its cultural place and popularity, many musicians, writers, filmmakers and artists reference or even pay homage to the western in their work. There are many examples of this, but one that I found to be a powerful and most interesting experience is Rosefeldt's installation, which I have briefly described below and refer to in the next chapter.

In 2009, Berlin-based artist Julian Rosefeldt developed an installation called *American Night*, which is a five-channel film installation that applied the stylistic devices of the western as a way to examine recent American history, and in particular to question America's role in the Iraq War. The installation presents the audience with a series of simultaneous western-genre vignettes that were primarily shot on one of Leone's original film sets in Almeria, Spain at Fort Bravo and in the Canary Islands. As noted earlier, the Leone film set can be visited by tourists and has primarily become a Spanish-based western movie theme park. What is interesting here is not only the use of the western genre to explore and expose the unreliability of popular memory and interpretation, but Rosefeldt's application of the characteristics associated with the western landscape. Throughout the entire installation, there is always at least one representation of the vast, lonely landscape. Since its opening at the German Museum in Berlin, this powerful, evocative and challenging installation has been shown around the world, including at the British Film Institute in London (2010) and in Australia at the Australian Centre for the Moving Image (2011), attracting many visitors, including myself. I went twice to the installation, purchasing the book of the exhibition, and I remain fascinated by it and hope to be able to experience it again.

However, such activities are not solely the realm of professionals, with audiences and fans actively engaging in creating their own homages to the western. While not isolated to the western, one can see hundreds of self-made parodies and touristic re-enactments of western movies on YouTube.

As Bazin notes, the western is 'a genre that can survive counterfeiting, pastiche, or even parody' (Bazin, 1971: 142) by musicians, artists, writers and filmmakers. And one in which, as viewers, fans, travellers, tourists and flâneuses, we actively participate.

From Frontiers to Pioneers: Australian Journeys

The Australian outback has been used not only in road trips and the bushranger movies discussed in the next two chapters, but also as another 'final frontier' of the New World (that is, Western-centric non-European countries colonised by white people). While the Anglo-Saxon Australians did not arrive in their new country with the same notions of Manifest Destiny as the Americans, we continue to celebrate a pioneering spirit through film in particular. Of the many pioneering movies, one of the most enduring is based on an iconic Australian poem, *The Man from Snowy River*.

The poem, written in 1890 by famous Australian poet Banjo Paterson, is based on the story of a valuable thoroughbred horse that escapes and joins the wild bush horses, with the poem focusing on the wild chase to recapture the horse and the boy who becomes a man. The star of the poem is a young, unknown bushman and his 'small and weedy beast', who defy the cautiousness of the other 'crack' riders and succeed in defeating the wild horses. The climax of the poem is a recounting of his wild ride down a steep mountainside:

> When they reached the mountain's summit, even Clancy took a pull,
> It well might make the boldest hold their breath,
> The wild hop scrub grew thickly, and the hidden ground was full
> Of wombat holes, and any slip was death.
> But the man from Snowy River let the pony have his head,
> And he swung his stockwhip round and gave a cheer,
> And he raced him down the mountain like a torrent down its bed,
> While the others stood and watched in very fear.
>
> He sent the flint stones flying, but the pony kept his feet,
> He cleared the fallen timbers in his stride,
> And the man from Snowy River never shifted in his seat –
> It was grand to see that mountain horseman ride.
> Through the stringybarks and saplings, on the rough and broken ground,
> Down the hillside at a racing pace he went;
> And he never drew the bridle till he landed safe and sound,
> At the bottom of that terrible descent.
> (extract from *The Man from Snowy River*, A.B. Paterson, first published in *The Bulletin*, April 1890)

This is also the climax of the 1982 movie of the same name, and the film clip still thrills and leaves me trembling with excitement and emotion. As recounted in the Introduction, it is this experience that led me to study the relationship between film, tourism and people in the first instance. Interestingly, my emotional response not only remains, but has increased over the years as I have laid more and more layers of meaning onto this poem and the movie, particularly through getting to know the landscape in which the movie was filmed.

As an avid horse rider and lover of the narrative of the poem and movie, I soon found myself participating as a guest and then working professionally as a guide on tours that were run by those who had worked with the horses on the movie, culminating in a guidebook, *Beeton's Guide to Adventure Horse Riding* (1984). Time and again I witnessed men trying to emulate the famous downhill gallop as presented in the movie – a risky endeavour. The actual hillside is truly frightening, with one stuntman breaking his leg during filming. Of course, this hill was not shown to these 'adventurers'.

From these beginnings, a new, particularly Australian, sector of tourism was born, that of a certain kind of High Country bush horse riding, with only three small businesses operating in this field prior to the movie, expanding to over 30 in the years following (Beeton, 2005a, 2008). In the 1990s I toured with over 20 of these operators (who all used *Man from Snowy River* imagery and language in their promotional material), producing the aforementioned guidebook, which gave me the opportunity to experience the breadth and depth of the influence of this movie on tourists, the tourism industry and the local communities involved.

Defying those who claim that film-induced tourism is short lived, 30 years on, in 2012, the actor who played the pivotal role of the young man from Snowy River in the movie, Tom Burlinson, led a second horseback tour revisiting the sites of the film (the first being held in 2011 as a one-off event). The booked-out tour comprised a wide range of people from Australia, Canada and the United States, many of whom were not even born when the movie first came out. Our trip was featured on national morning TV news for three consecutive days, with interviews with Burlinson, Americans who were on the tour and the tour operator. The members of the group re-enacted many scenes with Tom and our host Charlie Lovick, who was the Master of Horse and played one of the mountain men in the movie, including humming the iconic musical score as we cantered up the mountains.

Why does this movie remain so popular and continue not only to be available on DVD but also regularly shown on television (at least twice in 2012 in the US)? For the Australians on the tour, the primary interest related to the role of the original poem as part of our heritage, including its tale of the 'small person' winning out against a wealthy and privileged elite, the legends of the high country cattlemen and the countryside, as well as the movie itself. For the North Americans, the attraction was more about the romance in the movie, horses and notions of Australia as a 'final frontier' for such adventure. For many, the experience was highly personal, with one participant overcoming significant personal challenges to take part in what for her was a once-in-a-lifetime experience. This tour cost around double the price of a standard tour and has now become an annual event. Below is a brief photo essay of my experience of the tour.

Photo essay: *The Man from Snowy River* feature ride, 2012

The series of photos below is a selection of a few hundred that I took while on the tour; hence much of this reflection revolves around my choice of photos and what they mean to me.

As we rode up to the hut built for the movie, *The Man from Snowy River*, we encountered a group of people waiting to see us and Tom Burlinson. They had heard when they were in the nearby town of Mansfield that we would be there, and so took a day trip up to the hut (Figure 7.2). They not only photographed Tom, but also all of us on the trip, making us also feel like stars.

Figure 7.2 *Man from Snowy River* fans

We then posed individually with Tom outside the hut (Figure 7.3), which for me was a highlight as this is a strong image of the High Country and the story of the Man from Snowy River poem and movie.

Figure 7.3 With Tom Burlinson

After the photos, Tom signed the guest book in the hut (Figure 7.4), with this photo becoming even more important than a personal autograph as it is *'in situ'* in the context of the legend and movie.

Figure 7.4 The guest book

The following morning, the TV team from the Sunrise breakfast programme filmed a series of live interviews and segments during the weather forecasts, which we sat and observed, feeling more like privileged insiders than tourists (Figure 7.5).

Figure 7.5 Good Morning Australia!

This photo of me on my horse with the mountainous backdrop is special to me as it places me, as a horse person, into the landscape and legends (Figure 7.6).

Figure 7.6 The girl from Snowy River?

This experience not only enabled me to re-live aspects of the legend and movie with people directly involved in it, but also placed me back into this countryside, which was where my professional tourism life began. Consequently there were various layers to this experience, and the others on the trip each had their own meaning to apply to this experience.

Tourism Subtexts

This and the previous chapter barely scratch the surface of the significance of the western genre in film and television and its influence on many people's tourism experiences and journeys, along with its relationship to the landscape. As I noted in the introduction to this Part, the western provides us with an 'exemplar' in terms of the ongoing, universal relationship between film and tourism, along with my somewhat absurd and intense emotional connection and experience which, while not shared by all, does appear to cross many cultural boundaries.

While it can be argued that younger generations do not have the same connection to the western as those growing up during the 1930s to 1960s, the road movie, which reflects many elements of the western, remains one with which all audiences appear to relate, as discussed in the next chapter.

Also, the resurgence of the western, along with its continued use as a reference point for American (and Western culture) social history, indicate that it still resonates with remarkable force around the world.

One of the primary elements of the western, the landscape, presents the traveller/tourist with emotional connections to places that would otherwise not exist. Furthermore, numerous Australian films, while not specifically westerns in the sense of being American, display many of their attractions and attributes, including a frontier-based landscape, attracting a broader international audience. My own experience in Monument Valley (as well as in Australia) tends to lead me to lean towards a positive view of the role of the western movies and TV series in relation to tourism, and I am certainly aware of others such as Rothel (1990) who also confesses to be drawn to experience these places as a tourist.

The next chapter takes this discussion 'on the road' and away from horses as the primary vehicle, looking at road movies and their close connection to travel and tourism, particularly in relation to 'the journey'.

8 Travel and Transformation: Road Movies and Touristic Journeys

> Road movies portray a road of excess instead of a practical or functional road: travel for travel's sake, travel as an 'end' in itself.
> Laderman, 2002: 2

Arguably an offshoot of the western, the road movie genre emerged through American cinema and, simply put, cars and roads replaced horses and trails. According to O'Shaughnessy and Stadler (2008: online) the road movie was:

> ... developed in the era of cars and roads when the western landscape of prairies and horses was fading away. Once America is fully civilised, tamed, and modernised, the road itself becomes the new frontier: it is 'on the road' that freedom can be found.

They can also be seen as a product of the convergence of the 20th-century popularisation of two technologies – that of film and the automobile, both becoming accessible to the masses around the same time. They represented a form of personal freedom of movement and escape, literally in the case of the motor car (moving people) and figuratively in relation to films (moving pictures and emotions). In his authoritative publication on the road movie, *Driving Visions: Exploring the Road*, Laderman explains that, '[c]onceived together, automobiles and films dynamically reflect our culture as it becomes transformed ...' (Laderman, 2002: 3). Orr (1993: 129–130) sees the link between the car, the road and film as where '[t]he car as the expressive face of the peripatetic self, the instrument of its wandering, fits well with the movie camera'. The road movie presents us with society's achievements, while often sharply defining the social problems of the time (Cohan & Hark, 1997).

The development of the motor car and its place in cinema, while not confined to the US, is most often associated with it. Consequently, this chapter begins with a discussion of American highway development and road movies. From the early 20th century, Americans were pressing for a system of 'highways' or sealed roads to support not only the movement of people but also to provide for the motor car. Paxson (1946) considered this to be the final of three major coast-to-coast transport-related communication spreads, following the 19th-century railroad developments and dirt roads of the pioneers. In 1916 the Federal Aid Road Act was agreed to by the Federal Government, resulting in numerous highway developments, particularly during the Depression where road building was a major government employment support mechanism. By 1940 there was a strong system of highways across America; however, much of this work stagnated once the US joined WWII.

The American Interstate Highway system we know today and see represented in much of Western popular culture developed in a period of post-war recovery and growth, becoming a powerful symbol of progress and optimism as well as reinforcing the US notion of manifest destiny. It has been described as 'the largest public works program in history' (Cox & Love, 1996: 3). The Eisenhower administration introduced the Federal-Aid Highway Act of 1956 in June of that year, which authorised the development of 41,000 miles of high-quality highways tying the nation together, and was ultimately completed in 1976. Such a public works programme engaged the imagination of the nation, and further supported the development of the post-1960s' style of road movie.

While representing just over 1% of America's entire highway system, it is the interstate system that has captured the American imagination more than any other, carrying almost a quarter of all road traffic (Cox & Love, 1996). Such a vast highway network was 'made for tourism', while the road movie genre provides the tourist with a cultural lens through which to experience it, metaphorically and physically. Both contain elements of personal discovery and transformation through journey, even if it is purely imaginary. According to the US Department of Transportation:

> Roads are so much a part of our lives that they are, naturally, also a part of our cultural life. Although roads, and particularly the interstate system, are shown briefly in hundreds of films in which they provide, as in real life, transportation for the characters, roads are featured prominently in many others

Consequently, post-WWII filmmakers were soon faced with a vastly changed landscape, with the massive highway projects of the 1950s altering the great migratory routes of the Depression era and being transformed into the great tourist routes of the 1960s (Schaber, 1997).

The times are a-changin'

As with any attempt at classification, there are no firm boundaries when looking at movie genres. Road movies traverse other genres, including the buddy movie (such as *Thunderbolt and Lightfoot*, 1974), horror film (*Near Dark*, 1987), documentary (*Sherman's March*, 1985) and comedy (*Midnight Run*, 1988), along with glimpses of film noir aspects of futility and inevitable breakdown (Wood, 2007). So, while this is an extremely broad genre, we can see road movies as representing, reflecting and challenging the dominant social norms in times of change as well as actual movement among the disenfranchised and criminal elements, along with 'average' people breaking away from the mundane in the search for something new. These situations often culminate in one of two scenarios: finding oneself or annihilation. In particular, the road movie resonates with notions of freedom and social mobility, reinforced or reflected in the landscape (Eyerman & Lofgren, 1995).

Road movies also come from a longstanding literary tradition of the journey as narrative, such as Homer's *The Odyssey* and Mark Twain's *The Adventures of Huckleberry Finn* through to Kerouac's 1957 bestselling novel, *On the Road*, where the setting, social upheaval and change are central to the story. Narratives of social mobility were translated into movies such as John Ford's movie of Steinbeck's iconic novel, *The Grapes of Wrath* (1940), where a family joins a mass migration across America to California. The road presented an opportunity for them to recast their life and the potential to become someone else – someone 'new' (Eyerman & Lofgren, 1995).

While some argue that the road movie did not appear until the 1960s as a 'genre' per se, there were certainly many movies prior to then that can (and should) also be considered. Cohan and Hark (1997) agree; however, they acknowledge that there is a delineation between the movies made prior to and post 1960. The earlier films more often conclude with the road travellers being successfully reintegrated into the dominant culture, such as in *It Happened One Night* (1924), which relates the story of a wealthy socialite taking to the road as an escape from an unfulfilled yet privileged life, meeting the poor and then returning to her own culture enlightened; whereas in later films the protagonists tend to become further marginalised and isolated, many of whom never return (*Easy Rider*, 1969; *Thelma & Louise*, 1991).

We can draw parallels with the 1924 movie and how we behave as tourists – we immerse ourselves (or in reality, 'dip a toe into the water') in a foreign culture, adventure or lifestyle, but then return to our own lives, sometimes further enlightened as in *It Happened One Night* (1924). The similarities are even more evident when we consider that travel remains still a primarily middle-class pursuit. Even when we re-enact a more dangerous scene from a movie, such as some of those in *Easy Rider* (1969) and *Thelma & Louise* (1991), we tend to use our imaginations rather than a literal re-enactment, knowing we will return safely home, unlike in these movies.

Elements of the Road Movie

In order to understand the key elements that define a road movie, O'Shaughnessy and Stadler (2008) identify the primary characteristics of the road movie as where:

- the road provides the idea as well as reality of movement, connecting with the American notions of space and movement;
- movement becomes a goal in itself – the journey being more important than the destination;
- the movie explores concepts of social diversity along the road, providing snapshots of American life as well as social mobility, reflecting the American dream that it is possible to move up the social ladder;
- it is predominantly a male genre as it presents masculine ways of behaviour through its portrayal of freedom, lack of social ties and law breaking;
- it offers an explosive resolution for the viewer, typically ending with an acceleration and crash.

By comparing these elements of the road movie with those of the western, the similarities become clear, as seen in Table 8.1. While all of the examples cited combine the various elements to varying degrees, only one is used for each as an illustrative example. However, this focus on the physical elements of moving and travel neglects the emotional and spiritual transformational aspects of journeying, often brought out in road movies.

It is interesting that the examples that come to my mind for inclusion in the table are primarily movies for the road movies and TV series for the westerns, which most likely reflects my personal experience of these genres. Nevertheless, the TV series that for many represents the classic road movie genre is *Route 66* (1960–1964), with 115 episodes that followed the adventures of two friends, Buz and Tod, as they travelled in their Corvette along the

Table 8.1 Road movies and westerns

Element	Road movies		Westerns	
	Movie/TV series	Description	Movie/TV series	Description
Space and movement	Easy Rider (1960)	The highway provides a way to keep moving through a variety of iconic rural landscapes such as Monument Valley	Rawhide (1959–1966)	The droving trails provide a way to keep moving through various landscapes – primarily open grassland, mountains and rivers
Journeying	Forrest Gump (1994)	There is no 'destination', only the journey	Rawhide (1959–1966)	While there is a nominal destination, the entire series focuses on the journey on the Sedalia Trail
Social diversity and mobility	Grapes of Wrath (1940)	Depression-era family forced to travel after being made homeless. Many become little more than economic slaves; however, Tom Joad's family refuses to submit, swearing to fight injustice	Wagon Train (1957–1965)	Most characters are moving in order to improve their financial and social standing
Male genre	Easy Rider (1960)	Violence, risk taking, irreverent behaviour and motorcycles represent male activities	True Grit (1969, 2010)	Even though the main protagonist is a young woman, the focus is on male attitudes of revenge and lust (for money)
Explosive resolution	Thelma & Louise (1991)	Ends with a car chase, culminating in their decision to drive over a cliff to their death rather than be captured by the law. Challenges the primarily male domination of the genre	The Wild Bunch (1969)	Many western movies have explosive resolutions, but none more so than Sam Peckinpah's westerns. This movie ends with a sacrificial massacre of both the 'good' and 'bad' characters

iconic highway that connected America from Chicago to Los Angeles. The stated primary theme of the series was that of 'search, unrest, uncertainty, seeking answers, looking for a way of life', with the locations comprising 'the whole width and breadth of the US, with stories shot at the actual locations' (Alvey, 1997: 145). Alvey (1997) also notes that the true star of the series was America with its wide-ranging locations, and the series remains the only one to film on location in so many states of America (40 in total). The popularity of the series saw Corvette sales double in its first season.

Today, such a TV programme would be seen by tourism marketers as a great opportunity to promote the country, and might even try to influence the portrayal of certain places. However, such an approach was not considered at that time, and I have commented elsewhere that I believe such cynical marketing to be unnecessary and generally ineffective today, especially as most people are aware of such blatant manipulation.

Route 66, dubbed by Steinbeck as *The Mother Road*, was developed in 1926, following the dustbowl and pioneering era trails. Even without any conscious tourism promotion, Route 66 has entered the popular lexicon and mythology, with tourists continuing to search for remnants of this iconic highway in order to experience one of the most famous road trips in the world. As noted on the travel website, *The Road Wanderer*, '[t]o understand the history of Route 66 is to understand a little bit about ourselves, where we came from and where we hope to go in the future' (http://www.theroadwanderer.net/route66.htm). Of course, it had been popularised not only through the TV series but even earlier in the hit song of the same name written by actor and songwriter Bobby Troup and initially recorded in 1946 by Nat King Cole and subsequently by dozens of others, including Bing Crosby. As the saying goes:

Get your kicks on Route 66!

As noted previously, the landscape is generally cast as a central character of the road trip narrative, with the directors applying the use of phantom shots from the various vehicles, while the human characters often gaze out at the untouchable, intangible, yet powerful landscape. Eyerman and Lofgren (1995: 67) describe this as the situation where 'the road movie builds on both a physical and mental landscape'. This relationship is also reflected in the western genre, where Bazin (1971: 141) notes that 'the continuous movement of the characters, carried almost to a pitch of frenzy, is inseparable from its geographic setting'.

The Road, Travel and Tourism

> *Music and speed, combined with the ratio of the windscreen, made for an experience that was often more cinematic than the films I had to review ...*
> Petit, 2007: x

As noted in the introductory paragraphs of this chapter, the relationship between the road movie and travel or tourism is inextricable, with many tourism experiences being more about the journey than the destination, as with the narrative of road movies. The tourist's journey can also be metaphorical, culminating in personal change and growth not dissimilar to some of the road movie narratives:

> On the road, anything can happen, one is vulnerable but also open and, at journey's end, a new person has been manifested. (Eyerman & Lofgren, 1995: 67)

The current emphasis on tourist experiences, which has been informed in part by the concept of the *Experience Economy* as described by Pine and Gilmore (1999, 2011), parallels the genre of the road movie and its emotional metaphorical meanings, enabling the humble tourist (or traveller) to encounter life-changing incidents, often experienced through the lens of what for many is a series of numerous road movies in the tourists' experience. I vividly recall my first road trip in America to the Grand Canyon and New Mexico (along some of the original sections of Route 66) with a girlfriend, imagining we were Thelma and Louise and feeling incredibly free and liberated. While the movie *Thelma & Louise* presents the women as marginalised and brutalised by men, it is one of the few post-1960s road movies where women are placed in the lead roles, while maintaining a sense of freedom and equality through the movement through the landscape on the open road in spite of its explosive ending.

Yet, the nature of the experience of the protagonists in the film can be very different from that of the tourist, whose experiences are generally benign and controlled (Laderman, 2002) – we usually return home intact, rather than being killed, incarcerated, marginalised or suiciding. What seems to appeal to the tourist is the perception of risk and danger they can experience vicariously through their filmic references. Rascaroli (2003) sees the aspects of travel presented in the road movie being used as an opportunity for personal exploration, with notions of discovery and transformation, which is also central to many tourism experiences.

This underlines further similarities between road trips and tourism, particularly the notion of discovery and transformation. In fact, that first

American road trip I took was instrumental in a significant change in my personal and professional life, and some 15 years later my friend and I still talk about it as the best holiday ever. Even a night in a very cheap hotel with paper-thin walls, hard beds and bad food was a necessary element of our experience. This was not simply about travelling or tourism; due to our personal fandom references to movies, which included westerns (as discussed previously) as well as road movies, we came to experience our road trip in a particular way. These two film genres played a significant role for us in interpreting and framing our experiences by giving us a touchstone from which to explore these new places as well as ourselves.

The Other Road Movies: Europe and Australia

While originally an American construct, the road movie has been applied in varying degrees to movie narratives around the world, as the concept of journeying, change and discovery is universal, and is vividly reflected by the activities related to travel and tourism. Bemoaning the dearth of literature relating to non-American road movies, Rascaroli (2003) explains that the genre does exist beyond Hollywood, with European and Australian filmmakers in particular adapting the road movie to their own environments, both cultural and physical, arguing that such cross-fertilisation needs to be studied.

Europe embraced the road movie, but arguably more as an audience rather than as filmmakers, as Eyerman and Lofgren (1995) illustrate in their study of the American road movie and Swedish culture and cinema. They explain that Sweden's ideology of classless modernity excluded any discourse relating to the (American) notion of social mobility, so central to many road movies. Furthermore, notions of space, freedom and the open road are not as pronounced in the more densely populated and historically layered European landscape.

However, 'Europe' is a vast and varied continent, so any generalisations such as those above can be challenged. Certainly, Russia's vast landscape and traditions of travel and movement in countries such as Russia lend themselves to a particular form of road movie. Whether considering the pre- or post-Soviet era, the political environment differs from the 'classic' American notions of manifest destiny and personal discovery as reflected in their road movies. As Widdis (2010) explains:

> In the Soviet case, however, evolutions of the landscape as seen through the gaze of the traveller are inevitably more closely tied to the shifting ideological field with which filmmakers were forced to engage. (Widdis, 2010: 77)

Nevertheless, it appears that, from my very limited perspective and understanding, the post-Soviet era road movies such as the father and son journeys, *The Return* (2003) and *Koktebel* (2003), were similar to those in the United States that focused on times of social upheaval and change. Once again, we can see a difference between pre- and post-1960s road movies. While the pre-1960s European road movies are not as reflective of the American format, post-1960s movies tended to be more overtly influenced by the American genre (Rascaroli, 2003). For example, the movies of Rosselini (*Viaggio in Italia/ Voyage in Italy*, 1954), Fellini (*La Strada/The Road*, 1954) and Bergman (*Smultronstallet/Wild Strawberries*, 1957) were set on the road in Europe, with little connection to the American Hollywood format. However, from the 1960s we start to see European movies engaging more with the American genre, such as in Wim Wender's *Alice in den Stadten/Alice in the Cities* (1974) and *Im Lauf der Zent/Kings of the Road* (1976), albeit remaining particularly European, unlike Leone's spaghetti westerns which were firmly rooted in America. Rascaroli (2003: 73) affirms this, stating that both European and American directors 'use the motif of the journey as a vehicle for investigating metaphysical questions of the meaning and purpose and life'.

Often, the protagonists in the European road movie remain closer to the 'ordinary citizen', moving for practical reasons, including holidaying, rather than following the American line of rebels and outcasts. Rascaroli (2003) is also interested in the ways that travel films such as road movies have engaged with the changing European socio and geographical spaces and notions of national identity. She argues that, from around the 1980s, notions of mobility in terms of changing countries, nationalities and even cultures has become a reality for large groups of Europeans. As times change and uncertainty enters European politics and society, Eyerman and Lofgren argue that the road movie is increasing in popularity with filmmakers as well as audiences:

> The road movie is a genre tailored for tales and times of crisis – for downward as well as upward mobility – whether they be individual or collective. (Eyerman & Lofgren, 1995: 77)

The road movie has been regularly used in Australian narratives (in film as well as tourism promotion as discussed previously), where the vast landscapes hold a similar physical and metaphorical place in the Australian (Anglo) psyche as in America. Furthermore, Australians possess a similar positive attitude towards social mobility to that of the Americans. Supporting this notion, Murphy *et al.* (2001: 77) believe that, 'if the road movie genre had not developed in Hollywood, it probably would have originated from

Australia', with the main difference being that Australians cannot 'escape' across a border, being an island continent. As I have noted elsewhere:

> In classic American road trips such as *Easy Rider* (Dennis Hopper, 1969), *Forrest Gump* (Robert Zemeckis, 1994) and *Thelma & Louise* (Ridley Scott, 1991), as well as Australian movies such as *The Adventures of Priscilla, Queen of the Desert* (Stephan Elliott, 1994), *Wolf Creek* (Greg Mclean, 2005), *Last Ride* (Glendyn Ivin, 2009) and even *Mad Max* (George Miller, 1979), the 'road' (landscape or place) is a significant character, the 'place' significantly impacting on the characters' journey along with those they connect with and, subsequently, the overall story. (Beeton, 2010b: 115)

Three quite different movies that reflect Australians' relationship with the road (and outback) are the *Mad Max* trilogy (1979, 1982, 1985), *The Adventures of Priscilla, Queen of the Desert* (1994) and *Last Ride* (2009). Each, in its own way, plays a role in defining my own interpretation and touristic experience of travelling in the outback, with *Mad Max* being presented as a post-apocalyptic narrative where the road and landscape play a central role, both metaphorically and actually. The third movie in the trilogy, *Beyond Thunderdome*, takes the metaphorical into the touristic by 'reflect[ing] contemporary tourist and corporate discourses about space by focusing on the *representation* of place, rather than on place itself' (Falconer, 1997: 264).

While not as commercially successful as the other movies referred to, a powerful and emotional road movie, *Last Ride* (2009), presents the tale of a convict on the run through the outback who takes his 10-year-old son with him, while they get to know each other for the first (and last) time. The 'action' takes place in the Australian outback, with images of the vehicle and people being overwhelmed by the powerful, vast landscape – a recurring theme in the Australian psyche and often reflected in tourist narratives. Yet they are not strangers here – the father has relatives who are indigenous to the region from whom he has learnt about the land, which he now passes on to his son. For many Australians such a connection to the land is part of our psyche, even if not entirely realistic due to our highly urbanised society.

While engaging in a more contemporary discourse relating to gender, isolation and belonging, *The Adventures of Priscilla, Queen of the Desert* follows more of the pre-1960s road movie format, with the protagonists 'safely' returning to their lives, albeit dramatically changed.

Each of these movies presents a tough, expansive Australian countryside, far from the European notions of picturesque, yet each of these stories could hardly be set elsewhere, even though one of them (*Mad Max*) is not set in any specific (Australian) place. Interestingly, in spite of its supposed generic landscape, the region where the *Mad Max* trilogy was filmed has become a tourist attraction, particularly the deserted town of Silverton in outback New South Wales. This simple fact supports my thesis that tourists are not necessarily attracted by picturesque backdrops, but rather they seek out emotional experiences which they have often initially encountered at the cinema or even at home on TV.

The *Priscilla* movie, at times reminiscent of a Leone western with its operatic shots, spawned a series of specialised tours (such as Priscilla Desert Tours) and features on the Northern Territory's official tourist website (http://en.travelnt.com/about-nt/movie-territory/priscilla.aspx), as well as facilitating an increase in interest in small outback mining towns such as Cooper Pedy. While *Last Ride* has not directly affected tourism to a measurable degree, its portrayal of a sun-burnished landscape reflecting the powerful storyline elicits a powerful response in the viewer – one that I have found profoundly reflects and affects my personal interaction with the Australian landscape.

Connecting Australian road movies with the American western

While it is clear that the American road movie followed many of the narrative and metaphorical elements of the western, Murphy *et al.* (2001) believe that, in Australian storytelling, the bushranger films considered in the next chapter were the forerunners of the Australian road movie, inferring a connection between the American western and Australian bushranger and subsequent road movies. So, while he is referring to the primary role that the landscape plays in the American western, we can consider Bazin's comments regarding location in relation to US and Australian road movies as well as the western in that 'one might just as well define the western by its set ...' Bazin (1971: 141). This is nicely illustrated in Table 8.2, where the setting and role of 'place' in selected Australian road movies and the western genre is considered.

What is particularly interesting in this table is that many of the narratives could not be set elsewhere without changing the nature and emotional fabric of the film. Many of the locations are integral to the movie, such as the remote, small-town attitudes of the locals in *The Adventures of Priscilla, Queen of the Desert*, the modern indigenous knowledge in *Last Ride*, or the army based at 'remote' *Fort Apache*. The character of Rooster Cogburn (Wayne and Bridges) in *True Grit* (1969 and 2010, respectively) could only have been created through a backstory related to the American west.

However, in spite of my enthusiasm for physical and emotional immersion in places and films, not all film tourists need (or want) to immerse themselves in the reality of such harsh landscapes as in many of the movies

Table 8.2 'Place' as a character in Australian road movies and American/spaghetti westerns

Movie (year)	The set	Role of 'place'	Appeal/legibility	Touristic relationship
Australian road movies				
Mad Max trilogy (1979, 1982, 1985)	Silverton, New South Wales (outback Australia and deserted mining town)	Futuristic, post-apocalyptic world; land as enemy; foreign, barren landscape	The role of the road as metaphor is powerful, from a formal structure to dirt road and finally non-existent. Landscape not readily perceived (or meant to be seen as) as Australian	Has become acknowledged as Australian movie due to general promotion by film fans. Ghost town of Silverton and region became an attraction for fans and other tourists. Cars and other filmic memorabilia form part of a permanent exhibition at the Australian Centre for the Moving Image
The Adventures of Priscilla, Queen of the Desert (1994)	Various sites, Outback Australia	As a direct contrast to the city-based culture of the transvestite performance scene. Also representing conflict between cultural sensitivities	Liberation of attitudinal norms (for all characters)	The iconic scene on top of the bus with headgear streaming behind reflects a sense of joy and freedom that appeals to tourists
Last Ride (2009)	Various sites, Outback Australia	A place for displaced white people to flee to and through; a place of personal redemption and self-awareness	The land brings the personality of the characters into stark relief; the landscape is large, the humans at times insignificant. Both indigenous and western perspectives presented	The power of the land creates an interest to experience it and influences the tourist's relationship with the land

Westerns

Film	Location	Landscape	Themes	Tourism/Imagery
Stagecoach (1939)	Monument Valley, USA	A harsh, unforgiving, uncontrollable protagonist that is inaccessible and challenging	Good vs. evil, where the land as well as people (criminals, Indians) are overcome by the hero	Strong visual and emotional images for tourists to experience and take home as a souvenir
The Searchers (1956)	Monument Valley USA	A harsh landscape where the Indian (as enemy) is most at home	The land can only be understood by those close to it. For the protagonist it requires a harsh response	Confronting movie about race, ethnicity and fairness, contrasted with the sparse, harsh landscape. Almost encourages a touristic pilgrimage
Fort Apache (1948)	Corriganville Movie Ranch, USA	The fort is situated in a landscape inhabited by the native Indians	The land is a harsh protagonist for the members of the fort	Commentary on respect (or lack of) for Indian people with strong images of the unforgiving surrounds
The Good, the Bad and the Ugly (1966)	Almeria, Spain; Rome, Italy	The harsh land is the enemy and friend, depending on whether the characters wish to survive or kill	The land is as unmoving as the characters and their greed in this movie. Yet, there is a droll sense of humour and appreciation of the bizarre	Strong visual images – great for tourists to experience and then to get away from. Presents a strong vicarious relationship
True Grit (1969)	Buckskin Joe Frontier Town, California; Ridgway, Colorado, USA	Tough landscape for tough people	The woman must prove to be as tough as the men in order to survive	Strong visual and emotional images of a significant landscape
True Grit (2010)	Buena Vista Ranch, New Mexico; Texas, USA	Landscape remains central to the story		Strong visual and emotional images

referred to in the table. The famous buttes, mittens and plains of Monument Valley can be photographed at Fords Point without the tourist having to even step onto the land, which for some presents an experience more akin to their more removed viewing of the movies set there.

In an indication of the significant role the landscape plays in these movies, the filming of a sequel trilogy to the original *Mad Max* trilogy (*Mad Max: Fury Road*) was postponed indefinitely in 2010 due to heavy rains in the Broken Hill region altering the barren, ravaged landscape so central to previous stories into a lush, fertile place. At the time of writing, filming was planned to commence in 2012 but, once again, there were no guarantees and there were unconfirmed reports of the filming moving overseas.

Tourism Subtexts

On a more prosaic level, tourist sites are often promoted using the imagery and language of the road movie, particularly those involving expanses of forbidding country, be that desert, mountains, glaciers or 'badlands'. Interestingly, many of the tourist destinations where the attraction of the road trip (and movie) is used are the 'frontier' nations of America, Canada, Australia and New Zealand.

Tourism promotion

Some such tourism promotions include a 2011 Tourism Australia campaign based around individual road trips called *Great Australian Road Trips*, which included an online road trip video with slogans such as *set your spirit free*, or *discover more of the unexpected*, and so on. Tourism Victoria ran a very successful campaign for over 17 years around the slogan, *You'll Love Every Piece of Victoria*, which included numerous representations of road trips, journeys and personal discovery (... *or you can take the scenic route* ...).

Geographically the largest state in Australia, Western Australia, developed a road trip campaign in 2010 around the banner of *The Extraordinary Taxi Drive*, where 11 pairs of people from around the world each participated in one of 11 journeys throughout the state via taxi. The website includes information on the tourists, the taxi driver and their personal experiences, where they often talk about the 'journey' as opposed to the destination and reflect many of the life-changing aspects seen in the more positive, experiential road movies.

In 2011 New Zealand promoted tourism to its shores to its Australian neighbours by presenting a series of home videos and blogs from supposedly independent travellers taking road trips throughout the country. The TV advertisements built on their experiences as they travelled, often referring to life-changing experiences as well as the usual scenic sites.

While there will be examples of the road trip/movie being used in European destination marketing, it does not appear to be as prevalent, and such notions are rare in the Asian travel market, unless presented as spiritual pilgrimages.

Consequently, the filmic ties to travel and tourism via the road movie are complex, often providing the traveller with an emotional or psychological place from which to move forward throughout the travel experience. They also add excitement, colour and depth that may not instantly be there, particularly for the first-time visitor.

The road movie traveller

In her article on the road trip, published in the *Journal of Australian Studies*, Woodrow recounts a personal road trip, beginning her journey 'with a lifetime of memories built on road trips from movies, books and TV' (Woodrow, 1998: 162). The entire article is based on her desire to emulate the experiences (and perceptions) of characters from numerous movies and TV series, both Australian and American, and she openly acknowledges their influence:

> When I think of small towns in traditional road narratives I think of the man in a tinny farm truck with a bulging growth on his neck who runs down Wyatt and Billy in Easy Rider. (Woodrow, 1998: 164)

As we have seen in the past two chapters, both the western, road movies and other pioneering tales from the New World involve journeying and transformation, which are key elements of many travellers'/tourists' experiences. Whether desired or not, it is a rare person who can travel to another place and not experience some sort of shift or transformation, and one can argue that a visit to the cinema or the 'box in the corner' (TV) has a similar effect. Such 'shifts' do not have to be profound, and may be simply a move from one state to another – boredom to entertainment, sadness to laughter, ennui to exhilaration, busyness to reflection, and so on. Once again, we see the allegories here of movement, both physical and emotional, and tourism.

If we look at this in terms of the model introduced in Chapter 1 (Figure 8.1), the road movie engages the audiences in a highly cerebral activity where they actively interpret the narrative and then use this in their tourism or recreational activities, as I have done on numerous occasions, but most so with *The Man from Snowy River*. In fact, my 'use' of this movie, along with my American

156 Part 2: Travelling In, On and Through the Landscape: Voyeur or Flâneur?

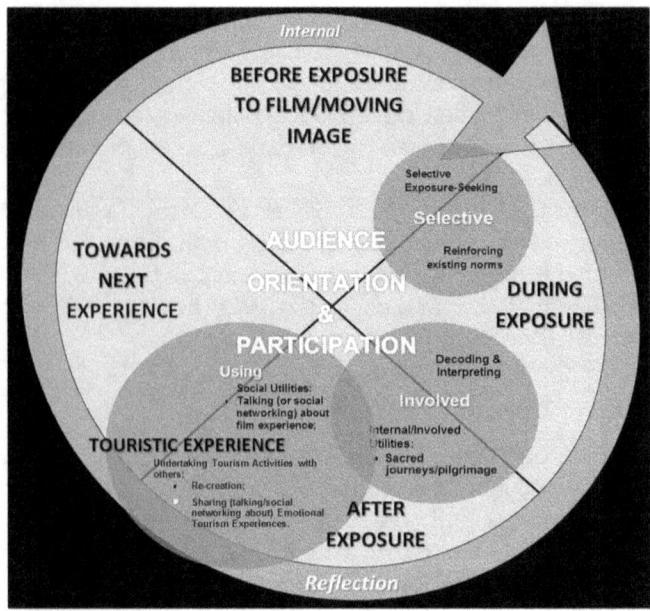

Figure 8.1 Modelling the relationship between audience and tourist activity

road trip, changed the direction of my professional as well as my personal life, and I find that I am still decoding, interpreting and using it today.

However, one major difference between some of the road movie narratives and tourism is that most tourists tend to belong to the middle or upper classes, reasonably wealthy and well educated, with the time, money and desire to travel. This is unlike many of the characters in road movies, especially post-1960, so we see tourists playing at being someone they are not, and probably do not really want to be. The opportunity to realise such fantasies is the backbone of tourism.

Furthermore, most tourism movements are from developed to undeveloped destinations. Consequently, the mobility that the tourist experiences is usually downwards in terms of wealth, class and education to experience more primitive and exotic cultures and societies. They then return to their lives with a better understanding of other ways of life, potentially enriched and changed by the experience. This is not unlike the storyline of the 1924 movie referred to earlier, *It Happened One Night*, where the privileged female star is able to return to her life, yet is changed by her experiences. In particular, backpackers and gap year students travelling on a budget fall into this category. We rarely see tourism experiences where the traveller is as excluded and marginalised as those in many road movies – that is not to say that tourists do not experience being an outsider, but they rarely suffer in the same manner as the stars of road movies.

While travel and tourism are primarily middle-class activities, some resort holidays provide occasions where lower class tourists have the opportunity to experience a higher class lifestyle, but they tend to be constructed rather than authentic experiences of wealth. They then return to their own lives with their preconceptions of wealth confirmed by these constructed experiences. While the focus of this book does not allow me to develop this socio-economic ('class') imbalance (or clash) further, it is important to be aware of the class and commoditisation issues surrounding travel and tourism.

Many road movies incorporate aspects of the maverick and even criminal 'on the run' into their stories. In the next chapter, we take elements of the western and the road movie genre as a framework from which to consider other stories of 'baddies', including the Australian Bushranger, the Italian (migrant) Mafia, Chinese Triads, and other criminal genres. This is also linked back to the tourism experience through the emotional representations, safe viewing distance (as audience and tourist) and glamorisation of these law breakers on film.

9 Baddies in the Old and New Worlds: Bushrangers, Gangsters and Crime On Screen

Another rich vein of storytelling and emotional imaging is that of the 'baddies' such as the Australian bushranger and the American gangster, which we consider in this chapter, along with other crime genres including the detective story. Many of these tales are closely linked to a specific place and presented in an often romanticised (or vicariously appealing) time. Such places often become tourist attractions and fan sites, as noted by Reijnders (2011) when he participates in such activities. They certainly evoke powerful emotional responses from audiences, who often became fans of many of the 'serialised' stories, especially in the detective genre where the lead character of the detective is central to the plot. But it is not only the 'goodie' (detective), but also the 'baddies' (bushrangers, gangsters and outlaws) who appeal to us in many complex ways, often linked to a national story or culture. They can also bear a close resemblance to the road movie genre, with the 'baddies' needing to move on – presenting a strong tie-in with travel and tourism.

The Australian Bushranger: Replicating the American Western?

While not solely limited to these countries, the Australian bushranger stories and the American western have numerous similarities, while also presenting certain stark differences. While Laing and Frost (2012) concur with the general view that westerns can only be set in the American west (see also Peterson, 2006), Frost concedes that there are western-style stories made and set elsewhere, including Australia. Movies such as *The Proposition* (2005), *Ned Kelly* (2003) and even *The Man from Snowy River* (1982/1988) tread a similar path to the American western with morally driven themes of pioneering, conflict and even a form of Manifest Destiny. Interestingly, most of the Australian bushranger movies and TV series are 'officially' classified as westerns (see the Internet Movie Database) while numerous commentators, including McGrath (2001) and Routt (2001) also liken them to the US western genre. This is particularly the case in terms of their relationship with the landscape, which in both genres becomes a major character and protagonist in the narrative as opposed to a benign backdrop.

However, as expounded later in this section, there are some major differences. Generally, the overall theme for the bushranger story is one where the criminal bushranger is an 'innocent' product of a corrupt colonial society, with the US western predominantly portraying the criminal from a more negative angle as a threat to personal freedom and development. As McGrath explains:

> From the beginnings of Australia's film industry, the 'bushranger film' was a standard adventure genre set in a settler-frontier context. Australians cherished bushranger legends in a range of popular media for their exciting storylines and national distinctiveness. Recognizing the familiar motifs of frontier adventure, conflict, escape, and shoot-outs, American film commentators described such films as Australian 'Westerns.' From the 1880s to the present, 'bushranger' characters of Australian frontier stories were recreated in a plethora of legendary bushranger novels for adults and children, popular plays, and commercial films. The most famous, Ned Kelly, robbed banks and **fought against the white 'squatters' and the police who acted for them** [own emphasis]. (McGrath, 2001: web)

As with many westerns and other American migratory stories, the landscape often frames the Australian pioneering and bushranger tales, as well as playing a distinct role. However, as opposed to other older cultures around the world (including Australian indigenous culture), the Australian landscape 'hasn't been incorporated into the symbolic order' (Gibson, 1983: 5) by the colonial settlers prior to the introduction of film as a major form of storytelling (and meaning-making). Furthermore, tourism in Australia developed alongside this, also in the era of the moving image (Beeton, 2005a). Consequently, the landscape, film and the Australian tourism experience are closely tied together in terms of images and emotions as well as some sort of 'symbolic order' or shared meaning as also discussed in the previous chapter. While our ancient and ongoing indigenous culture is intricately tied to the land, the films discussed in this chapter are Western-colonial derived.

Subverting law and order in Australian bushranger stories

The classic 'law and order' motif of the American western is often reversed and subverted in the Australian bushranger and settler stories, many of which represent the 'law' as corrupt and evil and the renegade or bushranger as the defender of humanity. Where America had gained independence from the British Empire by 1783, Australia remains a member of this colonialist power (the British Commonwealth) to this day. This is often reflected consciously and subconsciously in our stories, particularly by those that attempt to undermine notions of imperialism. This is clearly portrayed in the story, legend and mythology of our most famous bushranger, Ned Kelly, who is usually represented as a victim of circumstance and a political rebel rather than the horse thief, bank robber and murderer for which he was hanged. While I do not intend to address the ongoing controversy over *Ned Kelly the man* versus *Ned Kelly the myth* in this publication, the various movies that have been made tend to reflect and reinforce the accepted Australian folkloric, anti-colonialist storytelling elements.

Up until around 1914 the early Australian film industry developed a series of bushranger movies, following on from the success of what is arguably the first full-length movie in the world, and definitely the first filmic telling of the Ned Kelly tale, *The Story of the Kelly Gang* (1906). In these movies, the bushrangers 'do not control the hills: rather, for a time they express them' (Routt, 2001: 6). This relationship between man [sic] and the landscape is more reflective of the western's depiction of the American Indian or lone trapper rather than the Manifest Destiny of the American settlers trying to conquer and exert their will over the land. Interestingly, all of the Australian bushranger films were set in the period from 1860 to 1880, also a popular era for the American western and during the Gold Rush periods of growth and development in both countries. While Frost (2006) also sees parallels to Anglo-Celtic highwaymen and political tales, he acknowledges that 'Kelly's activities and his folklorisation resonate closely with those of American badmen ...' (Frost, 2006: 247). Due to my childhood inculcation (and interest) in the US western, I have tended to view these stories in a 'western' framework, gleaning my personal meanings from within this paradigm.

The bushranger movies, which focused on the legends of real-life bushrangers from that era including Ben Hall (1837–1965), Dan Morgan (1833–1865), Captain Thunderbolt (aka Frederick Ward, 1835–1870) and Captain Moonlight (aka Andrew Scott, 1842–1880) as well as Ned Kelly (1854–1880), proved extremely popular with an audience used to seeing itself represented through the eyes of others, primarily its colonial overlords, the British (Beeton, 2004). Sounding uncannily like a promotional tourist brochure for Australia, the publicity for the bushranger movie, *Captain Starlight* (1911) emphasised that this was:

> An Australian story essayed by Australian artists amidst Australian bushlife, in an Australian atmosphere. Cinematographed by Australian experts, and produced through Australian art and brains. Australia leads, and thereby establishes an important industry in Australia. (cited in Reade, 1970: 58)

The various iterations of the Ned Kelly movies reflect the development of Australian film over almost a century. As with many of the early forays into the movies outlined earlier in this publication, *The Story of the Kelly Gang* (1906) was produced by a theatrical entrepreneur (or showman), Charles Tait, who saw the film as a way for his theatre company to reach a wider audience. Produced in a time of great social upheaval, the movie was a success in England as well as Australia. Apart from some mediocre attempts in the 1950s, the next 'significant' screen version of the Kelly story appeared in 1970 in a British production, *Ned Kelly*, starring the Rolling Stones frontman, Mick Jagger. This movie placed the story within an English mythology, treating Kelly and his gang as modern-day versions of Robin Hood and his 'merry men', and was generally not well received in Australia. Finally, an Australian production, the 2003 movie, also called *Ned Kelly*, produced by Gregor Jordan, with Orlando Bloom, Geoffrey Rush and Heath Ledger in the lead role, sets the hero against a Protestant British establishment that recruits Irish police to brutalise Irish immigrants, a theme popular in the American as well as Australian psyche (French, 2003).

Table 9.1 from an earlier study (Beeton, 2004) compares the Kelly films' images of rurality with that of the contemporary tourism images, noting that often the images presented on film do not match what the tourism commissions are presenting. As these films are powerful representations of the Australian landscape and character, this can create a dissonance in the viewer/visitor's mind, at times expressed negatively. However, few tourist commissions have seriously considered such dissonance, preferring only to use films that support their agenda, ignoring others (and their audiences), at times to their detriment.

Apart from the 1906 movie when the Australian identity and a growing 'sense of self' was dominating this post-Federation era, the Kelly legend has

Table 9.1 Dominant tourism images in the Kelly movie eras

Movie (year)	Rural filmic images	Dominant Australian rural tourism images
Story of the Kelly Gang (1906)	The bush as a place to hide from and in. A place to be feared, where nature rules.	Light, warm, benign nature – European-style land (posters and postcards). Transport images with broad vistas (railways funded).
Ned Kelly (1970)	Threatening Australian bush reinforcing the tragic fate that awaits the hero. Lack of intimacy with the land. Pop idol element reduces rurality/authenticity.	Outback – desert, rock. National images of sun, sand and surf. Victorian state images very limited: – coastal (Fairy penguins); – regional (heritage focus).
Ned Kelly (2003)	Dark (most images in browns and greys, with overcast skies). No 'Australian' light. Rural landscape is foreboding, threatening and unforgiving to all. Barren, isolated farms. Stripped of any sentiment or idyll. Only one shot of Australian fauna early in movie.	National images of sun, sand and surf – bright and light. Victorian images: – panoramic vistas; – blue skies and sunshine – bright and light. Tourism Vic images of 'Kelly Country': – no images on website, just maps; – images in regional brochure – light and colour – blues, greens, autumnal. Tourism Vic images of Ned Kelly locations movie route – limited movie stills.

Source: Beeton (2004).

been primarily presented to reflect the myths, legends and cultural mores of international audiences of the US and the UK. As well as framing the stories for those international audiences, this reflects the influence they had on Australians' self-identity, as well as our cinema and storytelling. In terms of tourism, these stories have influenced the experiences of both international and domestic visitors to the historical sites of the Kelly story, which includes a rather 'hokey' animatronic 'Kelly Experience' in the small town of Glenrowan in the Australian state of Victoria. Bill Bryson's (2001) amusing account of his visit to this attraction presents a powerful example of an experience, partly created by and through the movies:

> Well, call me a Whimp, drop a brick shithouse on me, but I can honestly say that I have never seen anything so wonderfully, so delightfully, so monumentally bad as Ned Kelly's Last Stand. It was so bad it was worth every penny ... we were so delighted that we considered going in again. (Bryson, 2001: 166–167)

Some may see Byson's comments as negative; however, I found myself wanting to visit this 'theme park' that has inadvertently turned our most famous bushranger into an attraction producing great mirth, reinforcing the allure of humour (even if unintentional).

While the Kelly movies provide us with a valuable and interesting case to study, Table 9.2 returns to our broader discussion of the journey of the Australian bush (ranger and settler) stories and landscapes as told through film by summarising a selection of the better known stories.

As I have noted in another discussion of bushranger movies, 'film presented a powerful new medium that Australians could use to establish their Australian identity and express this to the rest of the world' (Beeton, 2004: 126). Such movies were internationally popular, and could well have challenged the growing influence of the western, except that the Australian government, fearful of their negative influence on the general populace, banned their production from around 1915, with some cinemas refusing to show them even prior to that time. It appears that the anti-authoritarian nature of these stories did not sit well during a time of impending war, as they presented audiences with a 'marginal history, just as the landscape was a marginal landscape' (Routt, 2001: 8).

While the burgeoning Australian film industry itself well could have survived the banning of the bushranger genre, for a range of reasons outside the remit of this publication, the industry went into decline from the late 1920s through to the 1970s, with most 'Australian' films being made by British and American companies, including *The Overlanders* (1946), *On the Beach* (1959), *The Sundowners* (1960), and even a version of *Ned Kelly* (1970).

However, as we moved through the 1970s, Australian-made film and television became more prevalent, with historical 'bushranger'-based TV series such as *Rush* (1974–1976) and Australian-produced movies including *Ned Kelly* (2003) and *The Man from Snowy River* (1982), along with a 'related' yet very different TV series filmed in Australia but produced by an American studio, *Banjo Paterson's Man from Snowy River* (1993–1996). That series was developed primarily for an American audience and reflects its US influence by being listed as an adventure and western, with a focus on the Americanised struggle between the cattleman and settler, and only passing references to bushrangers.

While the industry still has its challenges, Australian films, filmmakers and actors are highly regarded internationally, often producing well-received Australian movies and TV series connected to the bushranger genre, many of which remain focused on the Australian landscape. A recent Australian TV series, *Wild Boys* (2011), resurrected the traditional Australian bushranger story as a western, with a range of good-looking young actors in the roles, reminiscent of the American western, *Young Guns* (1988) which starred the extremely appealing Emilio Estevez, Kiefer Sutherland and Lou Diamond Phillips. However, the Australian story again subverts the classic western theme of the lawman bringing order to a wild place, with the law in this story primarily being corrupt, forcing the young men into a life of crime while caring for downtrodden family, friends and innocent acquaintances. This storyline has more in common with the Robin Hood tales from England, yet is clearly produced and marketed as a western. For example, the Internet Movie Database lists *Wild Boys* as a Western, Drama and Adventure, but the various movies and TV series about *Robin Hood* as Action, Adventure and Drama, along with Romance for the 1938 movie, *The Adventures of Robin Hood*, starring the romantic, swashbuckling Australian actor, Errol Flynn (IMDb, n.d.).

Such movies and TV series have played a powerful role in Australians' impressions of who they are and where they come from, and while some aspects are clearly modified and reinterpreted to tell a particular story, primarily they are well done, creating a strong sense of the Australian (Anglo) person and place. Again, we can see such emotional imaging playing out in the tourist experience, be that Bryson's kitsch experience at *The Kelly Experience*, or a more generic sense of being part of a heroic culture of independence and resilience. Certainly, Australians and others influenced by the stories (and movies) are making heritage pilgrimages to sites such as those related to Ned Kelly.

While I have argued above that the Australian bushranger stories are similar to the US western, yet also very different, American gangsters are often presented in a similar format to the western, where the motor vehicle replaces the horse and the dark city replaces the open badlands. Another genre using notions of good versus evil, the detective story, appears to be less related to the western genre, being more universal in its structure and cultural referencing. Nevertheless, the scenario of investigation, exposure and resolution (usually through an arrest) is universal. A brief discussion of the detective and gangster genres and their emotional touristic relationship follows.

Table 9.2 Australian bushranger and settler movies and TV series' relationship with landscape

Movie/TV series	Genre	Film location	Landscape and story	Storyline	Potential and actual touristic appeal
The Story of the Kelly Gang (1906)	Bushranger	Victoria, Australia	The bush as a place to hide from (to be feared) and in (to be embraced)	The good, downtrodden common man vs. a corrupt bureaucracy, where the landscape (bush) supports the downtrodden hero	Potentially strong as one of the first cinematic images of the Australian bush
Robbery Under Arms (1907, 1957, 1985) Captain Starlight (1911)	Bushranger	Victoria, New South Wales	The bush as a place of romance, daring and adventure	Based on novel by Rolf Bolderwood, Captain Starlight was a gentleman-robber	In spite of the number of versions of the story, it does not appear to have remained long in the Australian (or international) consciousness
Ned Kelly (1970)	Bushranger	South Eastern Australia	Threatening Australian bush reinforcing the tragic fate that awaits the hero	The bushranger was more 'Robin Hood' than a bush man; lack of intimacy with the land and the use of a foreign pop star in the lead role creates a sense of dislocation	Limited
Rush (1974–1976)	Adventure/drama	New South Wales, Australia	The landscape as enemy to gold prospectors, yet also can yield wealth for a few	Less romantic view of the Australian landscape – more of a pervading force than protagonist	Some heritage interest, adding a layer of storytelling to the Australian bush

Film	Genre	Location	Landscape depiction	Storyline	Tourism effect
Man from Snowy River (1982/1988)	Australian pioneer/western	Alpine National Park, Victoria, Australia	Australian bush culture – the land as nurturer and protagonist; final frontier adventure; man and horse striving together against the fickle environment	Reinforcement of an imagined bush heritage	International appeal of final frontier post the taming of the American west; tourists participating in adventure activities such as horse riding in the Australian high country
Banjo Paterson's Man from Snowy River (1993-1996) Snowy River: The McGregor Saga (US/UK release)	Australian pioneer/western	Kattemingga Movie Ranch, Victoria, Australia	Developing town where the land has been 'tamed', but it still lurks forebodingly in the background	Set 30 years after the famous adventure; final frontier style of stories similar to the early settler western stories – the farmer vs. the cattleman	Primarily American appeal as a final frontier; film set still stands on private property in rural Victoria, but unable to get permission to open to the public
Ned Kelly (2003)	Bushranger	Victoria, Australia	Dark, foreboding rural landscape	Bushranger as bush man; an innocent forced into crime, creating a rebel hero	Limited; had high expectations, especially in terms of 'star power' but did not eventuate
Wild Boys (2011)	Bushranger/western	New South Wales, Australia	The tough bush landscape is a place of refuge for those able to understand and respect it	Reinforcement of an imagined bush heritage as seen through American influence	Reinforces romantic appeal, legend and myth of bushrangers; may inform elements of the visitor experience

Mysteries and Detectives

As noted in the introductory paragraphs of this chapter, many detective stories have been presented in a serialised format in both movies and TV programmes. This probably has its genesis in the popular written stories on which they were based, as many were published in serial instalments in magazines, dime novels and the Dell Mapbacks described below. Furthermore, many stories are situated in real places, providing sites for fans and tourists alike to visit and experience.

Gunning (2005) explains the popularity of these detective films from the early 20th century in terms of his notion of 'spectacle' discussed earlier, noting that:

> The detective story, especially as practiced in France at the turn of the century, participates in a modern visual culture aware of the attractions of hiding as well as seeking, of the failure of insight as well as its successes. (Gunning, 2005: 87)

In fact, the first detective serial ever filmed has an interesting multicultural heritage. In 1908 the French film company, Éclair Films, adapted a popular series of 1980s American dime novels featuring the detective, Nick Carter (*Nick Carter, le roi des detectives*), starring Pierre Bressol. This is the first record of using the 'literary' tradition of episodic storylines in cinema (Popple & Kember, 2004). Unsurprisingly, they proved to be extremely popular, producing six episodes in 1908 and further 'new adventures' in 1909. Metro-Goldwyn-Mayer released a trilogy of Nick Carter films in 1939 and 1940. Wishing to capitalise on its popularity, but unable to afford the rights to produce a Nick Carter series, Columbia Pictures made the movie *Chick Carter, Detective* (1946) about his son.

Some decades on, wanting to capitalise on the popularity of James Bond (see Chapter 5), the Nick Carter character was refocused in the 1960s for the spy genre, with new spy stories unrelated to the original dime novels being produced. These included *Nick Carter va tout casser* (1964) and *Nick Carter et le trèfle rouge* (1965), both also dubbed into English for the US market. References in Europe and the United States to this popular series abound, including an example of Bond-esque tongue-in-cheek self-referential humour in the Carter movies, where in a particular scene in *Nick Carter et le trèfle rouge* (1965) the lead character finds a large collection of the Nick Carter dime novels and memorabilia.

Further iterations of Nick Carter continue today, demonstrating the success of applying episodic storylines to movies and TV series. We can see this in more contemporary stories, with the modern-day US CSI franchises, the British *Midsomer Murders* (1997–) and the Swedish *Wallander* (2005–) series, among dozens, if not hundreds, of others.

Another literary development that transferred to the screen were some of the popular Dell 'Mapbacks' series, which proliferated between 1942 and 1951 as a series of novels 'complete with crime map on back cover' (as stated on their front covers). These scene-of-the-crime maps were inspired by the real-life concept of police sketches (Schreuders, 1997). While many storytelling genres contributed to the series, including romance and adventure, out of the 577 Mapbacks, over half were crime stories. The format developed to incorporate Mapback paperbacks of MGM movies such as *King Solomon's Mines* (No. 433) and *Little Women* (No. 296), with their front covers featuring the movie stars, while others such as *Night And The City* (No. 374) and *Death In A Doll's House* (No. 356) were used to tie in with films. Many were based on the films which were initially based on a book, which creates an interesting paradox. It is not inconceivable to postulate that this concept of providing a map of the crime scene on the back cover has translated into a filmic device of mapping out crime sites, usually in the opening or final credits.

Agatha Christie had many stories published as Mapbacks that have also been filmed as movies or TV series, including *Appointment with Death* (Mapback No. 105 and movie from 1988) featuring Hercule Poirot, and *The Secrets of the Chimneys* (Mapback No. 570 and 2010 TV programme), as well as a number of TV adaptations of the Poirot series such as *Murder on the Links* (Mapback No. 454 and produced for TV in 1995) and *Sad Cyprus* (Mapback No. 529 and a 2004 TV adaptation). The exotic settings of many of Christie's stories continue to be presented in movies and TV series, including *Murder on the Orient Express* (2010) and *Death on the Nile* (2004). As with many of the Dell Mapbacks, fictional crime movies and TV stories were often based in identifiable, existing environments such as New York, London, the bucolic English countryside and so on, with fewer in purely fictional (or non-identifiable) places. Consequently, these stories contributed in no small way to people's images and emotional responses to real places that they could actually visit and where they could even experience a vicarious form of danger and excitement, which coincidentally is also a key tourism driver.

Any discussion of the detective genre must include acknowledgement of the role of Arthur Conan Doyle's Sherlock Holmes character and stories, which have been filmed countless times as movies, TV series and telemovies. The stories continue to influence not only detective films today, but even the writers of purportedly unrelated TV series such as the extremely popular medical-themed *House* (2004–2012), with the main character, House, closely resembling the Holmes persona as a drug-addicted genius solving insolvable medical cases with a stable, loyal friend and superiors he continually railed against as bumbling fools. This very brief description of *House* does not adequately convey all the nuances and parallels with the Holmes story, but I trust it serves to present an example of the power of Conan Doyle's tale and our fascination with the flawed, socially inept genius solving the insolvable.

While the traditional Holmes stories present a perspective of 19th-century England around the time of the Industrial Revolution, when travel was also becoming marginally more accessible, modern adaptations such as a series of BBC Wales produced telemovies set in the 21st century, *Sherlock* (2010–2013) place the stories in a contemporary London landscape. It seems the lure of Sherlock Holmes as a flawed genius transcends time, yet remains placed in a very recognisable England that we can visit in our minds as well as actually. And, of course there are many Holmes tours, especially around London, such as The Sherlock Holmes Walking Tour of London from Brit Movie Tours (http://britmovietours.com/bookings/sherlock-holmes-london-tour/).

An exemplar of the modern European model of serialised TV detective series is that of the popular Swedish series, *Wallander* (2005–2010), which has been re-filmed at the original site of Ystad on the south coast of Sweden by the BBC and re-presented in an English format of the same name (*Wallander*, 2008–2012), with UK star Kenneth Branagh in the lead role. As with many TV series where the audience engages personally over a relatively long period of time with the story, characters and places, this series has spawned a range of tourism-related business, including special tours and on-location re-enactments as well as memorabilia and souvenir sales. In his most interesting study, *Places of the Imagination*, Reijnders (2011) asks us why television detectives such as *Wallander* and *Inspector Morse* are so attractive to tourists, proposing that it is often due to the 'localisation' of such popular narratives, being set in identifiable communities and places. Such localisation presents numerous commercial tourism opportunities such as the aforementioned tours, but also manifests in associated filmic references which the local community may use as a frame of reference in their own lives. Reijnders illustrates this beautifully when he relates his witnessing of police officers in Ystad referring to real-life cases as 'being "a typical Wallander"' (Reijnders, 2011: 50). I have also seen evidence of this phenomenon at the height of the popularity of the Australian drama series, *Sea Change* (1998–2000) and at various places in the UK and US, where the communities at times virtually reinvent or reconstruct themselves in an unconscious self-parody – highly appealing to the lay-anthropologist tourist, which I find myself indulging in when fiction and reality collide in such an outstanding manner.

Gangsters, Mafioso and Triads

> *The American film gangster is an iconic figure of the industrial twentieth century in both its modern and postmodern forms, representing a culture of mobility, urban space, excess and individual licence.*
>
> Mason, 2002: vii

After reading my earlier chapter on the western, you will be aware of my fascination with Sergio Leone's spaghetti westerns and Ennio Morricone's musical scores and soundscapes. If *Once Upon a Time in the West* (1968), with its powerful and artistic imagery, innovative musical score and references to so many classic westerns, is my favourite western movie, you will not be surprised to know that *Once Upon a Time in America* (1984) is my favoured gangster movie. It follows a gang of Jewish street kids from childhood to adulthood in a complex, non-linear way that requires the audience to puzzle over various clues and signifiers (Hughes, 2006). Its epic narrative scale (over 30 years) and scope is almost overwhelming, and legend has it that this movie took so much out of Leone that it eventually killed him. He certainly did not produce any other movies prior to his death of a heart attack at the age of 60, five years after *Once Upon a Time in America* was completed.

In its negotiation of the links between the past and present, the movie presents a place in which the viewer and potential tourist can reasonably comfortably place themselves. Yet, this is not a comfortable film, portraying disconnection and separation, while throughout the characters simply desired to 'belong'. At the time, the movie was not a hit, due in part the cruel editing job done by an external editor who reduced its length which from 229 minutes to 144, seriously compromising the story, along with its violent rape scenes for which Leone had often been criticised. Nevertheless, it was hugely successful throughout Europe, illustrating the broad cultural appeal of this genre (Hughes, 2006). The movie has since been critically 'reappraised' and is now accepted as a powerful illustration of the genre, with some critics arguing that it is better than highly acclaimed gangster movie, *The Godfather* (1971) (Hughes, 2006).

This was a classic 'runaway production', being primarily filmed outside the US at Cinecitta Studios in Rome and on various Italian, French and even Canadian (Quebec) locations, with some US locations. Yet it remains staunchly American, creating a sense of New York that I cannot shake when I visit and the fog rolls over the Hudson River, even though I did not particularly 'like' the movie. Also, when experiencing Morricone's concert at the Adelaide Arts Festival in 2012, the haunting music from that movie transported me through time and space to my own touristic adventures in New York as well as the era and human struggles represented in the movie.

The appeal of the gangster to tourists

There certainly appears to be an insatiable human appetite for vicarious experiences of the 'bad', but the gangster is even more enigmatic than the detective, being tinged with certain elements of 'liberation from society' (Mason, 2002: vii) as experienced through the cinematic and television gangsters from *The Godfather* (1971) to *The Sopranos* (1999–2007), who are usually associated with the American Italian mafia. Tourists also seek forms of liberation from the constraints of their daily lives by becoming an 'other' person, often taking risks they would not normally take or simply through living in a higher level of luxury (and fantasy) than at home. Tourism provides a safe place from which to vicariously experience the dangers and contradictions of such liberation.

Quentin Tarantino is known for presenting a series of self-reflexive pastiches in his movies, with Lloyd Hughes arguing that he has 'come closest to writer Walter Benjamin's stated desire to create a text entirely composed of quotations' (Hughes, 2006: vii) in movies that are considered part of the gangster genre such as *Reservoir Dogs* (1991). In that movie he mixed other genres with the gangster genre, including black parody, horror and the B-movie while utilising texts from the posse in *The Magnificent Seven*, using colours for names as in *The Taking of Pelham 123* and references to the gangster lifestyle of *Goodfellas* (Mason, 2002). This is not unlike Leone's reflexive referencing of the American westerns in his spaghetti westerns, of which I suspect Tarantino is a fan.

The proliferation of gangster/mafioso tours such as *The Sopranos Tours* offered by dedicated companies such as the New York based *On Location Tours*, which employs guides who acted in the series, along with other generalist tour companies, is evidence of the attraction these stories have outside the cinema. As noted previously when discussing road movies, the emotional representations, safe viewing distance and the filmic glamorisation of such lawbreakers often ties in with the tourism experience.

In an effort to explain the continuing popularity of the gangster genre, Lloyd Hughes (2006) refers to two elements: the vicarious thrill of seeing the gangster get away with it, combined with the death of the gangster, restoring order after our vicarious journey of the imagination. Again, we do this when we travel – while we trust that the eventual 'death' will be figurative, we generally return to our own place of order after experiencing something of an exotic 'Other'. When we combine the two – movies and tourism – it can be a powerful experience indeed.

Asian triads in Hong Kong cinema

While I have focused here on the archetypal American gangster, the genre certainly exists in many other countries, albeit at times more reminiscent of Tarantino's brand of gangster of 'hipster killers accessorised with the patina and patter of cool, queasy violence cut to a breezy retro soundtrack …' (Hughes, 2006: 248) rather than a national cinematic genre. Nevertheless, movies portraying the Hong Kong triads have become a strong Asian gangster genre, providing the movie viewer with powerful, exotic images of the region. Chu (2003) explains that the popularity (and presence) of various film genres in Hong Kong developed alongside the region's political, economic and social environment, more often reflecting the time in which it was filmed as opposed to the period in which it was set. She refers to a number of local film critics who argued that the increasing popularity of the police and crime genre and strong violence in martial arts movies in the 1970s was a response to a series of police corruption scandals combined with a loss of confidence in the British and Chinese governments. From the mid-1980s, these themes of police and crime were replaced by triad and gangster films, with the criminals being the 'heroes' as in the US Hollywood stories. Wang Shen describes the hero-triads-police genre (*yingxiong pian*) as:

> 1. The protagonist … is a triad gangster while his mortal enemy – the police – is relegated to the background (or practically ignored); the so-called 'hero' is a thief with a conscience. 2. Intricacies of the plot give way to emotions and feelings. 3. Women play minor roles. 4. Style is uniformly consistent. (Cited in Chu, 2003: 69, as quoted in Law, 1997: 60–73)

It has been claimed that the Hong Kong triad gangsters (many of whom had controlling interests in the studios) pressured some producers for cameos in such movies (Hughes, 2006). I have also been told 'off the record' that this has also occurred in relation to the Italian mafia and movies, but we are moving into very murky waters by making such unsubstantiated claims, no matter how interesting they may be. However, even the fact that such tales abound illustrates the appeal of these movies, which can also be reflected in our emotional responses to certain places or images when travelling.

In many ways, the Australian bushranger legends, stories, movies and TV series are a pre-industrial Australian version of these fictionalised and highly glamorised stories of the American gangster and the Hong Kong triads. This section on gangsters began with a quote from Mason, and I'd like to finish with another:

> The film gangster, therefore, represents a seminal figure in the history of twentieth-century culture, forming the focus for a range of tensions that have dominated the discourses of industrialised society. (Mason, 2002: vii)

Tourism Subtexts

This is a particularly truncated story about some of the 'baddies' on the screen and their effect on us as viewers, fans and travellers. However, while being aware that this publication could fall into the trap of repetition in terms of emotion and travel, it is fascinating to consider as wide a range of genres as possible in relation to these points. Certainly, others have written in more detail and far more engagingly about the detective genre and tourism, and I commend Stijn Reijnder's book on this topic, which has assisted in guiding me through some aspects of this chapter, as well as providing another, albeit contentious, way for us to consider the places of our imagination as introduced in Chapter 1.

As a way to consider the tourism subtexts and relationships in this chapter it is worth revisiting the iterative model I presented towards the end of the first chapter (Figure 9.1), where the viewer engages in some sort of emotional way with the movie or TV programme/series which subsequently influences their emotional perspective of places or environments as they visit and experience them, often providing an interpretive framework from which to experience or contemplate their journeys.

Returning to the landscape as a tourist attraction, we can argue that, as the historical figures themselves are long gone, the landscape itself takes on an iconic or even celebrity status, with fans desiring contact with these places in lieu of the people. I introduced the notion that the site takes on celebrity status in my 2005 book, *Film-Induced Tourism*, arguing that '[t]he entire notion of celebrity and its transference from the actor to the places in the film is one that appears to be closely related to film-induced tourism

174　Part 2: Travelling In, On and Through the Landscape: Voyeur or Flâneur?

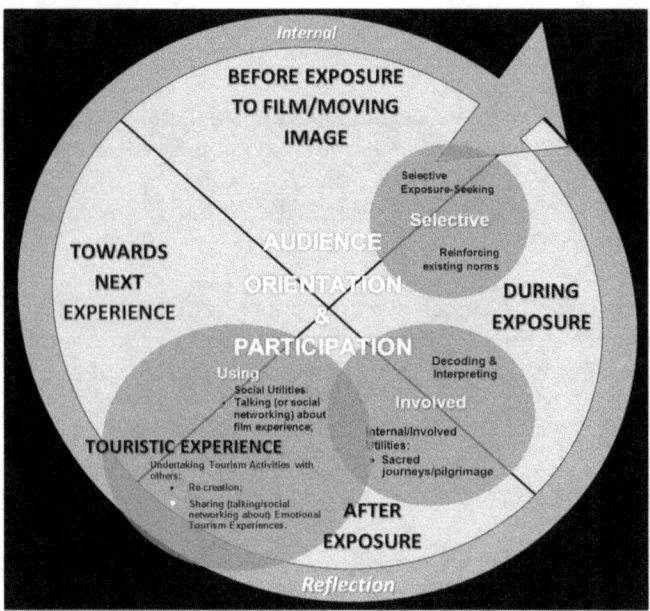

Figure 9.1 Modelling the relationship between audience and tourist activity

motivation' (Beeton, 2005a: 243). If we look at this in terms of Giles' (2002) PSI model discussed in Chapter 1, where fans seek out 'other encounters' that include imagined interactions, concluding with making an attempt to contact the celebrity, actually visiting the site of certain movie scenes can be a way of connecting with the celebrity status of the place or even landscape. While it may at first appear that I am drawing a rather long bow here, in fact I have listened many times to people boasting about having a special familiarity with certain places of filming. Sleeping in the same room as a star or eating at the restaurant where a gangster was shot provides a direct connection with a person, but visiting and experiencing places such as Monument Valley where the landscape overtakes the human celebrity status illustrates my point.

In terms of the 'baddies' stories introduced in this chapter, places are imbued with emotionally charged feelings and experiences, from mystery to violence, poverty to ostentation, impressing on the engaged viewer what is often a conflicting range of emotional responses, which can manifest when visiting these or similar places. In effect, tourists are trying to connect with real (and imagined) crime figures in a 'safe' manner via the film locations. Often in the shared stories of tourists, we hear 'it was just like being in a

Hercule Poirot plot', or 'it reminded me of *The Sopranos*', even when their actual experience has very little (if anything) to do with the story, film or TV programme. As discussed throughout this publication, these emotional representations often guide us and show us how to travel – literally, vicariously or figuratively.

Part 3
Imagining Places: Illusions and Dreams

Most of the tourism-based research into the relationship between film and tourism has tended to focus primarily on 'on-location' tourism – tourism to the places where a movie, TV series or range of films been filmed and/or set. However, as I have discussed previously (Beeton, 2005a), there is another aspect that has virtually been ignored, that of 'off-location' film tourism. Such tourism occurs at the film studio sets and sound stages, as well as at specially constructed tourist precincts or theme parks. They are often more accessible than the actual locations, being based in major cities such as the Hollywood studios and Boulevard in Los Angeles and Tokyo, or tourist destinations such as the theme parks in Orlando, Florida, Singapore, Hong Kong and the Australian Gold Coast. Even the external facades of the homes of the stars are available for public view.

This part of the book takes the notions of location and landscape discussed in Part 2 and wonders how places in the imagination can become places in 'reality' that can be visited and experienced and why we need such immersive experiences. Such ponderings bring us to consider the much-contested notion of 'authenticity'. While not engaging in an in-depth discussion, in the following chapter I bring the concepts of frontstage and backstage experiences into the world of the moving image based, studio-owned theme park. This goes some way towards illustrating the complexities and often very personal decision as to what may be 'authentic'.

As well as looking at the spaces and places created for fans and tourists along with other public sites, we consider the role of the moving image in art and events based around movies, such as film festivals. Of course, I am not an artist or art critic, so much of that discussion revolves around what I have experienced and how it affects me as a person, tourist and traveller.

10 Creating Place

> *The cinema does not just present images, it surrounds them with a world.*
> Deleuze, 1989: 69

While some commercial film studios provide the opportunity for tours on their premises, they are primarily working backlots and sets, and often are not open to the general public, especially when they are actually in use. Issues of confidentiality, pricing, security and copyright also mean that many 'live' (or 'hot') sets are not accessible, even when not being used. I experienced this with the (now closed for tourism) Fox Studios Backlot in Sydney when the *Mission Impossible II* (2000) soundstages were being built – half the Backlot was closed to visitors who had paid to experience a 'real' working Backlot, as promoted. Needless to say, many were disappointed. These tours are no longer available, closed primarily due to the lack of financial viability of the enterprise (Beeton, 2005a). In fact, the Fox Backlot tourist enterprise lost significant amounts of money for their partners, Lend Lease, as well as for Fox Studios themselves.

Furthermore, the process of film making is slow and does not provide the excitement and interest that visitors often want (or expect). Consequently, most studios do not offer such tours; rather, many have developed separate theme parks that re-present the film-making process in a more palatable, entertaining and emotionally appealing manner. Many have dispensed with the 'how we make films' information and demonstrations completely, offering immersive entertainment based on their movies, videos and TV series.

These studio-owned theme parks also provide a physical place for the fantasies they present on screen to exist in the 'real world' – or, at least, the world that human beings physically inhabit. Throughout this book, the primary focus has been on tourism and fictional movies and TV series, and how they engage our imagination and influence not only our travel experiences but also how we actually perceive and respond to our travel (and tourism) experiences. In order to explore this, I have unashamedly taken a personal, autoethnographic perspective by looking at some of the genres that have influenced me, such as the US western movies and TV series. However, there are many other genres and moving image related activities that also emotionally engage me, including science fiction, fantasy and animation as well as art installations and events.

Animation and Fantasy

Beyond the daily serve of rather simplistic (and repetitive) children's TV cartoons, when I first experienced the Disney cartoon, *Bambi* (1942), where he was calling for his dead mother, I became deeply engaged and connected to this format of popular culture, engaging in a highly emotionally manner with many of its characters. While more attuned to the Western culturally based sensibilities of Disney, some of the Japanese manga and anime also became part of my childhood, albeit in a highly mediated manner. In my younger years I found those about animals far more appealing, with *Kimba the White Lion* (1965–1967) and his big eyes being far more relatable than *Astro Boy* (1963–1966) with HIS big eyes! Today, with the rise of Asian popular culture, this interest has been rekindled and widened to include many of the beautiful and rather strange (to my Western eyes) anime stories. My tastes also incorporate Tim Burton and his fantastical worlds, including *The Nightmare Before Christmas* (1993), *Alice in Wonderland* (2010) and *Frankenweenie* (1982, 2012); while others including the *Harry Potter* movies as well as *Shrek* (2001) and the stop-motion animation of *Harvey Krumpet* (2003) never stop fascinating me. I am certainly not alone in this attachment, with adults as well as children engaging with many animated stories. One of my colleagues in the UK, Dr Brian Wheeller, is known for his postgraduate tourism lectures featuring *A Grand Day Out with Wallace and Gromit* (1989) and regularly refers to popular culture in his work (see Wheeller, 2004). Other colleagues in Japan are examining the anime and pop-cultural influences on travel and tourism in Japan, known as 'contents tourism' (Beeton *et al.*, 2013).

So, what has this to do with tourism, and how can fictional places such as those created in animated tales and fantasy stories become tourist attractions? Of course, some are set in 'real' places that are graphically presented, particularly much of the Japanese anime, but many fantasies are simply 'made up'. If anyone reading this has visited any of the Disney or Universal theme parks, you have the answer – these film studio based (owned) theme parks focus on re-creating the emotions and places of their fictional films. One of the most powerful examples of this is *The Wizarding World of Harry Potter* at Universal Studios' theme park in Orlando, Florida and Japan, where the entire place has been re-created from J.K. Rowling's mind and the visual representations in the movies. This is discussed in more detail later in this chapter, along with some other personal favourites.

If we trace the development of film studio owned theme parks and related sites, we can get some idea as to how this construction of fantastical places came about, and the reasons for its success. This provides a rather interesting framework in which to examine the relationship between fantasy and animation and tourism development.

Development of the (Studio) Theme Park

The term 'theme park' has become widely used to cover a broad spectrum of themed places, spaces and scapes, including amusement parks, museums, shopping centres, casinos and even cities, which tends to dilute the actual meaning – as Lukas (2008) argues, many of these places are simply themed spaces, not theme parks. Often the term has been used pejoratively to describe spaces that have been planned and constructed as opposed to organically grown, presuming some sort of superiority over the theme park. Yet, the theme park I am referring to is a place of emotion, activity and immersion and, while planned, it does not assume any other form of legitimacy other than simply being itself, unlike some of the 'theme park' places to which critics refer.

In this discussion, I use the theme park terminology quite specifically to refer to the immersive themed amusement parks, but I add a further subset, that of the film studio theme park, as my focus, which has many if not all of the early theme park elements. This is not surprising when we consider that the model of the modern-day theme park, Disneyland, had its genesis in the Disney studios, with people wishing to participate in the magic of movies.

From amusement parks and movie ranches to movie/TV theme parks

As the focus of this book is on the moving image, the theme parks I am looking at here are those developed by the film studios, of which Disneyland is acknowledged as the first. The concept certainly had its genesis in the amusement parks of Coney Island in the United States and Brighton Pier in the UK, as well as elements of the spectacle of the World's Fairs and open-air museums, yet its link to movies and TV took the concept into another realm altogether, where 'the Disney parks have become the physical embodiment of all that our company's mythologies represent to kids of all ages' (Wright, 2008: 6).

Movie ranches

As discussed in Chapter 7, movie ranches were sites near to the Los Angeles movie studios that could be used for location filming, particularly of western movies and TV programmes. However, fans also wanted to visit these ranches, not only to experience some of the filming magic, but simply to be in the places where their favourite actor, horse or story was realised. By the 1950s, many of the ranches had become major tourist attractions, welcoming tens of thousands of visitors each weekend, all needing to be entertained and transported back to the Wild West and other frontier places. Many of the elements of the movie ranches, including re-enactments of scenes from movies such as shoot-outs and punishments, street facades and costumed staff were incorporated into the theme park model, with professional actors being employed to perform, particularly as film star lookalikes. Disney's Frontierland and Main Street are reminiscent of such places, with their facades, corrals, cowboys and crooks.

I have discussed the famous Corriganville Ranch earlier in this book, but it is worth reproducing a description of the development of Corriganville from a movie location ranch to a themed park, which operated from 1949 until 1966:

> The park featured stunt men shows, visits to the movie lots, a working Western town, Indian craft displays, pony rides, stagecoach rides, and boating on the lake. During its heyday, the park attracted as many as 10–20,000 on weekends and was rated among the top ten amusement parks in the U.S. (Anderson, 1989)

While the first movie ranch to open to the public in the early 1940s is arguably the Jack Ingram – Motion Picture Ranch, promoted at the time as 'The only movie town in the world open to the general public' (Schnielder, 2007: 27), Corriganville presented a wide range of attractions and activities that brought these movie ranches closer to the future Disney theme park concept. Disney also purchased a movie ranch, the Walt Disney Golden Oak Ranch, in 1959 for segments of *The Mickey Mouse Club* which, as noted below, was closely linked to the development of the Disneyland theme park.

Disneyland

In the 1930s and 1940s, Disney studios were inundated with requests from people wishing to know more about the movie-making process, wanting to see how it was done; yet Disney believed that visitors would soon become bored watching an animator at work, so when the studios moved to Burbank, he proposed a 'magic little park' be set aside for visitors (Marling, 1994). This park included a main village, farm, western street and a train (one of Walt Disney's great passions), with an emphasis on family entertainment. Disney is quoted in the official publications on Disneyland, and in a display at the theme park, that, while sitting on a park bench watching his children play (Figure 10.1), he decided there should be:

> Some kind of amusement enterprise, where the parents and the children could have fun together. So that's how Disneyland started. (Extract from plaque at Disneyland, Anaheim, 2012)

In spite of the park at Burbank being rejected by the local council due to their somewhat misguided concerns of having a Coney Island style park with a 'carny' atmosphere in a suburban area, Disney's family-focused dream did not die, and he subsequently purchased land some 20 miles away at Anaheim, where Disneyland is today. While there are numerous histories and stories about Disneyland, from academic critiques to glossy coffee table books and blogs, my interest here is not in those stories but in the theme park's symbiotic relationship with film and television.

In order to fund the development of Disneyland, Walt Disney formed a partnership with the ABC Television Corporation to create and televise a variety show for children, *The Mickey Mouse Club* (1955–1959), with various reprisals in the 1970s, 1980s and 1990s. The 1950s programme aired from Monday to Friday, raising funds for the construction of the park as well as promoting ABC TV. The human stars of the TV show, the Mouseteers, first wore the now eponymous Mickey Mouse ears (IMDb). Furthermore, the opening of Disneyland, *Dateline Disneyland*, was telecast live in July 1955, complete with a range of technical glitches and misadventures we still see today on live broadcasts (Marling, 1994). In effect, the park was 'the first place ever conceived simultaneously with a TV series' (Sorkin, 1992: 206).

Figure 10.1 The park bench where Disney dreamed Disneyland

Disney now has film-related theme parks in many parts of the world, including Florida, Paris, Tokyo and Hong Kong, becoming the model for similar theme parks globally. Numerous other film studios have developed theme parks connected to, but separate from their film-making work, in particular Universal Studios and Warner Brothers with their Movie World in Australia. In particular, the Universal Studios theme parks are direct competitors to Disney (often competing in the same city such as Orlando and Los Angeles), yet have slightly different emphases, with Universal being more directly linked to its movies via high technology applications, while Disney focuses more on its heritage, characterisation and animatronics. Furthermore, through its numerous holdings such as the ABC TV network, Pixar Animation Studios, Touchstone Pictures, Miramax Films and Hollywood Pictures, the Disney Corporation has been able to develop its theme park experiences through leveraging its cultural power to 'tell stories in more ways than other theme parks can' (Lukas, 2008: 222). Universal also has numerous subsidiaries and partnerships, with one formed with Warner Brothers to develop *The Wizarding World of Harry Potter* theme park in Orlando and, more recently, Japan.

As well as the Disney, Universal and Warner Brothers theme parks, Asian film and tourism industries have developed their own theme parks, often based on the Disney model. Other movie theme parks include Movie Park Germany which has the tagline 'Wow, I'm in the Movies!' and Universal City Dubailand, with more being continually developed. While there continue to be those who are critical of the theme park, they continue to capture and engage the popular imagination across cultures and generations.

Creating the immersive experience: Technological development

In a studio-based theme park as opposed to an amusement-focused theme park like the Texan-owned Six Flags Parks, themed rides are more than rollercoasters, being highly immersive and emotional experiences, particularly when connected to a film or TV series. Emanating from his obsession with railroads, Walt Disney was fascinated with miniaturisation and models, in the 1950s planning a walk-through museum of miniature moving scenes (automata) based on his films as well as history, known as *Disneylandia* (Marling, 1994). While not coming to realisation due to the costs and operational challenges of using such small figures, the concept was applied in the development of the Disneyland animatronics and robotics, which remain an integral part of the parks.

Most of the technology applied to the theme park rides comes primarily from the motion picture industry itself, where compressing time and space into a few minutes yet telling a cogent story is elemental to filmmaking. One of the first examples of this was the *Back to the Future* ride at Universal Studios theme park in California, where in 1990 Doug Turnbull's technology combined 35 mm film with a flight simulator to create a movie-based theme ride (Hannigan,1998). This was also one of my own early experiences of an immersive ride when I visited the Universal theme park 10 years later in 2000, where it was still one of the most popular rides. It is this type of simulated experience, including 'dark rides', that differentiates the movie-based theme park from its amusement park competitors and studio backlot tours.

Not to be confused with the 'dark tourism' that is associated with travelling to places of death and tragedy, the term 'dark rides' refers to rides that use darkness and isolation to create emotional and psychological responses in participants. The concept has been traced back to the 1901 Pan American Exposition, where architect Frederick Thompson, inspired by Jules Verne's 1877 play, *A Trip to the Moon*, created a ride of the same name (Burrowes, 1998). He utilised the technology of the day, placing panorama and performance alongside the techniques of isolation and darkness in order to create a sense of travel and experience in the participants. According to Burrowes (1998), up to 30 passengers per 20-minute 'trip' paid 50 cents to board a cigar-shaped ship that 'flew' them to the moon, where they then disembarked and walked on the moon and through a series of caves to be entertained by a performance of moon creatures.

> The craft was a brilliantly lighted green and white cigar-shaped ship, 'the size of a small lake steamer' according to one account, with a large cabin in the middle and huge red canvas wings.
>
> At the sound of a gong and chains – the nautical motif that would partly define the space age – Luna started to gradually rock and then seemed to lift into the sky with its wings slowly flapping. The passengers, sitting on steamer chairs, saw first clouds floating by, then a model of Buffalo, complete with the exposition itself and hundreds of blinking lights. They could even see Niagara Falls. As they looked through the spaceship's railing, the city seemed to fall away, while the whole planet itself came into view. Then even Earth itself shrank into a dot. As Luna sailed on to the Moon, the voyagers saw a twinkling sky. Next, they sailed into a fierce electrical storm with lightning, thunder, and whistling wind, followed by a flight through a bluish atmosphere. Finally the passengers spotted the Moon, with the face of the Man in the Moon clearly visible. Next, Luna slowed, banked to the right, and soon struck something solid. It was the lunar surface.
>
> After the captain announced that their destination had been reached, the passengers walked off the spaceship and into an amazing scene. They

were greeted in a crater by 'Selenites,' sixty midgets with spiked backs, who escorted them past stalactites and 'crystallized mineral wonders' and then down an illuminated avenue to the City of the Moon. As they walked through the city, they were offered samples of green cheese by some Selenites and saw strange bazaars, souvenir shops, and mooncraft demonstrations. The journey ended in the castle of the Man in the Moon.

There, in a large throne room decorated with glass columns and bronze griffins, the king sat on a mother-of-pearl throne, giant bodyguards at his sides. He treated the earthlings to a view of his electric fountain, which showed all of the colors of the spectrum through splashing water, and to a dance performed by the maids of the Man in the Moon. Then the curtain fell and the show was over. (Burrowes, 1998: 34–35)

So, the dark ride is not necessarily 'dark', but instead uses interior design and enclosure to create a space that transports one to an 'Other' world and applies sensory effects to tell a story which in turn deepens the personal, emotional experience. The dark ride can encompass rides that operate on tracks (*The Revenge of the Mummy, Space Mountain*), float through water (*Pirates of the Caribbean, It's a Small World*), walk-through rides (*The Haunted House*) and simulation rides (*Star Wars, Back to the Future*). Many of the rides include additional sensory technologies that further deepen the experience, such as smells, sprays of water, puffs of air, heat and sound. Even for those rides not directly related to a movie or TV series, they all apply the cinematic modes of clever pacing, shifting scenes and storytelling.

In a most interesting (and popular) illustration of the intimate relationship between theme park rides and movies, Disney developed a series of movies to promote their rides and then used the movie imaging (such as the actors and more complex narrative) to further enhance the ride. This inversion is most evident with the *Haunted Mansion* and *Pirates of the Caribbean* as well as the *Country Bears* rides (Beeton, 2005a). I found it extremely comforting to find a robotic image of Captain Jack Sparrow in various situations as we moved through the ride, complete with Johnny Depp's particular good looks, cheeky characterisation and voice added to my experience, as not only could I follow a story during the ride, but I could also impose my own private narrative onto the experience.

As Strain (2003: 153) observes, '[t]he industry has come full circle, returning to the paradigm of George C. Hale's tours by combining film technologies with simulated vehicle motion.'

In other examples of movie narratives driving theme park experiences, Universal Orlando's *E.T. Adventure* takes visitors through the entire narrative of E.T.'s story, while the level of immersion experienced in the dark rides of

The Wizarding World of Harry Potter (which opened in June 2010 at Universal, Orlando and 2015 in Japan) reaches new heights. The key experience at *The Wizarding World of Harry Potter*, 'The Forbidden Ride', comprises not only the wild simulation ride from the 'top' of Hogwarts, but also the journey to get to it, merging two forms of dark ride to create the most immersive experience I have had. Here, the engineers have combined a dark walking ride with a rail-based dark ride with the seats being held above the track by a robotic arm, allowing them to pivot and tip most convincingly – certainly my arms were stiff and sore from 'holding on'!

Visitors start their immersion almost immediately, where the queuing process is incorporated into the experience (Figure 10.2). We enter Hogwarts and wander through the halls, where the portraits move and talk, and holograms of characters address us. In replicas of the rooms of Hogwarts Castle, such as the Headmaster's office, Prof Dumbledore welcomes us 'Muggles' and then in the Defence Against the Dark Arts classroom holograms of Harry, Ron and Hermione appear from under the Invisibility Cloak. Ron attempts a magic trick that goes wrong (of course), resulting in snow falling on us. The Sorting Hat and some of the talking portraits are then artfully used to

Figure 10.2 Creating place: Hogwarts Experience, Universal Studios. Clockwise from top left: Dumbledore's welcome (his hologram can be seen on the balcony); the paintings; ancient murals and paintings; The Sorting Hat; Harry, Ron and Hermione appear as holograms

provide us with safety reminders for the upcoming ride. All of these characters are holograms, using the original actors, not costumed theme park look-alikes, adding to the sense of authenticity and magic.

By the time we reach the 'ride', we are well and truly immersed in the world of Harry Potter, with high expectations of what the next experience may be. The sensory aspect increases exponentially with another move into the darkness on a 'magic bench' (which I thought was meant to be a broomstick), which moves and tips dramatically. We find ourselves following Potter on a wild ride down through windows and cliffs, being hit by the Whomping Willow into the Quidditch pitch, being squirted by spiders and breathed on by dragons, and pursued by many of Harry's enemies, including the Dementors and Voldemort himself. The ride uses all of the technology at its disposal, including animatronic dragons, projection screens, real sets, water sprays, breezes and puffs of cold air and, of course, sounds.

The entire experience is incredibly detailed and rich, and even after a return visit, I know I have missed much of the action and hanker to go back again. More importantly, during the experience, one can become convinced that this world and all of its magic and danger actually exists. In a matter of minutes we experienced not only the narrative of the ride, but also our own interpretations and emotions form our movie-watching (and book-reading) experiences. There was only one experience that excited me more. . . .

In another engaging use of technology, Universal has created a space for animated characters to directly interact with the audience, beyond simply using costumed characters. As I have already confessed, I am passionate about animation and have a very strong attachment to many of the characters I see on the screen, from Bambi and Mickey Mouse through to Wall-E, Ponyo and Donkey (from *Shrek*). So, it was hard to control my excitement when a costumed Donkey at Universal Orlando recognised me from the previous day, shouting out, 'There's my friend from yesterday!'. I did feel a little obsessive, and not such an invisible observer as I had thought, but I was still quietly thrilled. However, this hardly compared with my experience when I visited Universal Studios theme park in Singapore, where I witnessed the ultimate in bringing a cartoon character to life. Here, we could personally interact with the animated character itself, not a human in a costume! Donkey entertained us from the stage of a nightclub where he directly conversed with the audience, in real time.

I was so taken by this experience that I had no desire to know how it was done, as I had been allowed to believe that Donkey was real. However, when trying to describe the experience to others, I found I needed to understand a little more of the technology behind it. It is known as 'digital puppetry' and was developed in 1988 by the Henson Studios for use in *Sesame Street* (1969–), where the manually operated puppets interacted in real time with the digital puppet, Waldo C Graphic (Sturman, 1999). Basically, the puppeteer uses a computer or model to manipulate the image of the character as projected in real time onto a screen, which in the case of Donkey was a fine gauze screen with a nightclub set in the background, giving Donkey the appearance that he was in the club.

While this has also been used in the Disney theme parks in less dramatic ways, I did not consciously come across this technology until I visited Universal Studios in Singapore during the soft opening of the Sentosa Island resorts. Like the Harry Potter experience described previously, I long to experience this again, and was extremely disappointed when it was not available at Universal Studios in Orlando as recently as 2012, which was why I ended up hanging around taking photos of the 'costumed' Donkey who recognised me. So, even though I now understand a little more about the technology, I still wish to return in order to be 'tricked' again, bringing into stark relief the complications surrounding notions of 'authenticity' and experience discussed in this chapter.

When reflecting on these experiences, I continually become side-tracked by the sense of excitement and joy they brought me, along with a longing to experience them again. In these cases I am not merely an observer, and so immersed that it is even difficult for me to 'observe myself'. On reflection, I believe that in some way I want these animated worlds to be part of, or even all of, my own reality. This potentially correlates with my sense of being an 'outsider', or possibly some other disaffection towards my life. As I have responded this way for all of my conscious life, I suspect it is more about the former rather than the latter. However, I don't want to escape this world, I just want to the other one to be part of it. This, of course, is extremely personal and very difficult to express, but is an outcome of taking an autoethnographic approach to my research, which by its very nature is personal and reflexive. I also feel that there are others who are similarly affected and motivated to then live out their longing via fan events such as the various conventions, for example Comic-Con, re-enactments and travel to places of their imagination. Such considerations bring into questions notions of 'authenticity' and 'reality', which is considered in the next section.

I am reminded of Deleuze's (1989) reference to Fellini's comments that the child in us exists concurrently with the adolescent, old person and adult, where our experiences can be had and interpreted by all four personal entities. Certainly, my emotive child was evident in my experiences described above, but also from an adult's perspective and reflexivity.

So, rather than simply showing customers the mechanics and tricks of movie making, the studio-based theme park experience uses the cinematic effects and technology they have developed to tell the stories of the movies and television programmes. Much of this technology can be presented in far smaller spaces than some of the large sound stages used for filming and production.

> For Disney, Universal and other theme park operators, the glittering prize is the ability to 'downscale' theme park experiences, recreating in a $5–$20 million venue the essence of what they now produce in a $200 million complex. (Hannigan, 1998: 60)

As I noted in a previous publication, film studio theme parks have the ability to 'celebrate populist films that are set anywhere and can be viewed anywhere in the world, hence reducing the park's geographical appropriateness or its cultural relationships to the theme' (Beeton, 2005a: 184–185). They can also create 'real' places where there were none, as with animation and fantasy. This discussion brings us to thoughts on 'authenticity' and what it means in terms of tourism and the creative arts, in particular the moving image.

Authenticity?

Questions relating to the 'authenticity' of tourism experiences and products abound in the tourism literature, with travellers, tourists and researchers alike continually searching for their 'authentic experience'. The theme park has been heavily criticised for sanitising reality, with one of Disney's biographers, Richard Schickel coining the phrase 'Disneyfication', referring to:

> that shameless process by which everything the Studio later touched, not matter how unique ... was reduced to the limited terms Disney and his people could understand. Magic, mystery, individuality ... were consistently destroyed. (Schickel, 1986: 225)

Bryman (1999) developed this concept further, paralleling Rtizer's 'MacDonaldisation' by introducing the term 'Disneytization' into the modern lexicon to describe:

> [t]he process by which the principles of the Disney theme parks are coming to dominate more and more sectors of American society as well as the rest of the world. (Bryman, 1999: 26)

However, while he used this to infer a high level of structure in theming, differentiation of consumption, merchandising and emotional labour, and his term has been used to describe inauthentic places and experiences, movies and TV series are rarely 'authentic' or 'real', always having a created, imaginative structure. Films have their own particular forms of authenticity, in that they are constructed to be shown on a projected (usually flat) surface, using a range of 'tricks' to create an illusion of realty, which the audience buys into – they know that what they are seeing is not 'real'. If we think back to black-and-white film and TV, we even had to imagine the colours, yet I can still tell you categorically what they are on a black-and-white film. In fact, 'authenticity' is completely in the eye of the beholder. My earlier discussion regarding my very personal Harry Potter and Donkey experiences underlines this – for me, they are authentic experiences; however, I am sure there are others who would vehemently disagree.

As Sklan noted in 1964, the entire Disney process is about imagination and illusion, which in turn forms its own type of authenticity:

> In the theatre, the vital ingredient is not realism, but a blending of the real with the imaginary. The entertainer invites the audience to meet him half way. That is what has been successfully achieved at Disneyland. (Sklan, 1964: 12)

One way that we can place these anomalies within the authenticity literature can be to think about it in terms of Dean MacCannell's frontstage–backstage dichotomy, along with accepting that 'authenticity' is found through our imaginative processes. MacCannell (1973) claims that, by being allowed 'backstage' where outsiders can view the inner workings of an institution, tourists gain an 'authentic' experience. I have argued elsewhere that this is highly relevant to film-induced tourism, as 'front' and 'back' stage are theatrical and cinematic terms.

This form of tourist-based authenticity occurs after we have viewed the movie/TV programme and move out to experience it as the post-exposure phase in para-social interaction. There are various levels or stages of a backstage experience, and rarely does one actually get to 'deep backstage' – the truly 'authentic' experience (Beeton, 2005a). Cohen (1988) concurs that authenticity is negotiable and often different for each person (or tourist). It is their own perception of authenticity that is the key, so often what is authentic for a film tourist may simply be about being in the place where a star or character has been. In relation to the theme park:

> Issues of authenticity and reality become blurred and at times inverted in the theme park, and even more so in the film studio theme park that is a representation of what was an illusion in the first instance. (Beeton, 2005a: 189)

192 Part 3: Imagining Places: Illusions and Dreams

In an effort to disentangle what can become a rather circuitous discourse and develop a descriptive film studio theme park model, I have spent a great deal of time studying how models of authenticity such as those presented by Dean MacCannell and others have evolved, adapting them to the studio-based theme parks that I have been researching. MacCannell's (1973) model of authenticity comprised six 'stages', from a frontstage (public, constructed) experience through to backstage (private, authentic) experiences. Acknowledging the desire of tourists to experience the backstage, Pearce (1982) added elements of personal motivation and needs, creating a nine-fold classification. However, Pearce recognised that there remain inaccessible areas beyond these backstage experiences, such as rubbish collection areas and engine rooms. This is summarised in Table 10.1, where each level presents a different type of encounter.

When we consider audiences' reactions to film and television, these theories can assist us in understanding not only the range of individuals' experiences, but also how to respond to their wants and needs at the film studio theme park. In order to conceptualise the complex frontstage–backstage relationship between film, fantasy and tourism, some years ago I developed a film studio theme park model as presented in Figure 10.3, which has been tested against subsequent theme parks and remains relevant today, both as a physical and experiential representation.

The various regions outlined in the model include a frontstage that incorporates general public areas such as walkways, restaurants, amenities, rides and theatres, and a backstage which encompasses the actual film sets and sound stages of the studio, which not all of the studio-based theme parks

Table 10.1 Pearce's model of authenticity

Level	Type and place of encounter
1	Backstage people in a backstage region
2	Frontstage people in a frontstage region
3	Frontstage people in a backstage region
4	Backstage people in a frontstage region
5	Encounters with backstage people (region not important)
6	Encounters with frontstage people (region not important)
7	Backstage region (people not important)
8	Frontstage region (people not important)
9	Frontstage or backstage irrelevant

Source: Pearce (1982).

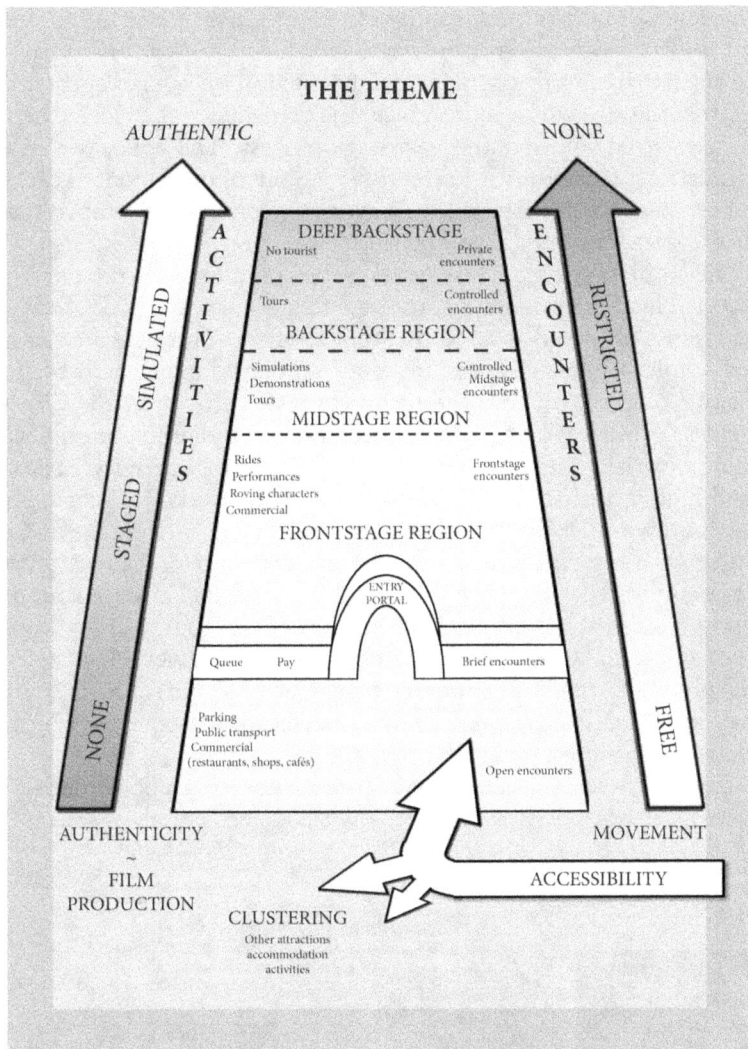

Figure 10.3 Studio theme park model
Source: Beeton (2005a: 190).

possess, but if not, they often have some working sound stages nearby. Two additional regions are shown which are physically situated before the frontstage in many studio theme parks, namely the general open space before entering the park and the entry portal itself. These are two distinct regions – one

194 Part 3: Imagining Places: Illusions and Dreams

engendering feelings of anticipation, the other a sense of arrival and welcome as one passes through the entry portal.

On the left-hand side of the model, the subjective level of authenticity is shown, moving towards a more 'authentic' experience the closer the visitor gets to the actual film-making backstage process. The opposite side of the model illustrates the diminishing level of freedom of movement as each experience becomes more controlled – allowing visitors to freely move around a working ('hot') film set is rarely feasible.

In the frontstage area, staff include the traditional theme park service employees, plus professional actors providing a meet and greet function as well as a sense of arrival at an 'Other' place where our movie dreams can be realised, while in the backstage area staff employed in the film production process can be present, from the technical staff through to the film actors themselves. While many film studio theme parks claim to present a 'real' backstage experience, it is often provided as a frontstage activity, easily accessible and highly mediated. A good example of this is the Universal Studios' Backlot tour, which includes a simulated flash flood, earthquake and a brief encounter with the animatronic shark from *Jaws*, along with a stunt show. In fact, many of the 'sets' are from past movies, including a sound stage purposely created for the *King Kong* section of the tour. Rarely do participants see any actual filming, supporting Walt Disney's view that they would find the process boring. Occasionally, I have seen filming in the theme parks, but they are usually short productions such as advertisements (Figure 10.4) and even they require a great deal of standing around.

So, such created events tend to reduce visitors' disappointment when a Backlot tour is not possible due to the various needs of actual filming, but

Figure 10.4 Filming advertisements in theme parks (Universal, Orlando)

tend to further blur notions of authenticity. Consequently, I needed to add a third region before the frontstage and backstage regions, which I refer to as a midstage, or simulated backstage. Finally, there remains an inaccessible backstage off-limits to the public, such as the labyrinth of service tunnels at Disneyland (Sorkin, 1992). In a film setting this equates with the 'real' working places of the film's creative and production staff as well as the invisible service aspects for visitors, referred to as deep backstage.

Even though there are studio tours at working studios such as Paramount Studios in Los Angeles, there seems to be less and less 'backstage' activities provided such as filming 'tricks' of the trade at the new generation of film studio based theme parks, based in places away from the studio (such as Universal Singapore, Disney Hong Kong, and so on).

Film, illusion and tourism

In effect, all of this discussion is closely linked to fandom, tourism and the tourist experience, where the visitors are seeking out opportunities to 'live the dream', often in place of their current lives. Many of our movies and TV series present illusions that create the place where such dreams are realised. The movie sets and studios created this illusion and film tourism sites perpetuate that illusion by providing a physical space where we can further experience the illusion of film, particularly in relation to fantasy and animation.

While not referring to the theme park, Deleuze goes some way to explaining why this format remains popular, and is more than simply a basic theme park, by explaining that 'even vaster circuits will be able to develop, corresponding to deeper and deeper layers of reality and higher and higher levels of memory or thought' (Deleuze, 1989: 68–69). Consequently, these theme parks perpetuate the 'authentic' illusion we experience on the screen (big and small) and create places for tourism.

A Framework for Studio Theme Park Development

As proposed and outlined earlier in this chapter, we can make historical, narrative and thematic connections between the movie ranches, studios, amusement parlours and studio-based theme parks. I have illustrated this in Figure 10.5, where all of these elements continue to influence one another.

Certainly, developing a theme park is one way to create a tourist destination where there may not have been one. However, there are other ways in which a destination or experience has been developed: some intentionally to

196   Part 3: Imagining Places: Illusions and Dreams

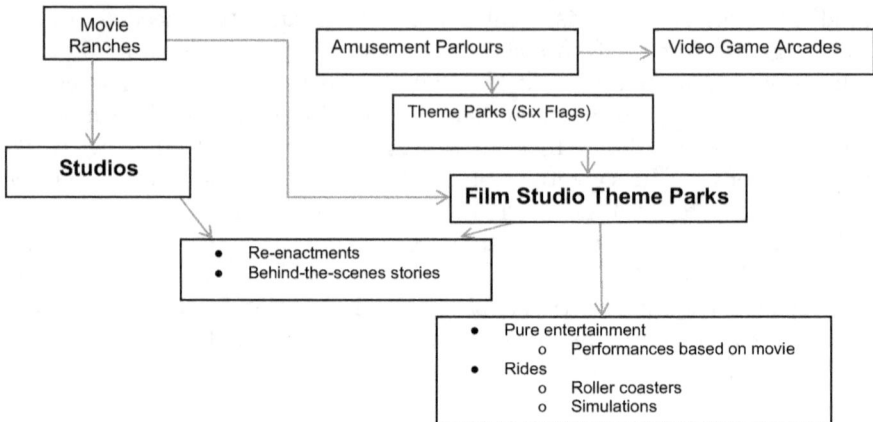

Figure 10.5 Studio theme park development

encourage tourists, such as 'walks of fame'; while others may attract film fans through the experience of a film festival or a repository of information such as in a museum or gallery. All of these will attract local visitors as well as tourists and add to the ambience and attractiveness of a particular destination, and are discussed in the following chapter.

11 Spaces and Places: Travelling for/to the Moving Image

In the previous chapter I considered the ways in which those theme parks owned and operated by the movie studios apply their technical and creative expertise to provide a place in the world for fantasy and illusion. There, visitors are able to engage in high levels of para-social interaction with fantastical creatures and imagined experiences in places converted from the imagination into reality. This chapter builds on this notion by looking further at a range of constructed experiences at specialised film tourism precincts, museums and art installations as well as festivals and events.

Follow That Star: Film Tourism Precincts

Closely associated to the theme parks and the moving image are the various film tourism precincts that have been established around the world, where visitors can engage with their para-social interest in the movie stars without necessarily meeting them, which for could ruin their illusion of 'knowing' them. This includes Walks of Fame, tours of the homes of stars and Movie Maps that (purportedly) show where the stars shop, eat and drink, as well as places they have stayed (and beds they may have slept in), along with filming locations.

All of these initiatives are closely tied to the tourism industry, and are often funded by local governments in order to increase tourism to their region. Some examples of this are the Hollywood Walk of Fame in the United States, the Avenue of Stars in Hong Kong (Figure 11.1), the Madrid Walk of Fame in Spain and the Bucharest Walk of Fame in Romania. These 'walks' are unequivocal about their links to tourism and local development, with statements on their respective websites confirming this, such as Hong Kong's

198 Part 3: Imagining Places: Illusions and Dreams

Figure 11.1 Tourists at Hong Kong's Avenue of Stars

aim '[t]o pay tribute to outstanding professionals of Hong Kong's film industry, to promote the tourism industry, and to consolidate Hong Kong's position as Asia's World City' (http://www.avenueofstars.com.hk/eng/home.asp), while Madrid's walk of fame was developed to supplement the city's *Calle del cine* (street of cinema) for the 25th anniversary of the Spanish Academic of Film (Anon, 2011).

Demonstrating an even more pragmatic, commercial approach to the film and tourism connections, the development of the Bucharest Walk of Fame was supported by a shopping centre, the tourism association and a local cinema. Even Anaheim in Los Angeles has a Walk of Fame, which of course includes local luminaries such as Walt Disney, along with other local sports people, musicians and community members as well as some movie stars.

The inspiration for these enterprises is the Hollywood Avenue of Stars, which has its own saga of its relationship with film stars, tourism, trash and development. First conceived in the 1950s by the Chamber of Commerce as a way to encourage visitors to the area, the first stars were set into the pavement on Hollywood Boulevard in 1960. However, during the 1960s and 1970s, many residents were moving out to the suburbs, resulting in a run-down area with all the concomitant issues of homelessness, illicit drug use and petty crime, which was in direct contrast to the glamour tourists associated with Hollywood and fully expected to experience. Overdue efforts in the 1980s to revive the Boulevard failed to address issues of public safety, and by the time I visited in the mid-1990s, the strip hosted many cheap t-shirt shops, tattoo parlours and homeless people, with little for me to do there apart from looking at and photographing the stars of the stars in the pavement, stare at the faux Chinese façade of Groman's Theatre and wander aimlessly with other tourists. Being a classic *flâneuse*, what I desired was to spend time soaking up the 'magic' of Hollywood in a nice cafe or bar, watching the passers-by, as well as experiencing the depth of the moving picture heritage on this famous boulevard. I wanted to feel some magic, but in reality

I was left slightly depressed and wondering how this could have happened to such an iconic place that was so 'alive' in my imagination.

A concerted effort from the Hollywood Chamber of Commerce, tourism operators and community groups in the late 1990s started to see a shift in the ambience of the area. The Hollywood Trust developed a self-guided walking tour with information on the history of the buildings (which also displayed interpretive plaques), identifying where specific stars' pavement stars are, providing the millions of visitors with reasons to stay longer (Beeton, 2005a). Buildings were being restored and a major retail area and permanent home of the Academy Awards developed at the intersection of Hollywood and Highland, where visitors would expect to see such things. In fact, I was surprised to learn that there was no 'home' of the Awards, but that the ceremony was held in various studio-based facilities, such as at Paramount Studios. This struck me as a major missed tourism opportunity as well as not having a place to celebrate and commemorate these significant awards. So, while we know there is enormous interest in the movies globally and Hollywood in particular, the Hollywood Walk of Fame has had to address many social as well as economic problems over its years of generation, degeneration and regeneration.

From the pavement stars of Hollywood Boulevard, one can take a guided tour of the homes of the stars, which in effect is a tour that passes the past homes of the stars (many have either passed away, over or on), and the locked gates of those still living in the area. Many of the home owners have had injunctions placed on their streets, banning the tour buses from pausing outside their homes. However, this does not seem to diminish people's fascination with places touched by stars as the tours continue unabated. On a recent movie tour I took in New Orleans, other participants insisted on seeing Brad Pitt and Angelina Jolie's house in the French Quarter. Needless to say the street view was of a locked doorway in the high wall. In many ways, the style of the French Quarter homes is perfect for those desiring privacy, with large internal courtyards away from prying eyes. Our guide did say that you know when they are 'in residence' due to the number of helicopters hovering over the area, trying to glimpse them.

Celebrity worship

What makes celebrity sites such as the Walks of Fame and tours of 'homes' so interesting to me is the way that they reflect (and support) our obsession with fame and celebrity. While it seems that Andy Warhol's oft-cited statement that 'in the future, everyone will be world-famous for 15 minutes' (Warhol, 1968) has become frighteningly true, with some of today's 'celebrities' simply being famous for being famous, we remain fascinated with traditional stars such as those in the film and music industries. From gazing on places where people used to live, or the locked gates and security fences of our current stars to hotels where they slept (especially while filming) and restaurants where the stars may eat and those they own, we continue to long for even the smallest connection with fame. I have noted elsewhere (Beeton, 2005a, 2007) that such fame also attaches to the filming locations themselves.

Psychologists John Maltby and colleagues have been studying the relationship between the celebrity and the fan, conducting a series of clinical studies examining what people would do for a star, identifying a clinical condition that has become known as 'celebrity worship syndrome' (Maltby *et al.*, 2003). They found that, contrary to earlier studies, there is a significant percentage of the population engaged in 'celebrity worship' as related to three personality types, where:

> Celebrity worship for entertainment-social reasons is associated with extraversion; celebrity worship for intense-personal reasons is associated with neuroticism; and celebrity worship reflecting pathological thoughts and behaviors is related to psychoticism. .... (Maltby *et al.*, 2003: 28)

This interesting study ties into the para-social theories that I have used as a framework for many of my discussions throughout this book. While we may rarely witness the third, more psychotic form of behaviour in relation to celebrities at the more touristic sites such as Walks of Fame, the entertainment-social elements are quite obvious, as they are part of our public persona, while I suspect the intense-personal reasons are also often present within our private selves, such as my own reactions to certain experiences like those I had with Donkey at the theme parks, my strong response to visiting the Spanish Riding School in Vienna, and even my numinous responses to places such as Monument Valley. While I am not sure if I would identify myself as 'neurotic', I must admit that the clinical meaning of the term does make some sense.

Maltby and his colleagues have continued to study the relationship between celebrity worship and many aspects of our lives, including some interesting work where they consider the relationship between religious orientation and celebrity worship (Maltby *et al.*, 2004), even looking at the connection between acceptance of cosmetic surgery and celebrity worship by Maltby and Day (2011). While they confirm the significance of our relationship with celebrities and the influence they can have on many people, I am yet to fully make a parallel distinction with film tourism per se, and suspect that I need to do a lot more study before even attempting to do so. Nevertheless, the power of celebrity does influence the way in which many of us experience filmic places and spaces, with hotels promoting rooms (or even beds) that the stars may have slept in, restaurants they frequent/ed and even food they consumed, such as the cupcakes consumed in *Sex and the City* in New York or the restaurant where Sally had her fake orgasm in *When Harry Met Sally* (1989). This restaurant was Katz's Deli, on E. Houston Street in New York, and the table at which the scene was filmed has a plaque on it that reads, 'Where Harry met Sally ... hope you have what she had!'.

Along with these places that have been touched by the lives of celebrities, there are also structured places such as museums and other repositories of moving image memorabilia that are popular with tourists and travellers as well as fans and film buffs. Furthermore, special events, film festivals and art installations also present us with further experiential opportunities.

Film Museums, Art and Events

While I am not sure if the Australian Centre for the Moving Image (ACMI) in Melbourne considers itself to be strictly a 'museum', avoiding such terminology in all of its promotional material, it does comply with the definition developed by the International Council of Museums (ICOM) that a museum is:

> a non-profit, permanent institution in the service of society and its development, open to the public, which acquires, conserves, researches, communicates and exhibits the tangible and intangible heritage of humanity and its environment for the purposes of education, study and enjoyment. (ICOM, 2007: 948)

The many elements that comprise ACMI are a powerful example of the range and influence of the moving image in our culture, and as such it is a major repository of Australian film and TV culture, memory and future. As they state in the 'Our Story' section on the ACMI website:

> the Australian Centre for the Moving Image (ACMI) celebrates, explores and promotes the cultural and creative richness of the moving image in all its forms – film, television and digital culture. (http://www.acmi.net.au/our_story.htm)

ACMI attracts local, interstate and international visitors, and is also a meeting place for film industry personnel, where one can often overhear ideas being pitched in the adjacent lounge. The various spaces and places within the centre provide an immersive experience in many aspects of the moving image, from viewing films in a state-of-the-art cinema through to researching the moving image from its early days through to digital media as well as participating in creative, often immersive, events and exhibitions.

The centrepiece of ACMI is its free, permanent exhibition, *Screenworlds: The Story of Film, Television and Digital Culture*, which encompasses the story of the moving image through an Australian lens, and has been one of my major inspirations for this book. In addition, there are two temporary exhibition spaces, an intimate one where I experienced the installation by Julian Rosefeldt, *American Night*, described in Chapter 7, while the large space has been used to mount blockbuster exhibitions such as the brilliant *Tim Burton* exhibition in 2011 and the ACMI-commissioned *Game Masters* in 2012, which was loosely linked to their 2008 *Game On* exhibition looking at the evolution of video games, as well as the world premiere of *DreamWorks Animation: The Exhibition* in 2014.

The exhibition of Tim Burton's work premiered at the New York Museum of Modern Art prior to touring to Australia and beyond. It was presented in Australia at ACMI from June to October, 2011 to great acclaim. The opening day saw a record visitation of around 2700 people, which was a major increase from the previously record-breaking *Pixar: 20 Years of Animation* exhibition (2007), which had just under 1000 visitors at its opening. Furthermore, there were many associated events which all sold out, including over 1500 people turning up to watch a live broadcast on a large screen of a masterclass by Burton.

Game Masters featured the stories of 35 leading videogame designers, comprising more than 120 playable games, including some of the original iconic arcade games. The exhibition was divided into three sections: 'Arcade Heroes', 'Game Changers' and 'Indies' which included the work of luminaries such as Masaya Matsuura. What particularly appealed to me was that this was an exhibition for novices (like myself), fans, gamers and industry professionals, which was no easy achievement. I particularly enjoyed listening to many of the interviews that were available on demand at many of the video stations throughout. I was also fascinated with the high level of immersion that visitors were able to experience, along with the knowledge and interest I gained from the exhibition which informs my comments on this form of moving image in the concluding chapter. There were other associated events such as a film programme with movies selected and introduced by leading videogame designers and the popular Thursday night free entertainment which included games-inspired music and performances.

The 2014 *DreamWorks Exhibition* was the biggest exhibition at ACMI (to date), presenting a celebration of 20 years of DreamWorks Studios animation. It featured over 400 items, with some of the concept drawings, models and original artwork never before shown in public. As with other large exhibitions, there were many associated events, such as movies, workshops, panel discussions and later night entertainment. As this studio developed the Shrek characters, along with other favourites including *Wallace and Gromit*, *Puss in Boots*, *How to Train your Dragon* and *Spirit: Stallion of the Cimarron*, this particular exhibition was one that I thoroughly enjoyed.

While I found the Burton exhibition to be exhilarating and enormously engaging, due in no small part to my personal passion, which was fuelled by assisting at the exhibition in a voluntary capacity, it was clear that many found *Game Masters* equally immersive, emotive and engaging, while *Dream-Works* tapped into a deep seam of fascination with animation. These exhibitions bring the visitor/fan right into the moving image making process, presenting a form of backstage experience beyond what is provided today in most theme parks. That said, often the theme parks will host museum-like exhibitions, such as the Lucille Ball tribute at Universal Studios in Orlando and the *Disney Gallery* with its historical presentation at Disneyland. However, during my visits to these theme parks, such exhibitions attracted only a small number of visitors, particularly in relation to the thousands walking past them.

As well as *Screenworlds* and the exhibition spaces, ACMI is the home of the Mediatech resource centre where visitors, professionals and researchers can freely access the National Film and Sound Archive. The centre also boats two state-of-the-art public cinemas which are used as the home of the Melbourne Cinémathèque, as well as film festivals, conferences, events and daily screenings. It is rich in information and interaction as well as providing a great deal of emotional engagement, enabling repeat visitation.

Other museums dedicated to cinema include some smaller, localised museums such as the Little Hollywood Museum in Utah and the Lone Pine Film History Museum in California. These types of museums are very specialised, providing a particular experience for dedicated fans, tourists and/or film buffs alike. Those with a broader remit such as ACMI include the New York Museum of the Moving Image with its range of artefacts and related exhibitions, the London Film Museum, the Film Museum in Berlin, the (Italian) National Museum of Cinema in Torino, and La Cinémathèque Francaise in Paris, which presents exhibitions, films on cinema screens and educational programmes as well as a library and archive centre. Its mission focuses on:

> preserving and restoring films and archives within its collections, programming major classics as well as complete retrospectives and tributes to filmmakers, actors, producers and film technicians, exhibiting precious pieces from its collections within the 'Passion Cinéma' permanent

exhibition, organising temporary exhibitions displaying the riches of its vault, and highlighting the ties connecting cinema to the other arts. (http://www.cinematheque.fr/fr/practical-information.html)

Surprisingly, there has not been a major, dedicated film/movie museum in Hollywood, even though one can visit various sets both at smaller 'museums' on Hollywood Boulevard and, of course, at the theme parks; however, the Academy Museum of Motion Pictures is slated to open in 2016 in Los Angeles, which may go some way towards addressing this.

Many of the exhibitions presented at ACMI have also been mounted at galleries and museums around the world as well as those dedicated to the moving image, such as the aforementioned *Tim Burton* exhibition which premiered at the New York Museum of Modern Art and has since been presented at the Seoul Museum of Art (2012) and La Cinémathèque Francaise (2013). *Game Masters* was shown at Le Papa Museum in New Zealand in 2013. At the time of writing, the *DreamWorks Exhibition* was still at ACMI, but it is slated to tour internationally.

Film and video art

I have described the Julian Rosefeldt *American Night* installation briefly in this chapter as well as earlier in the book, but there are many more examples of ways in which the moving image has been used in the art world. While I have rarely actively sought out such installations and exhibitions, I often find myself participating in a film or video art experience that has appeared within another exhibition or gallery. These days, it is not all that surprising, as '[i]n the first decade of the twenty-first century, it has become practically impossible to walk around the gallery district of a major city … without seeing a large number of artworks that consist of images that move' (Newman, 2009: 88).

Interestingly, these moving image installations are often the experiences that remain with me, returning to haunt and move me, rather than most static artworks. It may be the pure serendipity of uncovering works of which I was not aware (possible), or the power that moving images exert on me (probable), or I may simply have been extremely fortunate to come across some of the most remarkable in their genre (improbable). I suspect it is a fortunate combination of at least the first two, and at times the third. Nevertheless, artworks utilising the moving image are incredibly diverse and, as explained by Comer (2009):

> Artists have used the camera, the screen, and space in between. They have used magic lanterns, slide film, Super-8, 16mm and 35mm film,

video on monitors, video on multiple screens, video projected to a spectacular scale on urban buildings and downsized to the smallest of portable devices. (Comer, 2009: 8)

As well as at galleries visited while travelling, I have experienced many of these at ACMI, both in their permanent exhibition as well as touring exhibitions such as *American Night* and a more recent Australian work, *Mother Courage* (2013) by indigenous Australian filmmaker Warwick Thornton. Here, video of an aboriginal artist is projected inside the back of an open Volkswagen Kombi van, which in turn had been rendered as a part of the images presented in a continual plane from the film to the physical 'reality' of the van. It is not a simple experience to describe (common with much visual art – if we could tell the story in words, why use the visual?), but I returned to it many times over a period of a few months, strangely moved by feelings of alienation, confusion and the cultural ambivalence of a place so central to my being. This was not unlike my unsettled experience of *American Night*, playing into my own feelings of isolation that I noted in Chapter 10. Such emotions are very much part of the human condition, so I can only assume that others will experience a similar emotional pull. In these cases, the moving images have come to me, while they transport me elsewhere, such as the Australian outback through *Mother Courage* and America via *American Night* – what a generous gift from these artists.

Screenworlds also has a remarkable permanent three-dimensional immersive installation by Anthony McCall, *You and I, Horizontal II*, with streams of light in a pitch-black, hazy room creating various illusions. This has proven to be extremely popular with visitors, and during my time volunteering at ACMI, I loved to share this installation with them, as they were often tentative about entering a dark place. They all left in awe, and some returned many times, especially young adults and international tourists. McCall has related installations in New York (*You and I, Horizontal III*) and London (*Between you and I*). Previously, he described these light-based expressions as individual experiences, where:

> As long as you are in the room, you are within the film. Every point in the room presents a different aspect; it's necessary to walk around, to pass through the planes of light. It can't all be taken in at one glance. The film is in constant motion. It is composed out of the shifting relationships between each of the four planes: their speed of movement, the direction in which they travel, the orientation of each plane to the perpendicular, and the modulation of their surfaces. (McCall, 2003: 52)

So, these are some of my experiences of art that uses the moving image, which I have purposely made brief, as the field of visual arts is vast and requires far more study than I have been able to give it at this stage. However, suffice to say that, as a traveller, visitor, tourist or even resident, I love to engage with these works. It seems particularly the case when I travel, as I am in a more reflective/reflexive frame of mind and truly enjoy these experiences and the emotions they engender. I can also rediscover a certain emotional state when reflecting on them, and even visiting those in my local galleries – I feel once again like a flâneur or reflective traveller. Another thing that delights me is the often serendipitous 'discovery' of such experiences and artists.

Moving image themed events

Closely related to the above discussion are those events that are not focused on the preservation and display of artefacts and other touristic representations of the moving image, but more directly related to the viewing experience, such as events including film festivals and awards. These events can be large or small film festivals, and be industry focused as with the Cannes and Sundance Film Festivals, fan based including Science Fiction festivals, or purely as a way to introduce the filmgoer to a body of work such as the Italian or French Film Festivals in Melbourne, Australia. Of course, they are often a mix of some, if not all of these elements. Such events not only provide avenues and publicity for film and television, but are also tourism events in their own right, often attracting visitors from around the world.

Related to the more industry based film festivals are various awards as with the Palm D'Or at Cannes, as well as those events purely related to awarding accolades, such as the Academy Awards, the BAFTA Awards in the UK, various critics' awards, and the Australia Logie awards for television. The awards themselves can be voted on by industry, critics or fans, depending on the nature and aim of the particular award. While I rarely recommend Wikipedia as a reference site, there is an extensive list of awards from around the world under the headings of Critics' Awards, Significant Festival Awards, Industry Awards and Audience Awards (http://en.wikipedia.org/wiki/List_of_film_awards), while the Internet Movie Database lists thousands of film festivals and awards events (http://www.imdb.com/event/). Yet, as an indication of the pervasiveness of the moving image around the world, even these extensive lists are not exhaustive, with many specialised film festivals and awards being known only to those with a direct interest.

One such festival that I have been involved in for some years now that is not on these lists is the Ischia Film Festival, held on the beautiful and evocative Italian Island of Ischia, just off the Naples coast. What makes this festival of particular interest to me is that it hosts an 'International cinema competition dedicated to all the works that have promoted the *value of the territory* by *choosing the locations*' (http://www.ischiafilmfestival.it/; own emphasis). This includes works that not only give prominence in the film to the filming location, but also through enhancing the cultural identity of the region, which brings us back into the travel and tourism realm where cultural identity and image play a significant role. Furthermore, a Foreign Award is presented to movies that have paid tribute to Italian places. Previous winners include *The Passion of the Christ* (2004) by Mel Gibson, Ron Howard's *Angels and Demons* (2009), *To Rome with Love* (2012) written and directed by Woody Allen, and *Casino Royale* (2011) by Martin Campbell. All of these have subsequently generated tourism to many of the Italian locations they featured, and certainly have contributed to how visitors view and experience such places.

In conjunction with this, the festival runs a research-based conference on film tourism, 'Cineturismo', which is where my primary engagement resides, as a regular contributor/participant and occasional Honorary Chair of the Scientific Committee. Various conference themes include 'Movie-tourism: Fiction or Reality?' (2008), 'Location – Unreal Location – Common Places: Cultural Illusion and Truth in Movie Induced Tourism' (2010) and in 2011 the topic was 'Success and Potentiality of Cinema "Made in Italy" Compared to International Case-studies'. So we see filmmakers, tourists, film fans and researchers coming together at a beautiful place that has itself also featured in movies and has a certain amount of celebrity kudos attached to it due to the island's role in the early affair between Richard Burton and Elizabeth Taylor. In 1962 they were in Ischia filming the scenes on Cleopatra's barge for *Cleopatra* (1963), where they were photographed together, prompting the Vatican to accuse them of 'erotic vagrancy'. Such tales are still told to the visitor, and help to make this festival an entirely immersive film festival and tourism experience.

Surprisingly, the combination of these two events (film and tourism) is unusual, yet the synergies are very clear, presenting a way to engage the tourism industry, film industry and filmgoers simultaneously. I have personally found the experience extremely valuable and enriching, especially as a way to further understand the emotional connections between the moving image and tourism. At times, other film festivals have had small presentations on film and tourism in which I have been involved, such as the Venice and Rome Film Festivals in 2007, but such occasions seem rare and very dependent on individual champions such as regional film commissions.

In addition to such formalised, industry-based film festivals, there is a range of film events developed purely for fans which attract thousands of

208 Part 3: Imagining Places: Illusions and Dreams

visitors from around the world. These are often science fiction or other genre events, and include Trekkie Conventions (*Star Trek* TV series and movies), Dr Who Conventions (TV series), and even those based on comic characters at conventions such as Comic-Con. The para-social fascination these fans have with their fantasies is quite remarkable, going so far as to dress and speak in character, and it appears that many travel the world to follow these events. Japanese anime also has similar fan-based events, which will be studied in future publications relating to 'contents tourism'.

Illusions, Dreams and Travel

Elements of this section, from theme park and film technologies to art and the moving image and finally film festivals bring us to reconsider their place and role in the model proposed in Chapter 1 and reproduced in Figure 11.2.

All of them are highly involved, immersive occasions, where the tourist (traveller or fan) can engage in many para-social interactions within the 'using' realm. This can include simulated experiences (theme park rides), meeting characters (theme parks) and stars (film and fan festivals) and

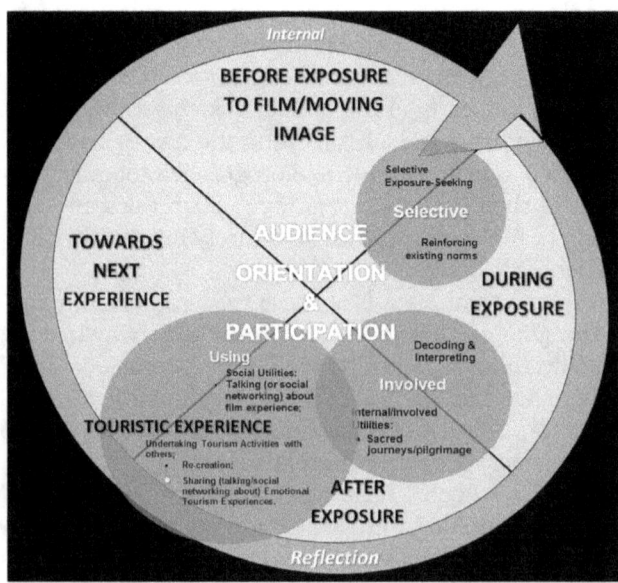

Figure 11.2 Modelling the relationship between audience and tourist activity

engaging emotionally in various moving image experiences at galleries and museums. In addition, the museums also provide an educational and learning experience which often informs other film events and experiences, including the act of watching a movie or TV programme. Ultimately, they also enlighten our travel experiences and relationships to places, people and events.

In spite of such clear correlations between fantasy and imagination, theme parks, precincts and themed events, they are not commonplace in film tourism research, and deserve far more serious study from the tourism perspective. In particular, the emotional responses created by film and then replicated, and even enhanced, at these studio-owned theme parks are significant and meaningful. While some of this is considered in the fan literature, it is not only the 'fanatic' who participates in these activities, but also the serendipitous traveller or tourist simply looking for additional activities and experiences.

12 Conclusion: Manifestations of Tourism Through Film and Television: Making (Some) Meaning from Moving Images and Moving People

Throughout this book, I've presented elements of the moving image, including movies and TV, in relation to their connection with travel and tourism, either literally, figuratively or emotionally. My aim has been to provide markers that illustrate the relationship between tourism and the moving image. I have focused primarily on created (fictional) film rather than the more non-fictional documentaries or even the specialised travel programmes and tourism advertisements using the moving image. This is due in part to the more intense responses we see in tourists when visiting places created via the imagination. Of course, there are many historical and memorial sites that also produce intense, numinous reactions in visitors (and pilgrims), but in the interests of clarity I have chosen to limit my focus to what has become, over the past 30 years, my main area of personal experience, interest, research and expertise.

Furthermore, due to their 'search' for the perfect light and colours with which to convey what they see as the touristic desirability of a place, tourism promotions, especially the 'glossy' travel magazines and TV programmes, tend to sanitise a place. To me, virtually all of the promotions for tropical islands are presented in such a way that they are interchangeable – a palm tree, sunset, hammock, expensive yacht and impossibly tanned people being served by exotic, beautiful 'natives' – whereas the moving image (in all its forms) often presents places in what can be seen as a 'grittier' and more 'realistic' fashion, even via fictional tales which can be based in real or imagined places. In many ways, such perceptions are the key to film (and moving image) related tourism, and as I have noted throughout this book, due to the emotional value we place on our filmic experiences, this is far more than simply looking at a nice image. However, such images do not need to be 'real' or 'authentic' in order to provide us with these powerful draws, and filmmakers are not required to present literal realities, yet those responsible for the promotional tourist brochures have been successfully sued for presenting images that create false and misleading expectations. This has been done via general consumer law as well as through the *1990 EU Directive on Package Travel for Visitors to Europe or from Europe*, which was updated in 2013 to revise the definition of 'package travel' to include more independent travel and incorporate the use of websites (Cordato, 2004; European Commission, 2013).

While the 1960s movies of Elvis Presley are set in constructed locations such as a clean and tidy Hawaii (*Blue Hawaii*, 1961; *Girls, Girls, Girls*, 1962, and so on) or New Orleans (*King Creole*, 1958), they have a 'heart', at the very least, and present us with a range of romantic emotional responses towards the locations that provided the basis for many baby boomers' primarily romantic dreams, especially in Hawaii. Yet, we cannot sue the estate of Elvis Presley or the studio for presenting us with misleading images and expectations of our visit to Hawaii. My own very personal responses to numerous visits to the Coco Palms Resort on Kauai where the wedding scene from *Blue Hawaii* (1961) was filmed attests to this. People continue to visit this ruin of a resort, which was partly damaged by Hurricane Iniki in 1992 and still not repaired, to re-create the wedding scene by reaffirming their own wedding vows with local celebrity Larry Rivera, who sang and performed with Presley. As a result, the ongoing saga of this now dilapidated, yet significant resort is one in which I am personally invested, especially considering that the person who started the MovieTour franchise, Bob Jasper, is now the caretaker.

Dramatic differences between the constructed promotional tourism programmes and the non-promotional application of the moving image, whether fiction or documentaries, can be seen in many places other than Hawaii, including those with additional intrigue and mystique such as Cuba. The many travel programmes and articles featuring what is still the exotic destination of Cuba present it in a romantic light – a place of past glory that retains its appeal through the original 1950s American cars and heritage buildings, most of which are in terrible state of repair, which does not come across in the promotions. Such attraction to faded beauty is not unlike the Coco Palms Resort discussed above, but on a far more serious and damaging scale due to the crippling poverty and overall hardship faced by the people of

Figure 12.1 Havana, Cuba – images of the imagination and reality. From the left, we can see a photo of a lovingly cared for car, women posing for tourists in the World Heritage heart of Havana, and finally the ruined residences one block away

Cuba who make their homes in these ruins. While trying to express the realities of the city, many of my own photos of Havana present it in a romantic light, yet movies such as *Buena Vista Social Club* (1999) provide quite a different perspective of the country, where famous artists and musicians had been forgotten by society, living in obscure poverty (Figure 12.1).

It was this documentary-based movie, not the romantic images of a luxurious past, that motivated me to visit, and I found myself meeting an old musician (Figure 12.2) who, in the 1960s, had entertained famous visitors at the island's most upmarket seaside resorts at Varadero, yet today could not even afford strings for his guitar. While this was a most moving encounter, it was not one out of the travel brochure.

Figure 12.2 Cuban musician, Ahmando Aguist

While the history of the movies presents us with a rich and powerful take on our lives and travel over time, it is not only the movies that affect us, so it is appropriate, as we draw towards the end of this book, to consider other formats of the moving image and its delivery.

Small Screens, Big Reactions: TV, Computers and Mobile Technology

While we have looked at many aspects of the moving image in this book, including its history, various genres and related tourist attractions and activities such as theme parks, I have only paid limited attention to the influence of the smaller screens, especially computers and mobile technology. I do at times refer to the para-social significance of TV series, especially in relation to the TV western, which is worth re-visiting before we briefly delve into the developing world of mobile technologies and moving images. In the movie, Network (1976) the character Howard Beale explains that:

> Television is not the truth. Television is a god-dammed amusement park. Television is a circus, a carnival, a travelling troupe of acrobats, storytellers, dancers, singers, jugglers, sideshow freaks, lion tamers and football players. (Howard Beale, *Network*, 1976)

Television developed in the 1950s, during a time of increasingly democratised 'mass' international travel, which is generally acknowledged as beginning with the introduction of the 747 'Jumbo' aircraft that could move hundreds of people quickly around the world. In addition, every night the world came to us in our living rooms, enhancing the desire to experience the world, while the development of the aircraft provided a way for us to do so. So, just as the beginning of cinema coincided with the development of more accessible travel such as via the railways, the development of mass entertainment through television is concomitant with that of mass tourism.

I reinforce the power of television in my discussion of the western TV series, where over 21 were being broadcast on prime time TV by the late 1950s, experienced from the comfort of our own homes. Consequently, the characters in these series became part of our home life, and as such we developed close para-social relationships with them over what was often many years. Their 'exotic' lives and the places in which they lived and travelled became familiar, yet beguiling. The big skies and open plains of the 'Wild West' were dramatic and resonated with personal as well as cultural meaning, especially for those (like me) trapped in the suburbia of the 1950s and 1960s.

Such relationships and audience responses do not only relate to the TV westerns, but to many popular series. Elsewhere, I have gone into detail regarding the touristic effect of the popular UK TV series, *Heartbeat* (1992–2009), on the small village of Goathland where it was filmed (Beeton, 2005a). The visitors are highly intrusive, often peering through the windows of residents' homes, trampling their gardens, parking on the common grazing land and overwhelming the few shops. These tourists had been experiencing the series in the privacy and intimacy of their living rooms for somewhere between 10 and 18 years (not including the continual series re-runs), feeling that they actually knew the village and its residents, even though it was a fictional series based in the 1960s. This resulted in the residents changing the ways in which they lived, with one of their responses to this ongoing intrusion (which continues today with some one million visitors in spite of the series finishing in 2009) being to move their living quarters to the rear of their homes (Beeton, 2000, 2005a). In this way they could eat, drink and be merry with some level of privacy. The Goathland Hotel, which retains part of its signage as the fictional Aidensfield Arms (Figure 12.3), developed a factsheet to hand out to visitors who were taking up much of the staff's time

Figure 12.3 Double entendre: The Goathland Hotel with its fictional Aidensfield Arms signage

(and energy), with repetitive questions about the place, the series and the locals – who tended to visit the hotel later in the day, after the day trippers had departed. Residents now do their local shopping early in the morning before the tourists arrive.

I personally experienced the effect of such powerful responses from the audience-turned-tourist when I stayed in a cottage that was used as the home of the lead character in the popular, award-winning Australian TV series, *Sea Change* (1998–2000). It is situated in a public camping ground (as it is in the story), and I found people taking photos of the cottage with powerful zoom lenses, as well as running up onto the veranda to peer through the windows. Such attention was most disconcerting, and made me feel highly exposed and stressed. I consequently suffered from extreme nightmares and began to feel that they were even taking part of my soul every time they 'stole' a photo of me, even though this was only for a few days. The manager of the caravan park acknowledged this problem, informing me about another woman staying there on her own (as I was), who left after one night due to such invasive activity. I have known this area for over 20 years, and there were occasions prior to this when I was the only person in the entire park, but I had not felt at all concerned. Also, as a professional tour guide, I was very used to having my photo taken, but not in this non-professional, personal situation. Gone was my idea of finishing writing up my study on *Sea Change* in the evocative atmosphere of the cottage! This experience has made me very aware of the photos I now take, particularly of other people's lives.

As the cottage is in a public caravan park, it was not possible to fence it off, so the management of the camping ground worked to address the issue by building paths that took people away from the cottage and constructing subtle earthwork 'barriers', as shown in the photos below. They also added a sign to the cottage that read 'Visitors are requested to respect the privacy of beach house residents', but one had to get rather (too) close to read it, as shown in Figure 12.4.

Figure 12.4 Privacy earthworks and signage for the *Sea Change* cottage

These examples of the powerful emotional relationships between TV series and the tourism experience are not unusual, with many more cases abounding of tourists inhabiting the increasingly numerous and varied fictional worlds of their TV heroes, often at a cost to the local residents. The Australian TV soap opera, *Neighbours* (screening continuously since 1985), is set in a suburban environment and filmed in the major city of Melbourne. Every day of the year, tourists are out searching for signs of the fictional suburb of Erinsfield. The daily *Neighbours* tour takes a group of (primarily English) fans to sites such as Pinoak Court where the external shots are filmed, known in the series as Ramsey Street. In order to give the visitors a sense of the street, the tour guide produces a street sign under which they can photograph themselves (Figure 12.5). This small court is so popular that the TV company pays for 24-hour security guards to protect residents' privacy as well as the properties themselves from souvenir hunters. The tour company also runs weekly trivia nights at an inner-city hotel, along with other *Neighbours*-related events, yet even they express surprise at the continued and consistent interest in their tour.

Such fascination is not simply a Western phenomenon, with TV tourism being extremely popular in many other cultures, such as in many Asian countries, with numerous Korean series including *Winter Sonata* (2002), *Dae Jang-geum (A Jewel in the Palace)* (2003–2004) and other Hallyu dramas (Kim & Wang, 2012; Su *et al.*, 2011; Lin & Huang, 2008), as well as numerous Japanese anime programmes where we witness fans visiting the places depicted via anime, as discussed in Chapter 10 and further explored in Beeton *et al.*, 2013. It is also worth noting another example I came across in Japan regarding the highly successful telemovie drama series, *Kita no Kunikara (From a*

Figure 12.5 *Neighbours* tour guide, tourists and the Ramsey Street sign

North Country) (1981–2001), set and filmed near the ski resort town of Furano on the island of Hokkaido. The tale follows the lives of two children torn between their divorced parents as they grow up in the Furano region, often living in harsh environments as each new home is constructed. The houses built for the series have won environmental design awards, further promoting the series and the sites, while blurring the line between fiction and reality. There is also a museum in Furano dedicated solely to the programme and its creator, Kuramoto Sou, who is a famous personality, writer and filmmaker in Japan. We are often unaware of these in the 'West' as they are primarily shown in Asian countries; however, this is a large and diverse international audience who are also the main tourists in the region. We usually only hear about Asian film and television through the expatriate communities, often followed by film festivals and special events, yet now YouTube is presenting another channel for the dissemination of popular culture to a far wider audience, such as K-Pop and J-Pop.

I believe that the influence of such programmes on our lives and our travel experiences is intense, and tells us a great deal about ourselves and our interest in the world that is often expressed through travel/tourism.

'Non-fictional' TV

As noted earlier, apart from a few limited examples in Chapter 2 on the early times of the moving image and my comments at the beginning of this chapter on the *Buena Vista Social Club*, I have avoided any in-depth discussion or analysis regarding the non-fictional genres in film and television. Nevertheless, documentaries, cooking programmes, 'reality' shows and travel programmes can all influence our approach to travel and tourism, often in ways similar to that of the more fictional stories I have focused on, as they can also create emotional responses.

Regardless of this, my primary interest remains with fiction, as I am fascinated with how these imaginary stories affect our own imaginations as we travel.

Computers and Mobile Technology

In the literature published to date, the focus of tourism has tended to be on the cinema and television; however, as we are considering the 'moving image' in this publication, we need to consider (albeit briefly) the place of computers and mobile technology within this discussion. While computers can display static images as well as moving images, we are most interested here in the relationship between sites with 'moving' pictures and the viewer.

Of course, TV series and movies can be downloaded and viewed on personal computers and other mobile devices, presenting us not only with many ways to view our standard programmes but, more importantly, where we view them. I can now watch episodes of *Heartbeat* on my iPad (or other device) while having a drink in the Goathland Hotel (Aidensfield Arms) and talking with the residents of that village, or sharing anecdotes with other tourists. This post on-air viewing has become a significant element of how ratings are now measured, with many programmes dramatically exceeding their initial screening figures. I can also post photos, videos and stories of my touristic experiences along with links to the series on my Facebook or other social media site and share with 'friends'.

From home movies to YouTube

Amateur travel movies have been filmed since the early days of cinema, especially once the technology became more portable from the 1930s (Nicholson, 2006). The archives of many families and their major life experiences, including travel, were recorded and hidden away in the family attic or cellar. However, it was the development of the personal video-recorder that enabled the general populace to record experiences and stories. Then the internet took these out of home storage onto the world wide web for all to see.

We are now seeing more non-professional, personal and individual moving image based sites and experiences presented via internet sites where moving images can be easily uploaded and shared, such as that of YouTube. Not only are audiences creating their own parodies on movies as noted in Chapter 1, but they are also filming their own touristic experiences and re-enactments, being fully engaged, active audience members and tourists. This continues to grow exponentially, but some that have appealed to me include a parody of the movie *Avatar* (2009), called *Avatar II: My Big Fat Pandora Versus The Deathly Hallows Striking Back at Muriel's Lethal Weapon: Unloaded*, which incorporates famous scenes from other moves (referred to in the title), with the characters represented by the Avatar characters.

It is not only the more contemporary movies and TV series getting exposure via YouTube, with another favourite of mine being a re-enactment of the opening credits of the 1960s TV programme, *The Andy Griffith Show* (1960–1968), by Tom Gregory from an online film guide, OVGuide (http://www.ovguide.com/). It is an amusing video, but also reinforces the longevity of this series, as does the annual Mayberry Days Festival based on the *Andy Griffith Show* characters and stories.

Furthermore, as surveillance researchers and artists such as Michelle Teran have noted, videos uploaded to YouTube can be geo-tagged and then appear on Google Earth, further strengthening our relationship between media and place (Gürses *et al.*, 2010), which again links us back to travel in yet another format.

Computer/video games

In the section on Film Museums, Art and Events in the previous chapter I outline my connection to the computer games presented at the ACMI *Game Masters* exhibition. While a highly complex and fascinating exhibition, my earlier discussion was a rather cursory account of the development of gaming, moving images and even tourism. In terms of the exhibition, people were travelling as tourists to visit the exhibition, but also many of the games represented 'real' places that we can travel to or experience.

There are some great examples of gaming events consciously tying in with tourism, such as in Japan where small rural towns are hosting gamer events that have some relevance to their local region, simultaneously encouraging game sales and tourism. At Shibu Hot Spring in the Nagano region, an event was held for the game *Monsutâ hantâ 3G (Monster Hunt 3)* (2011). Due to similarities with Yukumo Village, the fictional town created for the game, the world of the game was recreated, 'complete with structures and street facades from the game' (Capcom, 2012). This proved so successful for the game developer and distributor, Capcom, as well as the region, that the hot spring was again transformed into Yukumo for the release of *Monster Hunt 4* (2013).

The separation of games and films becomes more blurred as time goes on, as does their relationship with travel and tourism. For the game *Fantavision* (2000), Sony Computer Entertainment Inc. applied the phrase 'emotional gaming', which boasted complex narratives, detailed characters and many film allusions, redefining the term, 'interactive movies'. However, the technology was not sufficient to allow *Fantavision* to live up to this hyperbole (Newman & Simons, 2007). Nevertheless, the concept of emotional engagement and interaction with video games had been well and truly articulated. The highly popular *Grand Theft Auto (GTA)* franchise began its ascendency with *Grand Theft Auto: Vice City* (2002), which used the filmic and emotional gaming concepts to great effect by setting it in a recognisable Miami, Florida, which had been the location for the popular TV series *Miami Vice* (1984–1990). *GTA: Vice City* showcased 'the full abilities of Rockstar North [the production company] to neatly pastiche, paraphrase and reference the entire pop-culture moments into neat packages of consumer videogame' (Newman & Simons, 2007: 62). The game also used the voices of actors Burt Reynolds, Lee Majors, Ray Liotta and even one of the stars of the *Miami Vice* TV series, Phillip Michael Thomas (IMDb, n.d.). The *Grand Theft Auto* franchise has continued to set some of its most popular versions in recognisable cities, such as New York in *Grand Theft Auto IV* (2008), re-creating buildings such as the Empire State building, Chrysler Building, the Flatiron Building and the Brooklyn Bridge, along with the Statue of Liberty (Statue of Freedom in the game), and even some of the typical characters seen on the streets of New York (IMDb, n.d.).

Many games use broader film genres as well as specific places to create their emotional experiences, such as *L.A. Noire* (2011) set in 1940s Los Angeles with a very 'noir' storyline and context, and the western *Red Dead Redemption* (2010), set in a 1910 western town featuring traditional western storylines and language as well as the iconic landscape.

There are also games that have been developed as merchandising spin-offs from movies or TV series, and while often viewed a little sceptically, some such as *Spider Man 2* (2004) and *Peter Jackson's King Kong: The Official Game of the Movie* (2005) have been more successful, forging a balance between spectating and playing. Coincidentally, both of these games and their stories are set in New York, even though *King Kong* spends most of its time on the imaginary tropical Skull Island. The rendering of New York is powerful and the games present an emotional connection to place. I would not be surprised if people who had played such games see and feel a layer of New York that others may not.

Furthermore, as with the movies based on the theme park rides such as *Pirates of the Caribbean* (2003) (which also has related video games), there are movies that have been created to support or capitalise on the original video games, such as *Resident Evil*, which began as a Japanese video game (also known as *Bio Hazard*) developed in 1996 by Shinji Mikami, and now boasts numerous zombie-themed games and follow-up movies (*Resident Evil: Apocalypse*, 2004; *Resident Evil: Extinction*, 2007; *Resident Evil: Afterlife*, 2010; *Resident Evil: Retribution*, 2012; and *Resident Evil 6*, 2014) that support rather than replicate the games. The *Max Payne* (2001–2012) games, which are about a member of the New York Police Department with a complex back story, also have a number of movies based on them, which are more obviously location based than *Resident Evil*, while the storylines are more recognisably linked to the games.

I discuss various war-based games in Chapter 5, and while they may not directly connect with contemporary travel and tourism, games such as those based on famous battles in history certainly present us with something exotic, which is a cornerstone of travel and tourism motivation and desire. For example, the top 10 PC-based war games as identified on the About.com guide website include titles such as *Soldiers: Heroes of World War 2* where players can choose their affiliation (Britain, Russia, America, Germany) and

Medieval II: Total War, set in the 11th to 16th centuries, set in the Middle East, Europe and South America (http://europeanhistory.about.com/od/gamingresources/tp/aatppcwar.htm). After recently visiting Israel and passing through the Middle East, I can also see how these games could add a layer of meaning to those who play them and then visit the region.

Being Watched While Travelling

While I have commented on the potential of watching movies and TV series as well as playing computer games related to the places one is visiting while travelling, we are also in a society where we are being watched while we travel. In some parts of the world this is not only undertaken by commercial businesses, security companies and law enforcement agencies, but also filmmakers and performance artists. UK-based Austrian intermedia artist and filmmaker, Manu Luksch, obtained CCTV footage of herself in various environments, including the foyer of a theatre, shopping malls and other public spaces via the UK Data Protection Act (1998). The Act gives a person the right to request images of themselves from CCTV cameras, which she did, with varying degrees of success in spite of her legal rights enshrined in the Act (Gürses *et al.*, 2010).

All of the faces apart from her own had to be blocked out, presenting Luksch with rather disturbing yet interesting and strangely engaging footage, which she used to develop the science fiction movie, *Faceless* (2007). The movie is set in a world where the past and future do not exist, and everyone lives in a happy yet faceless 'present', until one woman recovers her face (Gürses *et al.*, 2010). This is a disquieting and quite profound film, but what is of interest to me here is the use of surveillance camera footage of people in public places who are often travelling to or from somewhere, to create a 'commercial' film. It is also another way that the moving image can inform our travels and experiences, providing a framework from within which we can literally and figuratively view our actions in public places.

While Luksch took a legal approach to obtaining the footage, others (primarily in the UK, as far as I can ascertain) are 'video sniffing', which entails using personal video recorders (PVRs) to pick up signals broadcast by wireless CCTV networks – they act out in front of these cameras, hijack it via their PVRs and edit it into a film. While this remains a rather grey legal area, and is considered illegal by most, films created in this manner have received some attention, with four being screened by BBC Channel 4 in 2008, and others at a festival, *Recoded: Landscapes and Politics of New Media*, held in Aberdeen, Scotland that same year (Dodson, 2008).

Luksch has also expressed interest in bringing others into her creative space, with projects that extend her *Faceless* approach such as the one she has mooted below:

> I would like to make all the recordings I collected in the process of making Faceless available online and invite people to create their own fiction from them, like a remix of image and meaning. The footage could be quite interesting material for others, since it is so difficult to get hold of. People could use it to tell new stories or use them for their own line of investigation. (Luksch, in Gürses *et al.*, 2010: 170)

This is certainly an area I wish to explore further, especially in terms of how such so-called subversive filming of people moving around in public spaces impacts on our own interpretations of travel and movement, which could be profound. As with the cinematic developments coming out of the Industrial Revolution, technological advances are providing new ways for us to experience today's popular culture, including entertainment, travel and tourism. In fact, these new ways are being adopted and adapted in such new and different ways that the links and interconnections are becoming highly intricate, but no less significant.

So What Does It All MEAN?

I have written quite a few thousand words to get to this final, important section; yet there is no meta-narrative or summation that can truly bring all the threads of travel, tourism and the moving image together into one neat package. To fully appreciate their relationship to, and influence on, travel and tourism, developments such as those discussed throughout this publication, and in particular those touched on above require more research and consideration.

The very nature of this rapidly changing scene requires us also to develop new ways in which to study and present our work. If the gestation period of this publication is anything to go by (years), I would suggest a more dynamic, user-generated web-based research site dedicated to this topic to be more appropriate, and hope that, by the time you read this, we (either myself and/or others) have something in place. The increasing application of Critical Studies methodologies to this field certainly provides us with ways to move forward. The reflexive nature of such approaches sits alongside my own lived-experience, autoethnographic approach presented throughout this publication. As Fullagar and Wilson (2012: 2) remind us, a 'plurality of critical approaches is important for maintaining a vital intellectual space for reflexive debate', and point out that we need to keep an open debate with researchers based in other paradigms. As noted in Chapter 1, many of the film/moving image and tourism-related studies from the Critical Studies field have not always engaged with the mainstream, often business-based, film-induced tourism research – a serious issue that my work in this publication attempts to address. As I noted throughout, I come from this tourism research paradigm, and my work is first and foremost informed by that literature, but over the past years I have come to want to understand and tease out the more subtle complexities of this field, and taking on more of the Critical Studies approaches and literature certainly supports this.

In this publication, I have strived to present the range of moving images in a way that may help to explain a little more about our very real and powerful connections between film, TV, games, video and so on and our actions when travelling as well as our reflections and emotional forms. In order to achieve this, I have consciously focused on those that have influenced (and continue to influence) me.

I maintain my primary premise that, as audiences, we actively and emotionally engage with the moving image, even if our response is negative or even simply indifferent. Then when we travel, this engagement not only informs our decision making (at times) but, more importantly, it provides further meaning to and connection with a place. This can also work in reverse – after visiting and actively/emotionally engaging with a place, we view films and other forms of moving images that are set or filmed there quite differently. I recently re-watched *The Italian Job* (1969), which was great fun but, while I had been to Italy many times, I had not been to Turin where it was set and filmed. While I loved the scenes and settings, they did not 'tug' on my emotions as other Italian movie settings do.

So, not only does film (or moving image) inform our travel experiences, but our travel experiences inform our film-watching experiences. Again, we can see a circular, iterative relationship here as, when I now visit Turin, I will recall the movie, its humour and action, and may even watch it again on my return, with quite a different emotional attachment.

As I said at the beginning of Chapter 1, tourism involves moving physically, metaphorically and emotionally, while we also continually engage with images that move – again physically, emotional and metaphorically. We have looked at these moving images in terms of various movie genres including silent cinema, the western, road movies, war and movies relating to unrest and propaganda, spy movies, gangsters, detectives, Asian pop culture, and fantasy and animation, along with other forms of the moving image, from panoramas to computer games and even related activities such as art installations, festivals and events. As technology develops, both the travel and moving image fields have benefited, often virtually simultaneously or concomitantly. This historical, technological relationship between moving images and moving people (literally and figuratively) has had received limited attention prior to the discussion in this publication.

For the last time, let us revisit the model I introduced in the first chapter illustrating the internal relationship between the responses and activities of the moving picture audience and the tourist (Figure 12.6), which is my attempt to illustrate the overarching processes we go through and the experiences we have.

I have expressed it as an iterative cycle that we move through as we experience a film or other form of moving image, which can include games and artistic installations, resulting in an endless parade of reactions, memories and experiences. While, in terms of tourism, we are interested in the aspects of the 'after exposure' and 'towards the next experience' sectors, I believe that I have demonstrated the importance of the other sectors, particularly the overlapping involvement aspects, as they all are part of our emotional landscape. The physical touristic activities are only a part of the film/moving image tourism experience, and as I noted above can come before we

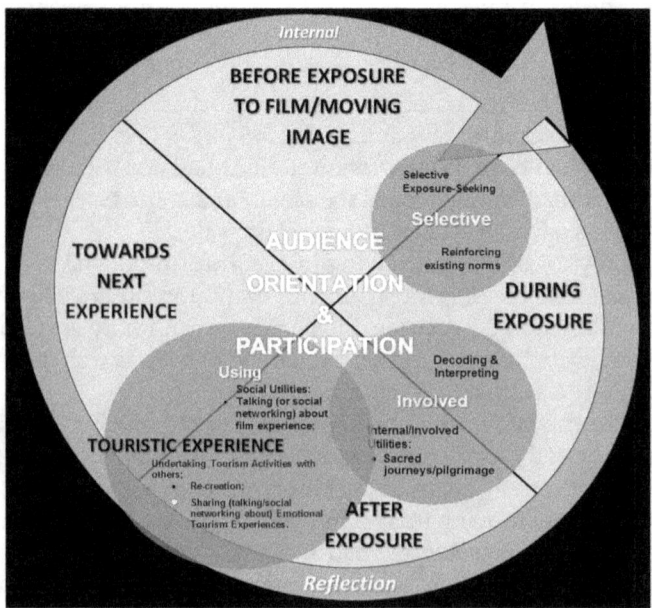

Figure 12.6 Modelling the relationship between audience and tourist activity

are exposed to a film, where we desire to re-visit our touristic experience via that film on returning home.

The concept of para-social interaction is certainly one way to further understand our own complex, personal reactions to the moving image and the stories they tell. Taking the lead of Kim (2011) who applied para-social interaction as a framework to his thesis on film tourism, I have proposed not only to consider this psychological framework, but to combine it with my own ethnographic studies to present a conceptual model of the relationship (and process) between film and audiences. I have also incorporated the excellent work by Reijnders (2011) and his circular process of imagination and perception in media tourism.

Back in the late 1990s, well before the high level of technological uptake we see today, the notion that there could be a para-social link between user-generated sites on the web and users was being mooted by researchers such as Eighmey and McCord (1998), who noted in their early research that, 'websites projecting a strong sense of personality may also encourage the development of a kind of parasocial relationship with website visitors' (Eighmey & McCord, 1998: 192) and they emphasised that those websites that were the most 'human' were preferred by users.

Ultimately, the meaning of what I have presented in this book is up to you, the reader. I have tried to communicate my thoughts and ideas as best I can by sharing some rather personal, autoethnographic experiences. I cannot control how you interpret and judge them, and nor do I wish to as it is always the unexpected insight or interpretation that moves us all forward towards a better, more complex understanding. I do hope that, as with all research, there are some points that have stimulated thought and discussion.

The Future: A Never-ending Story ...

For over 30 years I have been directly affected by film-induced tourism, initially as a tourist, followed by as a tour guide, then a student and now a researcher, writer and educator. Indirectly, my whole life has been a mash-up of popular culture, travel and tourism.

My studies outlined in this publication demonstrate that film and tourism have been directly and indirectly connected since the very conception of the moving image. The movies and TV programmes not only show us where to travel, but also provide us with some rather different templates as to what to do at these places as well as providing an emotional framework from which to make some sense of such personal travel experiences. As I have noted elsewhere in this book, Alain de Botton (2002: 9) points out that 'we are inundated with advice on *where* to travel to, but we hear little of *why* and *how* we should go...'. His comments and musings neatly intersected with my own emerging thoughts regarding film and tourism over 10 years ago, sowing the seeds of this publication. By using art and artists to express and guide his travel experiences, de Botton undertakes a journey not unlike those I have experienced via film or TV and which I have attempted to relay here.

Certainly, the more I learn about the moving image and tourism, the more there is to understand. This publication is, like my previous efforts, merely a speck in our field of knowledge, which I hope that for some will provide a jumping-off point for further research and study. However, I hope that the film buff, TV fan or even occasional viewer, along with the tourist and traveller, will also gain insights into their own relationship with the popular culture of today as expressed via the moving image and tourism, and as a consequence enjoy their experiences and reflections even more.

> It changes so suddenly. One moment it's paradise, the next it's trying to kill you. *The Man from Snowy River* (1982)

References

Adler, J. (1989) Origins of sightseeing. *Annals of Tourism Research* 16, 7–29.
Altick, R.D. (1978) *Shows of London*. London: Belknap Press.
Altman, R. (1996) The silence of the silents. *Musical Quarterly* 80 (4), 648–718.
Altman, R. (2006) From lecturer's prop to industrial product: The early history of travel films. In J. Ruoff (ed.) *Virtual Voyages: Cinema and Tourism* (pp. 61–76). Durham, NC: Duke University Press.
Alvey, M. (1997) Wanderlust and wire wheels: The existential search of Route 66. In S. Cohan and I.R. Hark (eds) *The Road Movie Book* (pp. 143–164). New York: Routledge.
Amad, P. (2006) Between the 'familiar text' and the 'book of the world': Touring the ambivalent contexts of travel films. In J. Ruoff (ed.) *Virtual Voyages: Cinema and Tourism* (pp. 99–116). Durham, NC: Duke University Press.
Amad, P. (2010) *Counter-Archive: Film, the Everyday, and Albert Kahn's Archives de La Panete*. New York: Columbia University Press.
American Red Cross (2005) *Rallying a Nation: American Red Cross Advertising During World War I*. Washington, DC: American Red Cross.
American Red Cross (2010) Red Cross will live on in celluloid history. *Red Cross Newsletter*. Washington, DC: American Red Cross.
Anderson, G. (1989) Corriganville history. *Favourite Westerns* 31.
Anderson, J. (2009) Ideas of North: Canada. In *Film + Travel, North America > South America* (pp. 103–123). Museyon Guides. New York: Museyon Inc.
Anon (2011) Madrid unveils its own walk of fame. *Buenos Aires Herald*, 28 June, 2011.
Ateljevic, I., Pritchard, A. and Morgan, N. (eds) (2007) *The Critical Turn in Tourism Studies: Innovative Research Methodologies*. Amsterdam: Elsevier.
Australian Centre for the Moving Image (ACMI) (2011) ACMI: Screen Worlds Exhibition. See http://www.acmi.net.au/screen_worlds_about.htm (accessed February 2011).
Auter, P.J. and Davis, D.M. (1991) When characters speak directly to viewers: Breaking the fourth wall in television. *Journalism Quarterly* 68, 165–171.
Barber, X.T. (1993) The roots of travel cinema: John L. Stoddard, E. Burton Holmes and the nineteenth-century illustrated travel lecture. *Film History* 5 (1), 68–84.
Baudelaire, C. (1986[1863]) The painter of modern life. In *My Heart Laid Bare and other Prose Writings*. London: Soho Book Company.
Bazin, A. (1971) *What is Cinema?* Vol. 2. Berkeley, CA: Regents of the University of California.
Beeton, S. (2000) It's a wrap! What happens after the film crew leaves? An examination of community responses to film-induced tourism. *TTRA National Conference – Lights! Camera! Action!* (pp. 127–136). Burbank, CA: Travel & Tourism Research Association.

Beeton, S. (2001) Smiling for the camera: The influence of film audiences on a budget tourism destination. *Tourism, Culture and Communication* 3 (1), 15–26.

Beeton, S. (2004) Rural tourism in Australia – has the gaze altered? Tracking rural images through film and tourism promotion. *International Journal of Tourism Research (Special Issue: Rural Tourism)* 6, 125–135.

Beeton, S. (2005a) *Film-Induced Tourism*. Clevedon: Channel View Publications.

Beeton, S. (2005b) The case study in tourism research: A multi-method case study approach. In B. Ritchie, P. Burns and C. Palmer (eds) *Tourism Research Methods. Integrating Theory and Practice* (pp. 37–48). Wallingford: CABI.

Beeton, S. (2007) The good, the bad and the ugly: CSR, film and tourism. Two cases of filming in a small community. *Tourism Review International* 11 (2), 145–154.

Beeton, S. (2008) From the screen to the field: The influence of film on tourism and recreation. *Tourism Recreation Research* 33 (1), 39–47.

Beeton, S. (2010a) The advance of film tourism. *Tourism and Hospitality Planning and Development* 7 (1), 1–6.

Beeton, S. (2010b) Landscapes as characters: Film, tourism and a sense of place. *Metro (Special Feature Section on Landscape and Location in Australian Cinema)* 166, 114–119.

Beeton, S. (2011) Tourism and the moving image – incidental tourism promotion. *Tourism Recreation Research* 36 (1), 49–56.

Beeton, S., Bowen, H. and Santos, C. (2005) State of knowledge: Mass media and its relationship to perceptions of quality. In G. Jennings and N. Nickerson (eds) *Quality Tourism Experiences* (pp. 25–37). Oxford: Elsevier Butterworth-Heinemann.

Beeton, S., Yamamura, T. and Seaton, P. (2013) The mediatization of culture: Japanese contents tourism and pop culture. In J.-A. Lester and C. Scarles (eds) *Mediating the Tourist Experience* (pp. 139–154). Ashgate: Franham.

Bell, C. and Lyall, J. (2005) 'I was here': Pixilated evidence. In D. Crouch, R. Jackson and F. Thompson (eds) *The Media and the Tourist Imagination: Converging Cultures* (pp. 135–142). Abingdon: Routledge.

Benjamin, W. (1972) A short history of photography. *Screen* 13 (1), 5–26.

Benjamin, W. (1998[1936]) *The Work of Art in the Age of Mechanical Reproduction* (transcribed by A. Blunden). Los Angeles, CA: UCLA School of Theatre, Film and Television. See https://www.marxists.org/reference/subject/philosophy/works/ge/benjamin.htm (accessed April 2011).

Blom, I. (2007) The first cameraman in Iceland: Travel film and travel literature. In L. Porter and B. Dixon (eds) *Picture Perfect: Landscape, Place and Travel in British Cinema Before 1930* (pp. 68–81). Exeter: The Exeter Press.

Booth, A.R. (1991) The development of the espionage film. In W.K. Wark (ed.) *Spy Fiction, Spy Films and Real Intelligence* (pp. 136–160). London: Frank Cass.

Borton, T. and Borton, D. (2015) *Before the Movies: American Magic Lantern Entertainment and the Nation's First Great Screen Artist, Joseph Boggs Beale*. Indiana University Press: Indiana.

Bramwell, B. and Lane, B. (2014) The 'critical turn' and its implications for sustainable tourism research. *Journal of Sustainable Tourism* 22 (1), 1–8.

Brewster, D. (1856) *The Stereoscope: Its History, Theory and Construction*. New York: Morgan and Morgan.

Britton, R.K. (2010) Landscaping the revolution: The political and social geography of Cuba reflected in its cinema. In G. Harper and J. Rayner (eds) *Cinema and Landscape* (pp. 177–188). Bristol: Intellect.

Bronner, S.E. (2011) *Critical Theory: A Very Short Introduction*. Oxford: Oxford University Press.
Bryman, A. (1999) The Disneyization of society. *Sociological Review* 47 (1), 25–47.
Bryson, B. (2001) *Down Under*. London: Black Swan.
Buchmann, A., Moore, K. and Fisher, D. (2010) Experiencing film tourism: Authenticity & fellowship. *Annals of Tourism Research* 37 (1), 229–248.
Burrowes, W.E. (1998) *This New Ocean: The Story of the First Space Age*. Toronto: Random House.
Buscombe, E. (2006) *100 Westerns*. British Film Institute Screen Guides. London: BFI Publishing.
Caldwell, G. (ed.) (2006) *Burton Holmes Travelogues. The Greatest Traveler of His Time, 1892–1952*. Cologne: Taschen.
Campbell, J. (1949) *The Hero with a Thousand Faces*. New York: Pantheon Books.
Capcom (2012) The Monster Hunter hit trajectory. *Capcom Investor Relations*. See http://www.capcom.co.jp/ir/english/hit/02.html (accessed July 2013).
Chaplin, C. (1964; electronic reader version, 2011) *My Autobiography*. Harmondsworth: Bodley Head, Penguin.
Christie, I. (2007) The Anglo-Boer War in North London: A micro study. In L. Porter and B. Dixon (eds) *Picture Perfect: Landscape, Place and Travel in British Cinema Before 1930* (pp. 82–91). Exeter: The Exeter Press.
Chu, Y. (2003) *Hong Kong Cinema: Coloniser, Motherland and Self*. Abingdon: Routledge Curzon.
Cohan, S. and Hark, I.R. (1997) Introduction. In S. Cohan and I.R. Hark (eds) *The Road Movie Book* (pp. 1–14). New York: Routledge.
Cohen, E. (1988) Authenticity and commoditization in tourism. *Annals of Tourism Research* 15 (3), 371–386.
Cohen, J. (1999) Favourite characters of teenage viewers of Israeli serials. *Journal of Broadcasting and Electronic Media* 43, 327–345.
Collins, D. (1987) *Hollywood Down Under. Australians at the Movies: 1896 to the Present Day*. London: Angus and Robertson Publishers.
Connell, J. (2012) Film tourism – evolution, progress and prospects. *Tourism Management* 3 (5), 1007–1029.
Comer, S. (2009) Editor's note. In S. Comer (ed.) *Film and Video Art* (pp. 6–11). Millbank: Tate Publishing.
Cordato, A.J. (2004) Are you a target for consumer claims? *The University of New South Wales Centre for Continuing Legal Education Tourism and Leisure Law Seminar 2004, Sydney*.
Cousineau, P. (1998) *The Art of Pilgrimage. The Seeker's Guide to Making Travel Sacred*. San Francisco, CA: Conari Press.
Cox, W. and Love, J. (1998) *The Best Investment a Nation Ever Made: A Tribute to the Dwight D. Eisenhower System of Interstate and Defense Highways*. Diane Publishing: Darby.
Crofts, S. (1989) Re-imaging Australia: Crocodile Dundee overseas. *Continuum: Journal of Media & Cultural Studies* 2 (2), 129–142.
Crompton, J.L. (1979) An assessment of the image of Mexico as a vacation destination and the influence of geographical location upon that image. *Journal of Travel Research* 17 (4), 18–23.
Croy, W.G. and Walker, R.D. (2003) Rural tourism and film-issues for strategic regional development. In D. Hall, L. Roberts and M. Mitchell (eds) *New Directions in Rural Tourism* (pp. 115–133). Farnham: Ashgate.
DCITA (Department of Communications, Information Technology and the Arts) (2003) *National Tourism Strategy*. Canberra: DCITA.

de Botton, A. (2002) *The Art of Travel*. London: Hamish Hamilton.
Deleuze, G. (1989) *Cinema 2: The Time-Image* (trans. H. Tomlinson and R. Galeta) Minneapolis: University of Minnesota Press.
Denzin, N.K. (1997) *Interpretive Ethnography: Ethnographic Practices for the 21st Century*. Thousand Oaks: Sage.
Dietz, P.E., Matthews, D.B., Van Duyne, C., Martell, D.A., Parry, C.D.H., Stewart, T., Warren, J. and Crowder, J.D. (1991) Threatening and otherwise inappropriate letters to Hollywood celebrities. *Journal of Forensic Sciences* 36, 185–209.
Disney Studio Services (2011) *Golden Oak Ranch*. See http://studioservices.go.com/goldenoakranch/index.html (accessed September, 2011).
Dodson, S. (2008) The secret art of video sniffing: Real life stars of CCTV. *The Guardian*, 28 April. See http://www.guardian.co.uk/culture/2008/apr/25/3 (accessed June 2013).
Dubisch, J. (2004) Memory, motion and the (re) construction of history on a motorcycle pilgrimage. In S. Coleman and J. Eade (eds) *Reframing Pilgrimage: Cultures in Motion* (pp. 105–132).
Earnest, P. (2010) The International Spy Museum responds, in Ronald Radosh, Scoping out the International Spy Museum. *Academic Questions* 23 (3), 293–296.
Eighmey, J. and McCord, L. (1998) Adding value in the information age: Uses and gratifications of sites on the World Wide Web. *Journal of Business Research* 41, 187–194.
Endy, S. (2004) *Cold War Holidays. American Tourism in France*. Chapel Hill, NC: University of North Carolina Press.
European Commission (2013) *Proposal for a Directive of the European Parliament and of the Council on Package Travel and Assisted Travel Arrangements. Amending Regulation (EC) No. 2006/2004, Directive 2011/83/EU and Repealing Council Directive 90/314/EEC*. Brussels: European Commission.
Evans, E.A. (2003) In the sandals of Pharaoh: James Henry Breasted and the stereoscope. Occasional Paper, 12 July. Association for the Study of Travel in Egypt and the Near East. Oxford: Worcester College, Oxford University. See http://mcclungmuseum.utk.edu/research/reoccpap/stereoscope.htm (accessed February 2011).
Evans, E. (2007) Character, audience agency and trans-media drama. *Media, Culture and Society* 30 (1), 197–213.
Eyerman, R. and Lofgren, O. (1995) Romancing the road: Road movies and images of mobility. *Theory Culture Society* 12 (53), 53–79.
Falconer, D. (1997) 'We don't need to know the way home': The disappearance of the road in the *Mad Max* trilogy. In S. Cohan and I.R. Hark (eds) *The Road Movie Book* (pp. 249–270). New York: Routledge.
Feilitzen, C. and Linne, O. (1975) Identifying with television characters. *Journal of Communication* 25, 51–55.
Fielding, R. (1970) Hale's Tours: Ultrarealism in the pre-1910 motion picture. *Cinema Journal* 10 (1), 34–47.
Foucault, M. (1976) *The Birth of the Clinic*. London: Tavistock.
French, P. (2003) Ned Kelly. *The Observer*. Sunday 28th September, 2003.
Friedberg, A. (1993) *Window Shopping: Cinema and the Postmodern*. Berkeley, CA: University of California Press.
Frost, W. (2006) Braveheart-ed Ned Kelly: Historic films, heritage tourism and destination image. *Tourism Management* 27 (2), 247–254.
Fullagar, S. and Wilson, E. (2012) Critical pedagogies: A reflexive approach to knowledge creation in tourism and hospitality studies. *Journal of Hospitality and Tourism Management* 19, e2: 2–6.

Geraghty, C. (1991) *Women and Soap Opera*. Cambridge: Polity Press.
Gernsheim, H. and Gernsheim, A. (1969) *The History of Photography: From the Camera Obscura to the Beginning of the Modern Era* (2nd edn). New York: McGraw-Hill.
Gibson, R. (1983) Camera natura – landscape in Australian feature films. *Framework* 22 (3), 5–10.
Giles, D.C. (2002) Parasocial interaction: A review of the literature and a model for future research. *Media Psychology* 4 (3), 279–305.
Gjorgievski, M. and Trpkova, S.M. (2012) Movie induced tourism: A new tourism phenomenon. *UTMS Journal of Economics* 3 (1), 97–104.
Graml, G. (2004) (Re) mapping the nation Sound of Music tourism and national identity in Austria, ca 2000 CE. *Tourist Studies* 4 (2), 137–159.
Grau, O. (1999) Into the belly of the image: Historical aspects of virtual reality. *Leonardo* 2 (5), 365–371.
Grieveson, L. and Kramer, L. (2003) Storytelling and the nickelodeon. In L. Grieveson and P. Kramer (eds) *The Silent Cinema Reader* (pp. 77–86). Abingdon: Routledge.
Griffiths, A. (2006) Time traveling IMAX style: Tales from the giant screen. In J. Ruoff (ed.) *Virtual Voyages: Cinema and Tourism* (pp. 238–258). Durham, NC: Duke University Press.
Grihault, N.I.C.K.I. (2003) Film tourism-the global picture. *Travel & Tourism Analyst* (5), 1–22.
Grünewald, R.D.A. (2002) Tourism and cultural revival. *Annals of Tourism Research* 29 (4), 1004–1021.
Gunning, T. (1986) The cinema of attraction: Early film, its spectator and the avant-garde. *Wide Angle* 8 (3/4), 63–70.
Gunning, T. (1989) 'Primitive' cinema: A frame-up? Or the trick's on us. *Cinema Journal* 38 (2), 3–12.
Gunning, T. (2005) Lynx-eyed detectives and shadow bandits: Visuality and eclipse in French detective stories and films before WWI. *Yale French Studies* 108, 74–88.
Gunning, T. (2006) 'The whole world within reach': Travel images without borders. In J.Ruoff (ed.) *Virtual Voyages: Cinema and Tourism* (pp. 25–41). Durham, NC: Duke University Press.
Gürses, S., Luksch, M. and Teran, M. (2010) Trialogue on interventions in surveillance space: Seda Gürses in conversation with Michelle Teran and Manu Luksch. *Surveillance & Society (Special Issue on Surveillance, Performance and New Media Art*, ed. J. McGrath and R. Sweeny), 7 (2), 165–174.
Hackley, C. (2007) Auto-ethnographic consumer research and creative non-fiction: Exploring connections and contrasts from a literary perspective. *Qualitative Market Research: An International Journal* 10 (1), 98–108.
Hannigan, J. (1998) *Fantasy City: Pleasure and Profit in the Postmodern Metropolis*. Abingdon: Routledge.
Harris, C., Wilson, E. and Ateljivic, I. (2007) Structural entanglements and strategy of audiencing. In I. Ateljivic, A. Pritchard and N. Morgan (eds) *The Critical Turn in Tourism Studies* (pp. 41–56). Amsterdam: Elsevier.
Hills, M. (2002) *Fan Cultures*. London: Routledge.
Hills, M. (2005) Patterns of surprise: The 'Aleatory Object' in psychoanalytic ethnography and cyclical fandom. *American Behavioral Scientist* 48 (7), 801–821.
Hirschman, E. (2000) *Heroes, Monsters & Messiahs: Movies and Television Shows as the Mythology of American Culture*. Kansas City: Andrews McMeel Publishing.
Holbrook, M.B. (2005) Customer value and autoethnography: Subjective personal introspection and the meanings of a photograph collection. *Journal of Business Research* 58 (1), 45–61.

Holt, N.L. (2001) Beyond technical reflection: Demonstrating the modification of teaching behaviours using three levels of reflection. *Avanti* 7 (2), 66–76.
Holt, N.L. (2003) Representation, legitimation and autoethnography: An autoethnographic writing story. *International Journal of Qualitative Methods* 2 (1). Article 2, www.ualberta.ca/~iiqm/backissues/2_1final/htm/html/holt/html [accessed November 7, 2007].
Horne, D. (1992) *The Intelligent Tourist*. McMahons Point: Margaret Gee Publishing.
Horton, D. and Wohl, R.R. (1956) Mass communication and para-social interaction: Observations on intimacy at a distance. *Psychiatry* 19, 215–229.
Houghton Mifflin (2000) *The American Heritage® Dictionary of the English Language* (4th edn). New York: Houghton Mifflin.
Hughes, H. (2006) *Crime Wave. The Filmgoers' Guide to the Great Crime Movies*. London and New York: I.B. Taurus.
Hughes, H. (2008) *Stagecoach to Tombstone. The Filmgoers' Guide to the Great Westerns*. London and New York: I.B. Taurus.
Hughes, L. (2006) *The Rough Guide to Gangster Movies*. London: Rough Guides.
Hutchings, P. (2004) Uncanny landscapes in British film and television. *Visual Culture in Britain* 5 (2), 27–40.
ICOM (International Council of Museums) (2007) *Museum Definition*. See http://icom. museum/who-we-are/the-vision/museum-definition.html (accessed March 2013).
IMDb (n.d.) *Internet Movie Database*. See: http://www.imdb.com/ [web based database].
Irvine, C. (1914) Doings at Los Angeles. *Moving Picture World* 22, 198.
Iso-Ahola, S.E. (1984) Social psychological foundations of leisure and resulting implications for leisure counseling. In E.T. Dowd (ed.) *Leisure Counseling: Concepts and Applications* (pp. 97–125). Springfield IL: Charles C Thomas Pub Ltd.
Jamal, T. and Hollinshead, K. (2001) Tourism and the forbidden zone: The underserved power of qualitative inquiry. *Tourism Management* 22, 63–82.
Jansson, A. (2002) Spatial phantasmagoria: The mediatization of tourism experience. *European Journal of Communication* 17 (4), 429–433.
Johnson, L.K. (2008) Spies in the American movies: Hollywood's take on Lese Majeste. *Intelligence and National Security* 23 (1), 5–24.
Kim, S. (2011) The production and consumption of experience: Inter-Asian responses to small screen tourism in Korea. Unpublished PhD thesis, Leeds Metropolitan University.
Kim, S. and Wang, H. (2012) From television to the film set: Korean drama *Daejanggeum* drives Chinese, Taiwanese, Japanese and Thai audiences to screen-tourism. *International Communication Gazette* 74 (5), 423–442.
Kindem, G. (1979) Pierce's semiotic and film. *Quarterly Review of Film Studies* 4 (1), 61–70.
King, G. and Krzywinska, T. (2002) Introduction. In G. King and T. Krzywinska (eds) *Screenplay: Cinema/Videogames/Interfaces* (pp. 1–32). London: Wallflower Press.
Koppes, C.R. and Black, G.D. (1990) *Hollywood Goes to War. How Politics, Profits and Propaganda Shaped World War II Movies*. Berkeley, CA: University of California Press.
Laderman, D. (2002) *Driving Visions: Exploring the Road Movie*. Austin, TX: University of Texas Press.
Laing, J. and Frost, W. (2012) *Books and Travel: Inspiration, Quests and Transformation*. Bristol: Channel View Publications.
Levy, M.R. (1979) Watching TV news as para-social interaction. *Journal of Broadcasting* 23, 69–80.

Levy, M.R. and Windahl, S (1984) Audience activity and gratifications: A conceptual clarification and exploration. *Communication Research* 11 (1), 51–78.

Lin, Y.-S. and Huang, J.-Y. (2008) Analyzing the use of TV miniseries for Korea tourism marketing. *Journal of Travel & Tourism Marketing* 24 (2–3), 23–227.

Lomine, L. (2005) Tourism in Augustan society. In J.K. Walton (ed.) *Histories of Tourism: Representation, Identity and Conflict* (pp. 71–87). Clevedon: Channel View Publications.

Lukas, S.A. (2008) *Theme Park*. London: Reaktion Books.

MacCannell, D. (1973) Staged authenticity: Arrangements of social space in tourism settings. *American Journal of Sociology* 79 (3), 357–361.

Macionis, N. (2004) Understanding the film-induced tourist. In W. Frost, G. Croy and Beeton, S. (eds) *International Tourism and Media Conference Proceedings* (pp. 86–97). Berwick: Monash University Tourism Research Unit.

MacKenzie, J.M. (2005) Empires of travel: British guide books and cultural imperialism of the 19th and 20th centuries. In J.K. Walton (ed.) *Histories of Tourism: Representation, Identity and Conflict* (pp. 19–38). Clevedon: Channel View Publications.

Maltby, J. and Day, L. (2011) Celebrity worship and incidence of elective cosmetic surgery: Evidence of a link among young adults. *Journal of Adolescent Health* 49, 483–489.

Maltby, J., Houran, M.A. and McCutcheon, L.E. (2003) A clinical interpretation of attitudes and behaviors associated with celebrity worship. *Journal of Nervous and Mental Disease* 191, 25–29.

Maltby, J., Day, L., McCutcheon, L.E., Martin, M.M. and Cayanus, J.L. (2004) Celebrity worship, cognitive flexibility, and social complexity. *Personality and Individual Differences* 37, 1475–1482.

Marling, K.A. (1994) *As Seen on TV: The Visual Culture of Everyday Live in the 1950s*. Cambridge, MA: Harvard University Press.

Manvell, R. (1974) *Films and the Second World War*. South Brunswick, NJ: J.M. Dent.

Mason, F. (2002) *American Gangster Cinema: From Little Caesar to Pulp Fiction*. Basingstoke: Palgrave MacMillan.

Mazow, L.G. (1992) *Panoramic Sensibilities in Nineteenth- and Twentieth-Century American Painting, 'An Endless Panorama of Beauty: Selections from the Jean and Alvin Snowiss Collection of American Art,'* Palmer Museum of Art: Pennsylvania.

McCall, A. (2003) 'Line Describing a Cone' and related films. *October* 103, 42–62.

McGrath, A. (2001) Playing colonial: Cowgirls, cowboys, and Indians in Australia and North America. *Journal of Colonialism and Colonial History* 2 (1). See http://muse.jhu.edu/journals/journal_of_colonialism_and_colonial_history/toc/cch2.1.html#articles2.

Mick, D.G. (2005) 'I Like to Watch,' President's Column in *ACR Newsletter*. Spring 2005. See www.acrwebsite.org/print.asp?artID=214.

Miller, D.M.S. (2008) Disaster tourism and disaster landscape attractions after Hurricane Katrina: An auto-ethnographic journey. *International Journal of Culture of Tourism and Hospitality Research* 2 (2), 115–131.

Mintz, S. and Roberts, R.W. (2010) Introduction: The social and cultural history of American film. In S. Mintz and R.W. Roberts (eds) *Hollywood's America: Twentieth-Century America Through Film* (4th edn) (pp. 1–28). Malden, MA: Wiley-Blackwell.

Moody, P. (2007) The marketing of landscapes in British silent cinema. In L. Porter and B. Dixon (eds) *Picture Perfect: Landscape, Place and Travel in British Cinema before 1930* (pp. 19–28). Exeter: The Exeter Press.

Mordue, T. (1999) Heartbeat Country: Conflicting values, coinciding visions. *Environment and Planning* 31, 629–646.
Mordue, T. (2001) Performing and directing resident/tourist cultures in Heartbeat Country. *Tourist Studies* 1 (3), 233–252.
Moser, J.E. (2001) 'Gigantic engines of propaganda': The 1941 Senate investigation of Hollywood. *The Historian* 63 (4), 731–752.
Murphy, F., Venkatasawmy, R., Simpson, C. and Visosevic, T. (2001) From sand to bitumen, from bushrangers to 'bogans': Mapping the Australian road movie. *Journal of Australian Studies* 25 (70), 73–84.
Museyon (2008) *Film + Travel: Asia, Oceania, Africa*. New York: Museyon Inc.
Museyon (2009) *Film + Travel: North America, South America*. New York: Museyon Inc.
Nacify, H. (2006) Lured by the East: Ethnographic and expedition films about nomadic tribes – the case of *Grass* (1925). In J. Ruoff (ed.) *Virtual Voyages: Cinema and Tourism* (pp. 117–138). Durham, NC: Duke University Press.
National Film and Sound Archive (2011) *Red Cross Activities During and After WWI (c. 1919)*. NFSA title number: 76092. See: http://aso.gov.au/titles/historical/red-cross-first-world-war/
Nelson, K.E. (1996) *A Thumbnail History of the Daguerreotype*. Cecil, PA: Daguerreian Society. See http://www.daguerre.org (accessed April 2011).
Nelson, R.S. (2000) The slide lecture, or the work of art 'history' in the age of mechanical reproduction. *Critical Inquiry* 26 (3), 414–434.
Newman, J. and Simons, I. (2007) *100 Videogames*. British Film Institute Screen Guides. London: BFI Publishing.
Newman, M. (2009) Moving image in the gallery since the 1990s. In S. Corner (ed.) *Film and Video Art* (pp. 86–121). Millbank: Tate Publishing.
NFO New Zealand (2003) *Lord of the Rings Market Research Summary Report*. Prepared for Tourism New Zealand, NFO World Group, 4 April 2003.
Nicholson, H.N. (2006) Through the Balkan states. Home movies as travel texts and tourism histories in the Mediterranean, c.1923–39. *Tourist Studies* 6 (1) 13–36.
Niver, K.R. (1967) *Motion Pictures from the Library of Congress Paper Print Collection, 1894–1912*. Berkeley, CA: University of California Press.
Noy, C. (2003) The write of passage: Reflections on writing a dissertation in narrative/qualitative methodology. *Forum of Qualitative Social Research* 4 (2) [online journal].
Noy, C. (2004) 'The trip really changed me'. Backpackers' narratives of self-change. *Annals of Tourism Research* 31 (1), 78–102.
Noy, C. (2007) The language(s) of the tourist experience: An autoethnography of the poetic tourist. In I. Ateljivic, A. Pritchard and N. Morgan (eds) *The Critical Turn in Tourism Studies* (pp. 349–370). Amsterdam: Elsevier.
O'Hehir, A. (2011) A moral compass that points to the west. *Weekend Australian*, 8 January.
O'Regan, T. (1996) *Australian National Cinema*. New York: Routledge.
Orr, J. (1993) Commodified demons II: The automobile. In J. Orr (ed.) *Cinema and Modernity* (pp. 127–154). Cambridge: Polity Press.
O'Shaughnessy, M. and Stadler, J. (2008) *Media and Society*. South Melbourne: Oxford University Press.
Paris, M. (1995) *From Wright Brothers to Top Gun*. New York: Manchester University Press.
Paxson, F.L. (1946) The highway movement, 1916–1935. *The American Historical Review* 51 (2), 236–253.
Pearce, P.L. (1982) *The Social Psychology of Tourist Behaviour*. Oxford: Pergamon Press.

Pearce, P., Filep, S. and Ross, G. (2011) *Tourists, Tourism and the Good Life*. New York: Routledge.
Peterson, J.L. (2006) 'The nation's first playground': Travel films and the American West, 1895–1920. In J. Ruoff (ed.) *Virtual Voyages, Cinema and Travel* (pp. 79–98). Durham, NC: Duke University Press.
Petit, C. (2007) Preface. In J. Wood (ed.) *100 Road Movies* (pp. x–xii). London: British Film Institute.
Pine, B.J. and Gilmore, J.H. (1999) *The Experience Economy: Work is Theatre and Every Business a Stage*. Boston, MA: Harvard Business Press.
Pine, B.J. and Gilmore, J.H. (2011) *The Experience Economy* (revised edn). Boston, MA: Harvard Business Press.
Popple, S. and Kember, J. (2004) *Early Cinema; From Factory Gate to Dream Factory*. London: Wallflower Press.
Radosh, R. (2010) Scoping out the International Spy Museum. *Academic Questions* 23 (3), 287–297.
Rascaroli, L. (2003) New voyages to Italy: Postmodern travellers and the Italian road film. *Screen* 44 (1), 71–91.
Reade, E. (1970) *Australian Silent Films: A Pictorial History of Silent Films from 1896 to 1929*. Melbourne: Lansdowne Press.
Reeves, B. and Greenberg, B. (1977) Children's perceptions of television characters. *Human Communication Research* 3, 113–117.
Reijnders, S. (2011) *Places of the Imagination: Media, Tourism, Culture*. Farnham: Ashgate Publishing.
Rewtrakunphaiboon, W. (2009) Film-induced tourism: Inventing a vacation to a location. *BU Academic Review* 8 (1), 33–42.
Riley, R.W. (1994) Movie-induced tourism. In A.V. Seaton (ed.) *Tourism. The State of the Art* (pp. 453–458). West Sussex: John Wiley & Sons.
Riley, R. and Van Doren, C.S. (1992) Movies as tourism promotion: A 'pull' factor in a 'push' location. *Tourism Management* 13 (3), 267–274.
Riley, R., Baker, D. and Van Doren, C.S. (1998) Movie induced tourism. *Annals of Tourism Research* 25 (4), 919–935.
Roberts, R.W. and Welky, D. (2010) A sacred mission: Oliver Stone and Vietnam. In S. Mintz and R.W. Roberts (eds) *Hollywood's America: Twentieth-Century America Through Film* (4th edn) (pp. 281–300). Malden, MA: Wiley-Blackwell.
Robinson, D. (1996) *From Peep Show to Palace: The Birth of American Film*. New York: Columbia Press.
Roesch, S. (2007) *There and Back Again: Comparative Case studies of Film Location Tourists' on-site Behaviour and Experiences*. Doctoral dissertation, University of Otago.
Roesch, S. (2009) *The Experiences of Film Location Tourists*. Bristol: Channel View Publications.
Rosengren, K.E. and Windahl, S. (1972) Mass media consumption as a functional alternative. In D. McQuail (ed.) *Sociology of Mass Communications* (pp. 166–194). Harmondsworth: Penguin.
Rothel, D. (1990) *An Ambush of Ghosts: A Personal Guide to Favorite Western Film Locations*. Madison: Empire Publishing.
Routt, W.D. (2001) More Australian than Aristotelian: The Australian bushranger film, 1904–1914. *Senses of Cinema* 18. University of Melbourne. See http://sensesofcinema.com/2001/feature-articles/oz_western/.
Rubin, A.M. and Perse, E.M. (1987) Audience activity and soap opera involvement: A uses and effects investigation. *Human Communication Research* 14, 246–268.

Rubin, A.M. and Step, M.M. (2000) Impact of motivation, attraction, and parasocial interaction of talk radio listening. *Journal of Broadcasting and Electronic Media* 44, 635–654.

Rubin, A.M., Perse, E.M. and Powell, R.A. (1985) Loneliness, parasocial interaction, and local television news viewing. *Human Communication Research* 12, 155–180.

Ruoff, J. (1998) Around the world in eighty minutes: The travel lecture film. *CineAction* 47, 2–11.

Ruoff, J. (2006a) Show and tell: The 16mm travel lecture film In J. Ruoff (ed.) *Virtual Voyages: Cinema and Tourism* (pp. 217–237). Durham, NC: Duke University Press.

Ruoff, J. (ed.) (2006b) *Virtual Voyages: Cinema and Tourism*. Durham, NC: Duke University Press.

Ryan, C. (ed.) (2007) *Battlefield Tourism: History, Place and Interpretation*. Amsterdam: Elsevier.

Seaton, P. (2007) *Japan's Contested War Memories: The 'Memory Rifts' in Historical Consciousness of World War II*. London: Routledge.

Schaber, B. (1997) 'Hitler can't keep 'em that long': The road, the people. In S. Cohan and I.R. Hark (eds) *The Road Movie Book* (pp. 17–44). New York: Routledge.

Schickel, R. (1986) *The Disney Version: The Life, Times, Art and Commerce of Walt Disney* (revised edn). London: Pavilion.

Schneider, J.L. (2007) *Corriganville: The Definitive True Story of the Ray 'Crash' Corrigan Movie Ranch*. Victorville, CA: Corriganville Press.

Schramm, K. (2004) Coming home to the motherland. In S. Coleman and J. Eade (eds) *Reframing Pilgrimage: Cultures in Motion* (pp. 133–149). New York: Routledge.

Schreuders, P. (1997) *The Dell 'Mapbacks'*. Rotterdam: 010 Publishers.

Seaton, A.V. (1998) The history of tourism in Scotland: Approaches, sources and issues. In R. MacLellan and R. Smith (eds) *Tourism in Scotland* (pp. 209–239). London: International Thomson Business Press.

Simpson, P. (ed.) (2002) *The Rough Guide to Cult TV: The Good, the Bad and the Strangely Compelling*. London: Rough Guides/Haymarket Customer Publishing.

Sklan, M.A. (1964) *Walt Disney's Disneyland*. Burbank, CA: Walt Disney Productions.

Smith, V. (1996) War and its tourist attractions. Tourism. In A. Pizam and Y. Mansfield (eds) *Crime and International Security Issues* (pp. 247–264). Chichester: Wiley.

Smith, V. (1998) War and tourism. An American ethnography. *Annals of Tourism Research* 25 (1), 202–227.

Sorkin, M. (1992) See you in Disneyland. In M. Sorkin (ed.) *Variations on a Theme Park* (pp. 205–232). New York: Noonday Press.

Stever, G.S. (2009) Parasocial and social interaction with celebrities: Classification of media fans. *Journal of Media Psychology* 14 (3), 1–39.

Steward, J. (2005) 'How and where to go': The role of travel journalism in Britain and the evolution of foreign tourism, 1840–1914. In J.K. Walton (ed.) *Histories of Tourism: Representation, Identity and Conflict* (pp. 39–54). Clevedon: Channel View Publications.

Strain, E. (2003) *Public Places, Private Journeys. Ethnography, Entertainment and the Tourist Gaze*. New Brunswick, NJ: Rutgers University Press.

Stranieri, V. (2000) Sinister control, demonic possession? Not! Don't assume we are stupid. *Australian Screen Education Online* 24.

Sturman, D.J. (1999) *A Brief History of Motion Capture for Computer Character Animation*. Paris: MediaLab. See http://www.siggraph.org/education/materials/HyperGraph/animation/character_animation/motion_capture/history1.htm (accessed February 2013).

Su, H.J, Huang, Y.-A., Brodowsky, G. and Kim, H.J. (2011) The impact of product placement on TV-induced tourism: Korean TV dramas and Taiwanese viewers. *Tourism Management* 32, 805–814.

Tooke, N. and Baker, M. (1996) Seeing is believing: The effect of film on visitor numbers to screened locations. *Tourism Management* 17 (2), 87–94.

Torchin, L. (2002) Location, location, location: The destination of the Manhattan TV Tour. *Tourist Studies* 2 (3), 247–266.

Travel Today (2007) Japan soap to lure tourists. *Travel Today*, 12 September, p. 1.

Turnbull, S. (2009) Imaging the audience. In S. Cunningham and G. Turner (eds) *Media and Communication in Australia* (pp. 65–78). Sydney: Sydney, Allen and Unwin.

Turner, J.R. (1993) Interpersonal and psychological predictors of parasocial interaction with different television performers. *Communication Quarterly* 41, 443–453.

Tzanelli, R. (2007) *The Cinematic Tourist: Explorations in Globalisation, Culture and Resistance*. London: Sage.

Urry, J. (1990) *The Tourist Gaze: Leisure and Travel in Contemporary Societies*. London: Sage.

Urry, J. (2002) *The Tourist Gaze* (2nd edn). London: Sage.

Urry, J. and Larsen, J. (2011) *The Tourist Gaze 3.0* (2nd edn). London: Sage.

Veeder, G.K. (1990) The Red Cross Bureau of Pictures, 1917–1921: World War I, the Russian Revolution and the Sultan of Turkey's harem. *Historical Journal of Film, Radio and Television* 10 (1), 47–70.

Walton, J.K. (2005) Introduction. In J.K. Walton (ed.) *Histories of Tourism: Representation, Identity and Conflict* (pp. 1–18). Clevedon: Channel View Publications.

Warhol, A. (1968) *Exhibit Catalog*. Stockholm: Moderna Museet.

Westwood, S. (2005) Out of the comfort zone: Situation, participation and narrative interpretation in tourism research. *The First International Congress of Qualitative Inquiry*. University of Illinois at Urbana-Champaign, CD ROM.

Wetta, F.J. and Curley, S.J. (1992) *Celluloid wars: A Guide to Film and the American Experience of War* (No. 5). Westport: Greenwood Publishing Group.

Wheeler, B. (2004) 'Cheese, Gromit – we'll go somewhere where there's cheese' – Wallace and Gromit's *Grand Day Out*: Imagery, metaphor and postgraduate tourism teaching. In J. Tribe and E. Wickens (eds) *Critical Issues in Tourism Higher Education* (pp. 17–23). ATHE Publication No. 4. Eastbourne: Association for Tourism in Higher Education Publications.

Widdis, E. (2010) 'One foot in the air?' Landscape in the Soviet and Russian road movie. In G. Harper and J. Rayner (eds) *Cinema and Landscape* (pp. 73–88). Bristol: Intellect.

Wohlfeil, M. and Whelan. S. (2012) 'Saved!' by Jena Malone: An introspective study of a consumer's fan relationship with a film actress. *Journal of Business Research* 5 (64), 511–519.

Wood, J. (2007) *100 Road Movies*. London: British Film Institute.

Woodrow, I. (1998) Road trip. *Journal of Australian Studies* 25 (58), 162–169.

Wordsworth, W. (1805) *The Prelude of 1805 in Thirteen Books*. DjVu Editions, Global Language Resources Inc.

Wright, A. (2008) *The Imagineering Field Guide to Disneyland*. New York: Disney Editions.

Zacher, C.K. (1976) *Curiosity and Pilgrimage: The Literature of Discovery in Fourteenth Century England*. Baltimore, MD: Johns Hopkins University Press.

Index

Academy Awards, 199, 206
ACMI – *see* Australian Centre for the Moving Image
Akiro Kurosawa, 117
Almeria, 115–116, 130, 134, 153
Almeria Western Film Festival, 130
animation, 63, 132, 180–181, 184, 188, 195, 202–203, 223
anime, 52, 180, 208, 216
anthropology, 1, 2, 7–8, 24, 26, 51
Anti-British film, 82
anti-war, 79, 92, 98, 102
Asia, 3, 4, 1, 85, 97–98, 102, 103, 118, 155, 173–174, 180, 184, 198, 216–217, 223
Australian Centre for the Moving Image, xiii, 6, 33, 34, 152, 201–203, 2–5, 319
authenticity, 2, 24, 63, 126, 163, 177, 188, 189, 190–195
autoethnography, 27, 31–35, 69–72, 90, 109, 120–123, 189, 222, 225
Avenue of Stars, 197, 198

British film, 83, 93, 108
British Film Institute, 134
Burton Holmes, 52, 53–54, 60, 64, 66, 74, 99
bushranger, 4, 108, 109, 134, 151, 157, 158–161, 163–165, 173

Cambodia/Kampuchea, 90, 101–102, 106
celebrity, 17, 20, 23, 32, 38, 62, 68–69, 87, 95, 173–174, 199, 207, 211
celebrity worship syndrome/CWS, 20, 62, 199–200
Charles Marquis Warren, 118, 199
cinema of attractions, 39–40, 111

civil unrest, 60, 61–62, 66, 68, 69, 75, 90, 92, 100–102, 109
Coco Palms Resort, 32, 211
Coen Brothers, 115, 132–133
Cold War, 90, 91, 92–96, 100, 104, 105
Comic-Con, 189, 208
communications studies, 7, 16
computer games, 34, 62, 105–106, 219–221, 223
contents tourism, 9, 24, 180, 208
corporate social responsibility, 23
critical studies, 27, 222–223
curiositas, 13–14

dark rides, 185–187
Dell Mapbacks, 167, 168
detective stories, 167–170, 171, 173, 223
digital puppetry, 188–189
Disney, 51, 129, 180, 182, 184, 186, 189, 190–191, 194, 198
Disneyland, 32, 50, 51, 125, 129, 181, 182–184, 195, 203
DreamWorks, 202–204

Ennio Morricone, 116–117, 130, 131, 133, 170, 171
espionage, 87, 91, 92–96, 106
European cinema, 81–83, 148–149

fans/fandom, 17, 19, 20, 27–28, 30, 59, 70–72, 127, 128–133, 134, 137, 148, 152, 158, 167, 173–174, 177, 182, 189, 195–196, 200–201, 202, 203, 206–207, 209, 216
film commission, 88, 224

Index

film tourism precinct, 4, 197–199
flâneur, 15, 62, 107–108, 110, 125, 206
flâneuse, 107, 109, 134, 198
Fox Backlot, 179

Game Masters, 202–204
gangster movies, 75, 93, 108, 170–172
Great Depression, 76
Gulf War, 61, 65, 99, 100

Hale's Tours, 49–51, 53, 186
hero's journey, 112–113
House Committee on Un-American Activities/HCUAA, 92–93

IMAX, 7, 15, 42, 65
impacts, 7, 23, 26
International Spy Museum, 92, 95–97
inversion, 118
Ischia Film Festival, 206–207

James Bond, 93–95, 97, 167
Japanese war films, 85
John Ford, 96, 114–116, 118, 122, 132
Julian Rosefeldt, 184, 204

Lumiere Brothers, 37

mafia, 157, 171, 172
Manifest Destiny, 93, 113, 123, 132, 134, 142, 148, 159, 160
migration, 12, 103–104, 143
Mini-Hollywood, 116, 129
Monument Valley, 114–117, 118, 121–122, 125, 132, 140, 145, 153, 200
movie map, 56, 197
Movie Park Germany, 184
movie ranch, 128–132, 182
  Big Sky Movie Ranch, 119, 127, 129
  Corriganville Movie Ranch, 119, 120, 128, 129, 153, 182
  Famous Players-Lasky Movie Ranch, 126, 127, 130
  Golden Oak Ranch, 126, 129, 182
  Iverson Movie Ranch, 126, 129
  Jack Ingram Motion Picture Ranch, 128, 182
  Kattemingga, 130–131, 166

  Melody Ranch, 127, 129, 133
  Monogram Ranch, 127, 128
MovieTour, 211
museum – *see also* International Spy Museum, 33, 34, 101, 106, 129, 134, 181, 184, 197, 201–204, 109, 217

national cinema, 75, 86, 172
numinous, 70, 120–122, 200, 210

Pacific war, 84–85, 105–106
Paramount Studios, 33, 195, 199
para-social interaction/PSI, 17–20, 28, 174, 197, 200, 208, 213, 225
para-social relationships, 17, 19–20, 118, 213
participant-observation, 31, 51, 54
phantom rides, 37, 48–50, 60
picturesque, 40, 42, 45, 46, 50, 66, 108, 150, 151
pilgrimage, 11, 19, 32, 62, 63, 69–74, 85, 87, 89, 90, 100, 104, 128, 153, 155, 164
Pol Pot, 101
postwar recovery, 62, 92, 142
postwar tourism, 64, 87
propaganda, 61, 67, 75, 76, 77–80, 81–85, 92, 95, 98, 99, 102, 223
PSI – *see* para-social interaction
psychology, 1, 2, 7, 16, 21

Quentin Tarantino, 117, 127, 133, 171, 172

Red Cross Travel Film Series, 81
Route 66, 146, 147
runaway production, 32, 77, 87, 114, 116, 131, 170

Sam Peckinpah, 118, 145
science ficton, 62, 105, 180, 206, 208, 221
semiotics, 21
Sergio Leone, 114–118, 119, 129–130, 133, 134, 149, 151, 170–171
simulacra, 24, 42
Spaghetti Western Orchestra, 116, 132

The Grand Tour, 11–12, 40, 55–56
The Mickey Mouse Club, 129, 182, 183

The Wizarding World of Harry Potter, 33, 180, 184, 187–188
Tiananmen Square, 100
Tim Burton, 33, 180, 202, 204
tourism commission, 108, 161
tourism marketing, 9, 23, 108
tourism promotion, 9, 96, 108, 146, 149, 154–155, 210
tourist gaze (*see also* virtual mobile gaze), 10, 14–16, 24, 62, 63
travel lecture, 34, 40, 47, 48, 52–55, 56, 57, 60, 61, 65–68, 74
travelogue, 9, 24, 34, 47, 50, 52, 53–54, 56, 58, 60, 66–67, 68
triad, 157, 172–173
TV western, 118–119, 126, 213, 214

Universal City Dubailand, 184
Universal Preparedness Productions, 78
Universal Studios, 33, 50–51, 180, 184–185, 187–189, 194, 203

video sniffing, 221
Vietnam War, 61, 98–9, 102
virtual mobile gaze (*see also* tourist gaze), 14–15, 42, 62, 63, 107
virtual travel, 40, 48, 84

walk of fame, 107, 198–199
Warner Brothers, 50, 58, 104, 126, 184
WWI, 27, 66, 68, 72, 76–78, 80, 83, 86, 102
WWII, 27, 61, 76, 78, 79, 81, 83–84, 85, 88, 92, 95, 102, 103, 105, 111, 142

For Product Safety Concerns and Information please contact our EU Authorised Representative:

Easy Access System Europe

Mustamäe tee 50

10621 Tallinn

Estonia

gpsr.requests@easproject.com

www.ingramcontent.com/pod-product-compliance
Lightning Source LLC
Chambersburg PA
CBHW070600300426
44113CB00010B/1329